# SERVICE STRATEGY IN ACTION

John

Thank you so much

for our workshop together

I hope you'll find this

book inspiring

Wolfgang

# SERVICE STRATEGY IN ACTION

**A PRACTICAL GUIDE FOR GROWING YOUR
B2B SERVICE AND SOLUTION BUSINESS**

# Christian Kowalkowski and Wolfgang Ulaga

ISBN-13: 9780692819104
ISBN-10: 069281910X

# CONTENTS

# PREFACE

These are times of fast transformation and change. With growing digital disruption across industries, the emergence of new business models, Industry 4.0, IoT-based services, and the mounting pressure to deliver better business outcomes for customers, much has been written about *what* servitization of industries means and *why* firms need to move into the service space. Yet, in times where increasingly 'everything' is considered as a service, decision-makers still need to understand *how* to master this profound transformation and decide which concrete actions they must take to carry out this change.

With this book, we fill the gap of long needed practical guidelines for navigating the transition from a product-centric to a service- and solution-savvy business model. To achieve profitable growth and stand out among competitors in today's global markets, it is no longer enough to simply make great (service) products. Companies must start to think more strategically about service, determine how to compete through innovative services and solutions, and create more value for (and with!) customers if they want to deliver business outcomes that truly matter.

We wrote this book for senior executives and experienced managers in industrial companies and professional services organizations, who want to design and implement a service-growth strategy that will deliver results. We adopt a unique perspective by blending managerial relevance with academic rigor to take you on a hands-on twelve-step journey to profitable service growth. We share the concepts and frameworks that we developed based on sound research and many years of experience working with hundreds of managers in industrial and professional services companies. Our proprietary road map will help you break out of a narrow product-centric logic and discover how to determine if your company is "fit-for-service," make the most of your existing services, innovate and create value-added services and solutions beyond your products, embed a true service-centric culture in your organization, drive change and align your service strategy with corporate goals, transform your product-centric sales force into a service-savvy sales organization, design an organizational structure that promotes service growth, and align your interests with distributors and partners.

This book is the fruit of multiple research projects and numerous practitioner workshops we facilitated across the globe. Over the years, we published more than thirty-five articles in scientific and managerial journals, including *Harvard Business Review* and the *Journal of Marketing*, and two books (in French and Swedish) on service strategies. Yet, this exciting journey would not have been possible without the help of executives and managers we were blessed to work with in a vast variety of industries and companies, such as, ABB, AGC, Air Liquide, Areva, ASML, Biomet, Bühler, Carrefour, Cargill, Caterpillar, Dalkia, DSM, Electrolux, Ericsson, Evonik, General Electric, GEA, Gemalto, Hempel, Holcim, Husqvarna, John Deere, EMC, KBA-NotaSys, KGHM, Kemira, Linde, Mammoet, Markem-Imaje, Maersk Damco, Merck Chimie, Metso, Neopost, Neste Oil, Nexans, Nilfisk, Ooredoo, Outokumpu, Outotec, Post-NL, PPG, Rexel, Rio Tinto, Rockwool, Saab, Safran, Saint Gobain, Sandvik, Scania, Schindler, SERCO, SHV, Siemens, SIKA, Skanska, SKF, Syngenta, Tetra Pak, Thales, ThyssenKrupp, TNT, Toyota Industries, Vallourec, Veolia, Volvo Group, and Xylem.

We would also like to thank our coauthors, colleagues and researchers we have worked with over the years: Federico Adrodegari, Klaus Backhaus, Sergio Biggemann, Mary Jo Bitner, Sundar Bharadwaj, Eva Böhm, Thomas G. Brashear Alejandro, Staffan Brege, Per-Olof Brehmer, Stephen W. Brown, Danilo Brozović, Per Carlborg, Frederic Dalsace, Carlos A. Diaz Ruiz, Bo Edvardsson, Andreas Eggert, Heiko Gebauer, Marcella Grohmann, Anders Gustafsson, Jens Hogreve, Maria Holmlund, Frank Jacob, Bart Kamp, Gerald Karsenti, Mario Kienzler, Daniel Kindström, Athanasios Kondis, Mattias Lindahl, James Loveland,

Jane Maley, Mekhail Mustak, Stefan Michel, Winter Nie, Fredrik Nordin, Rogelio Oliva, Glenn Parry, Chris Raddats, Risto Rajala, Jakob Rehme, Chloe Renault, Nicola Saccani, Tomohiko Sakao, Erik Sandberg, Jaakko Siltaloppi, Alexey Sklyar, David Sörhammar, Michael Steiner, Werner Reinartz, Anna Salonen, Bård Tronvoll, Florian von Wangenheim, Charlotta Windahl, Lars Witell, Stefan Worm, and Marcus Zimmer.

While we hope that our book proves helpful and thought-provoking, we do not expect that it will provide a final answer to all challenges on your journey to profiting from service growth. We are sincerely interested in your comments and reactions and hope that our book will initiate a fruitful dialogue among our community on this topic we all are so passionate about. Please share your ideas on www.ServiceStrategyInAction. com or follow us on Twitter on @Serv_Strat to continue the conversation with your peers and with us. May we *cocreate* the journey of profiting from service growth together!

Christian Kowalkowski
Associate Professor of Industrial Marketing
Linköping University (Sweden) and Hanken
School of Economics (Finland)

Wolfgang Ulaga
AT&T Professor of Services Leadership and
Co-Executive Director Center for Services Leadership
W. P. Carey School of Business
Arizona State University (USA)

Linköping and Tempe
February 2017

# INTRODUCTION

Today, many firms set out to navigate the transition from a goods-centric to a service-savvy business model. Increasingly, having world-class products is no longer enough to combat commoditization and stem rampant erosion of margins in many markets. More than ever, to keep competition at bay and sustain growth, companies must redefine what they do for (and with) customers and venture into adjacent spaces, providing value-added services and customer solutions.

This book is about *service growth*. It has been written for companies that have their historical roots firmly grounded in product-centric logic. The key challenge for the vast majority of these companies is not to shed their historic product base and become service providers—that is, to move from product *to* service. Rather, the fundamental challenge for these firms consists of finding smart ways of growing beyond their historic goods-centric core. As we will see, by finding new ways of combining goods and services into what we call "hybrid offerings," many companies today chart a path for growth through service and customer solutions in increasingly competitive markets.

For over a decade, we have accompanied numerous firms on their journeys from focusing on manufacturing and selling products to providing service and customer solutions in a broad array of industries and markets. In our discussions with many executives and analyses of various companies and markets, we found that the imperative of moving toward a service-centric business model reaches far beyond the traditional goods-centric manufacturing firm in business-to-business markets. Becoming truly service-centric also represents a formidable challenge to firms in fast-moving consumer industries or companies already operating in traditional service contexts. Think of retailers in consumer markets, distributors serving B2B customers, or even companies in financial services. As one manager excellently explained, "In our industry, we sell 'financial products.' The word says it all. We offer a standard mortgage, slap an interest rate on top of it, and sell the package off the shelf. We are in the business of box-pushing."

When service-growth strategies work, the payoffs are impressive, and firms often discover that their new activities make more money than products. But for every success story, numerous cautionary tales remind us that this move involves more than a few cosmetic adjustments. Without giving this strategic initiative serious thought, and without methodologically managing the change process, our research has found that the transition is doomed to fail and companies struggle to turn a profit from their service growth initiative.

This book has been written for the manager who has to think about the service strategy of the firm and how to implement it. It leverages our practical experience and brings together the lessons learned from hands-on work with managers through workshops and their own projects. It is also the result of more than a decade's sound research on the key success factors of service-growth strategies. Together, we conducted multiple research projects, interviewed and surveyed hundreds of managers, and published numerous articles in the scientific and managerial press. This has allowed us to understand the road map that a goods-centric firm needs to navigate to master the transition to a more service-centric business model and mind-set.

## Roadmap for Service Growth

Our intention in this book is to provide decision makers in product firms with the tools they need to craft a competitive service strategy and put it into practice. Readers can employ the twelve-step road map in figure 0:1 and use methods and frameworks for each step in their own firms to navigate the transformation into service.

**Figure 0:1**
**The Roadmap for Service Strategy in Action**

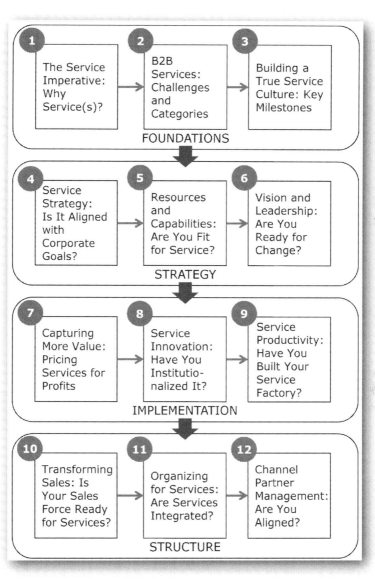

The first part of the book tackles the very foundations of a service business: why to move into services and how to understand services and a service culture. The second part deals with strategic issues: how to craft an overall service strategy, how to determine if the firm is ready for service transformation, and how to lead the change. Then we discuss how to come to grips with implementation: how to manage the service portfolio, develop new services, and build the service factory. Finally, we show how to build the structure needed: transforming the sales force, integrating service into the organization, and aligning with channel partners. More specifically, each chapter deals with the following issues:

In chapter 1, we explain why service is such a powerful growth engine for companies regardless of industry sector and market. We discuss the underlying drivers for service transformation and show the most important internal and external motivations that every company needs to consider.

In chapter 2, we define more precisely what we mean by "service" and discuss fundamental characteristics that make service strategies hard to implement for many product firms. Recognizing that services are heterogeneous activities, we provide a classification framework for business services. This allows for a more thorough understanding of the growth opportunities at hand and how firms can combine products and services in intelligent ways—what we refer to as hybrid offerings.

Chapter 3 addresses how a service culture deviates from a manufacturing mind-set. We examine the role of service on a companywide level and provide a framework for stakeholder mapping. Finally, we present the seven deadly sins of service-myopic firms and discuss how to avoid them.

Chapter 4 focuses on how to craft the service strategy. It begins with scrutinizing common arguments against service-led growth. We then discuss how to redefine the mission of the company, addressing questions like these: Is your DNA goods-centric or service-centric? How do you determine the right market position? How do you manage the commodity magnet?

Chapter 5 reveals unique resources and distinctive capabilities needed and provides a diagnostic-tool framework for determining whether your firm is fit for service. While manufacturers frequently struggle to compete with pure-service players, they can be in a unique position to grow revenues through hybrid offerings if they learn how to leverage resources and build capabilities for service growth.

Chapter 6 presents a change management framework and discusses visionary leadership, top managers' roles as change agents, and how to manage internal resistance to change. Building on the established eight-step process for leading change, we discuss how firms can manage the service transformation.

Chapter 7 shows how to build the service portfolio, how to get more mileage out of existing services, and how to move from free to fee. It also reviews the pricing options managers have at hand and presents a framework to guide the crafting of compelling value propositions.

Chapter 8 discusses how to institutionalize service innovation. First, we show how service innovation differs from conventional product innovation and what this means for product-centric firms. Then we explore how to identify new service opportunities and provide managers with a service innovation framework.

Chapter 9 demonstrates how to build the service factory—that is, how to industrialize the implementation of service, how to manage the specificities of service, and how to address service productivity challenges. We also show how to work with the service blueprinting method, which can be used both strategically and at a microimplementation level.

Chapter 10 reveals how to build a service-savvy sales force—the skills needed, the necessary steps to take, and the implications for the sales organization. Businesses must foster personality traits in favor of service and understand how to implement service strategy at sales force level.

Chapter 11 provides fundamental guiding principles for how to integrate services in the organization, including the relationship between product and service units and central and local ones. Recognizing that different organizational structures have their distinct pros and cons, we discuss how businesses should organize to accomplish service growth and control.

Chapter 12 provides a structure and strategy framework for aligning with channel partners and accessing the feasibility of the current channel structure arrangement. It provides guidance for how to define a dealer strategy and discusses how to manage value constellations in complex business networks.

The proprietary twelve-step road map we present in this book provides a unifying framework—supported by best practices from a variety of businesses, industries, and countries—for how to navigate the transition from a goods-centric to a service-savvy business model. At the end of each chapter, we provide a set of questions that allow you to think through how your company is positioned on the road map for service growth.

# CHAPTER 1

## THE SERVICE IMPERATIVE: WHY SERVICE(S)?

*A business absolutely devoted to service will
have only one worry about profits.
They will be embarrassingly large.*
—*HENRY FORD*

Everywhere in the world, we are evolving toward a service economy. In all developed countries, services occupy a paramount place in the economy, frequently passing the threshold of 70 percent of GDP; in countries such as the United States, the United Kingdom, and France, it has risen to almost 80 percent, whereas Germany is just at the threshold with 69 percent, and India still far below it with 52 percent.[1] In addition, advanced services are increasingly important for companies classified as manufacturing industries. Even in countries that have historically concentrated their efforts on manufacturing, services maintain a sustained progression. For example, in China, the services sector accounted for 22 percent of GDP in 1980; by 2014, this had increased to 48 percent. The government has clearly stated its desire to accelerate the growth of the part that services play in its economy.

From the workshops we have led in China, it becomes clear that the Chinese market is maturing and that companies no longer experience double-digit growth through product sales. Instead, services are ways to build customer relationships and get productivity improvement. The more the Chinese economy moves into a maturity stage with little or no growth, the more the service imperative becomes relevant. Also, when increasingly going abroad, Chinese firms will have to play the service game. For instance, $60 billion telecom group Huawei has achieved meteoric growth and, together with Ericsson of Sweden, now dominates the telecom network managed-services market. The growing number of acquisitions by Chinese investors now also includes firms in the services sector, such as healthcare, finance, media, and entertainment.[2] A recent example is the $6 billion acquisition of electronics distributor Ingram Micro by aviation and shipping conglomerate HNA Group.[3]

Today, services represent a powerful growth engine in most industries, including fast-moving consumer goods and retailing. Let's consider two examples. As part of a companywide ambition to reignite growth and accelerate innovation, fast-moving consumer goods giant Procter & Gamble created an entirely new division, Agile Pursuits (AP), to venture into franchising. AP allowed Procter & Gamble to explore entirely new business models it had never used before as a way to leverage several of its most powerful brands (such as Mr. Clean or Tide) for creating better customer experiences and securing growth across its billion-dollar brands. For example, the company focused on one blockbuster FMCG brand, Tide, to launch Tide Dry Cleaners in 2008, a franchise of retail outlets operated under the iconic Tide[4] laundry detergent brand, providing both wet- and dry-cleaning services, including drive-through valet and twenty-four-hour service. Today, forty-four locations served customers in seventeen states across the United States. By moving from a focus on packaged goods to serving customers in the dry-cleaning market, P&G redefined the customer job from a broader perspective. Instead of focusing on excellence in manufacturing, marketing, and selling a fast-moving consumer product, the company found new ways to deliver a service experience. This implied for the company to learn how to set up and run a "people business." P&G had to learn how to master a service-centric business model, which is very different from its traditional expertise in manufacturing and selling fast-moving consumer goods.

Second, Phoenix-based PetSmart's service growth initiative shows that the transformation is not limited to manufacturers of consumer goods; traditional service firms, such as retailers, can successfully grow deeper into value-added services by adopting a truly service-centric approach. Jim and Janice Dougherty opened their first two stores, called PetFood Warehouse, in Arizona in 1987. Today, PetSmart is North America's largest specialty retailer of services and solutions for the lifetime needs of pets. Over the years, the company has successfully evolved from a pet supply store to a service-centric company. Beyond the sale of specialty pet supplies and services such as grooming and dog training, the retailer today operates cat and dog boarding facilities and pet daycare centers. PetSmart operates approximately 1,430 stores and about two hundred in-store facilities with PetsHotels and Doggie Day Camps. Many PetSmart outlets also contain veterinary offices under the Banfield Pet Hospital brand.[5] While the $8.3 billion leveraged buyout by a group led by private equity firm BC Partners in 2015 led to drastic changes in the organization, investments for services has remained high.[6]

Cleary, over the years, PetSmart, much like P&G, has redefined the customer job the company engages in. Instead of pursuing a goods-centric logic—that is, focusing on pushing boxes from the retail shelf into customers' shopping carts—PetSmart holistically addresses the needs of the pet as a family member and, of course, the needs of the pet owner. During the years of the financial crisis, PetSmart sales went from $4.7 billion in 2007 to $5.1 in 2008 to $5.4 in 2009. While PetSmart was hit in its discretionary hard goods sales—its customers weren't buying the extra toy as they were leaving the store nor the extra leash or dog bed—PetSmart found that its service-savvy business model was more resilient within a downswing. Services, which included pet training, grooming, boarding, and adoption services, added an extra $527 million to the company's balance sheet in 2008, a figure that rose to $808 million of total sales of $7.1 billion in 2014.[7]

The P&G and PetSmart examples show how service infusion is an attractive route to growth. Similarly, business-to-business manufacturers see these low-hanging fruits and increasingly shift their business logic from a profit equation based on equipment sales and internal cost cutting to an approach based on revenue and margin growth through value-added services. As such, manufacturers across many industries seek to expand beyond their traditional core business through service growth. Yet, while the perspectives are indeed promising, the challenges of overhauling a firm's existing business are significant. The case of Xerox group illustrates this underlying trend (see exhibit 1).

## Exhibit 1
### Xerox: From Selling Office Equipment to Optimizing Business-Process and Document Management—and Back Again

Founded in 1906, Xerox is an $18 billion company that, during the last decade, has transformed itself from a technology company—a manufacturer of photocopiers and printers—to a service provider. In 1958, Xerox invented a breakthrough technology, allowing it to build a desk-sized photocopier that could make several-fold more copies per day than competitors but at a price seven to eight times higher than the competition. Competitors were pursuing a "razor and razor blade" business model— charging for the machine at a modest markup over cost and charging separately for support and services. The company had to innovate with a new business model to succeed—that is, leasing the machine for ninety-five dollars per month instead of buying it. The business model imposed most of the risk on the tiny Xerox; only beyond the first two thousand copies each month would the customers pay four cents per copy. However, users averaged two thousand copies per day, generating revenues beyond even the most optimistic expectations. The new business model powered compound growth, turning the $30 million Xerox into a global enterprise with $2.5 billion in revenues by 1972.

In the coming decades, the main competition would come from a host of Japanese firms that entered the low end, where Xerox was weak. The Japanese competitors could sell products cheaper than Xerox could manufacture, which created a burning platform and impetus to change. Furthermore, digital commerce and communication increasingly threatened its core business of photocopiers and printing.

When turnaround CEO Anne Mulcahy took the helm in 2001, Xerox was teetering on the verge of bankruptcy. Almost immediately, she launched a drastic restructuring plan, which included the launch of a revamped services unit, to help steer Xerox away from bankruptcy and

4

pursued a wide-scale service transformation, which current CEO Ursula Burns has, until recently, continued. Between 2000 and 2009, the company reduced its workforce from ninety-five thousand to fifty-four thousand employees. Xerox acquired Affiliated Computer Services (ACS), the world's largest diversified business process outsourcing company, for $6.4 billion in 2010. The acquisition—the largest in Xerox's history—catapulted the company's presence in the $500 billion business-services market and added seventy-four thousand staff members to Xerox's fifty-four thousand. The new Xerox sought to help customers manage their document and business process operations and the associated costs as efficiently as possible. A consequence of the new strategy is that it sold its clients fewer products: some big industrial customers went from having fifty thousand to twenty-two thousand Xerox-made machines. "That was counterintuitive for a business built on selling more and more products," according to Andy Jones, director of Xerox's European outsourcing operations.

For several years, the fastest-growing business for the 146,000-employee company has been business process outsourcing services. In 2014, 56 percent of total revenue came from the services segment; the share was 23 percent in 2009, before the acquisition of ACS. In fact, only 15 percent of the group's revenues come from equipment sales nowadays; eighty-five percent is annuity-based revenue that includes contracted services, maintenance, supplies, rental, and finances. The service transformation has enabled longer contracts, customer intimacy, and better resilience to downturns.

Back in 2013, Ursula Burns, chairperson and CEO, told investors that the "shift to services-led growth portfolio is paying off." Nonetheless, in 2016, the company decided to split into two companies: the hardware-centric Xerox (e.g., high-end color and customized print) and the service-centric Conduent (e.g., business transformation, automation, and analytics). It was "taking further affirmative steps to drive shareholder value," and separation rationale included sharpened management focus, simpler organization, and more distinct investment propositions with differentiated financial profiles, growth drivers, and business prospects. In fact, in order to succeed with service-led growth, firms must exploit the synergistic benefits of offering products and services. Research shows that without such positive spillover effects, increased shareholder value is unlikely to materialize. In the case of the two new companies, time will tell if Xerox can once again reinvent itself.

*Sources:* Chesbrough (2010); Fang et al. (2008); *Financial Times; Wall Street Journal;* Xerox

## What Drives Service Growth?

The shift toward service orientation is not a recent trend. Over forty years ago, Theodore Levitt, renowned professor of marketing at Harvard Business School, was already encouraging major industrial groups in the United States to develop services around their products and to recognize that they were already service providers. Levitt rightly underlined that every goods-centric company must also provide service to survive.[8]

In business markets, manufacturers must provide a host of services that simply enable sales of goods. For example, a manufacturer of industrial refrigeration equipment could not sell its goods to retail store chains unless the company also provided on-site services accompanying and facilitating the sale. Professional buyers would bypass the supplier if it did not provide installation and repair services or fast intervention in case of equipment breakdown. While goods-centric firms have always provided such services, what is new is the sense of urgency that has become palpable in the executive boardrooms. Over the past years, service growth has indeed risen from the backseat of corporate strategy to the top of management's agenda. Growing revenues and margins beyond the firm's traditional product-centric business thus have increasingly become a burning platform.

A case in point is Boeing, the Chicago-based, $96 billion aerospace company that builds jetliners, fighter jets, rockets, and satellites. According to CEO Dennis Muilenburg, "Substantial services growth is core to Boeing's strategy." Having less than 10 percent services market share at its civil and defense businesses, there is "ample room to grow" by moving away from the ups and downs of product sales and tapping into the stable and lucrative revenue stream of services throughout the multidecade lifetime of aircrafts. Boeing aims to more than triple service sales in ten years, from about $15 billion in 2015 to $50 billion by 2025.[9]

There are two fundamental motivations of why goods-centric firms seek service-led growth. Companies either pursue service-growth strategies from a defensive stance in a move to protect their existing turf and solidify their ongoing business, or they view service as a proactive weapon to actively move to acquire new customers, break into competitors' accounts, and access greater volumes and bigger margins. These moves are fueled by a number of fundamental trends that we summarize in figure 1:1. Here, we discuss three main factors rooted in firms' external environments and three drivers related to companies' internal motivations.

**Figure 1:1**
**Why Believe in Services? Key Drivers for Service Growth**

| External Factors Tied to the Environment | Internal Motivations from the Company |
|---|---|
| • Saturated and commoditized markets<br>• Customer pressure<br>• Proliferation of competition | • Exploit product and technology expertise<br>• Capture customer relationship value<br>• Open new market opportunities |

## External Factors Tied to the Market Environment

Several external factors favor the emergence and growth of service activities in business markets. Above, we cite all three particularly important ones: flat markets with eroding profit margins for manufactured goods sold, customers becoming more professional and increasingly outsourcing noncore activities, and proliferation of competition from both incumbents and new entrants.

### Saturated and Commoditized Markets

A growing number of industries see themselves confronted with a saturation of demand in core product areas. It means that they cannot grow their installed base further. This is particularly evident in mature markets where companies seldom make greenfield investments anymore due to stagnated or even declining demand. Consider a mature industry, such as pulp and paper, a typical case in point. For years, pulp and paper manufacturers have downsized capacities and closed mills in Europe and North America. At the same time, major companies redirected investments to countries such as Brazil and China. North America has been a mature market since the mid-1990s; since then, few investments in new capacities were made, and more than five hundred machines have been phased out. A similar development can be seen in Europe. Despite this evolution, the demand for service has increased, a trend that has benefited companies like Finland's Valmet, the global market leader of papermaking lines. Since the 1990s, the company's service revenues have more than tripled, and services such as maintenance, rebuilds, and performance optimization will continue to be the company's most important target of development.[10]

Capturing greater revenues and profits through value-added services is particularly important in situations where the number of new units sold is by far outnumbered by the installed base of goods sold. In many markets, the installed base is more than tenfold the size of annual product sales. Table 1:1 shows examples of some markets that we have studied. For example, Otis, the world's largest elevator and escalator company, annually sells one hundred thousand elevators and escalators and performs maintenance on more than 1.9 million machines. Of the firm's $13 billion revenue, the majority comes from service.[11]

The process of commoditization has accelerated in recent years. Increasingly, profit margins for equipment sales are razor thin, and manufacturers of material-handling equipment and ATM machines generally earn next to nothing through their product sales. This evolution toward the sale of commodities results in falling prices and rampant erosion of profit margins. As a managing director in the material-handling industry pointed out, "If you measure in real time the price today and the price five years ago, the price has fallen for everything."

Table 1:1
Relationship between New Unit Sales and Installed Base

| Industry | Annual Unit Sales | Installed Base | Installed Base Factor (IBF)* |
|---|---|---|---|
| X-Ray Imaging Equipment[1] | 160 | 7,000 | 1:44 |
| Elevators[2] | 100,000 | 1,900,000 | 1:19 |
| High-Voltage Transformers[3] | 920 | 15,500 | 1:17 |
| Forklift Trucks[4] | 12,500 | 159,000 | 1:13 |
| ATM Machines[5] | 2,750 | 20,038 | 1:7 |

*Installed base factor (IBF) = number of installed goods already in use divided by the annual new unit sales (1 = national sales 2010; 2 = company-specific global sales 2014; 3 = global sales 2010; 4 = national sales 2009; 5 = national sales 2009)

When purchases are made solely on price, products become interchangeable, and the results are a vicious cycle of downward-spiraling margins. For example, the ATM density in South Korea is the highest in the world with 2,907 ATMs per million people.[12] Russian retail banks can now buy from Korean manufacturers and obtain lower prices than they would domestically, benefiting from price wars originating abroad. In order to break the vicious cycle of downward-spiraling margins, companies have to find new profit generators such as more sophisticated cash-management solutions.

When facing commoditization, the most common mistake companies make is failure to understand the changing market conditions and adapt accordingly. In particular, premium-player incumbents tend to cling on to their conventional product-centric profit formula—even when it is turning into a burning platform that is no longer supported in the market. Service growth has proven to be a viable response when crafting an effective commoditization strategy. Margins in services frequently greatly surpass the margins realized in sales of products; a cross-industry study found that the margins in services surpass those of products by two to five times (see table 1:2).[13] Even in industries where healthy product margins have been sustained, such as the elevator industry, margins on maintenance services are 25 to 35 percent, compared with 10 percent for new equipment.[14] However, the margin leverage can be even higher; the director of a French manufacturer revealed to us that the operational margins realized in services for his company frequently surpass by six to eight times those of products.

Table 1:2
Margins in Product and Service Businesses

| Industry | Margins in Product Business | Margins in Service Business | Margin Leverage (Service Margin/ Product Margin) |
|---|---|---|---|
| Machine Tools | 1–12% | 5–15% | 2 |
| Metallurgy Equipment | -3–6% | 15–20% | 4 |
| Paper Machines | 1–3% | 10–15% | 5 |
| Power Equipment | 2–5% | 15–20% | 4 |
| Rail Vehicles | 3–6% | 8–10% | 2 |

Source: Monitor Group (2004)

*Customer pressure*

The growing professionalism of customers means that they put the heat on their suppliers. Customers not only ask for more services or seek to outsource activities; more and more, they want to pay for achieved performance instead of buying goods and services. As many customers are reducing their supplier base, they expect more from their remaining suppliers such as a more complete product-service portfolio. With more professional purchasing departments, customers expect their suppliers to help them cut production costs and increase productivity. Customers are even looking for support in how to better serve their customers successfully. Taken together, this customer pressure necessitates that suppliers revisit their market strategies, either pursuing commoditization (submitting to cost pressure and lowering margins) or differentiation (proactively building a business around value-added services and hybrid offerings that help the customer run its business process).

For over two decades, outsourcing has been a major trend in many industries, facilitated by benchmarking and other innovations in performance measurement. Requirements for profitability and continuous cost reductions, along with the need for flexible access of production facilities and technological developments, have driven the development and equipped suppliers with many new service business opportunities. By outsourcing noncore processes to suppliers and transforming capital expenditure (CAPEX) to operational expenditure (OPEX), companies reduce cost structure and gain flexibility, especially in times of crisis. In order to stay relevant, product firms have to seize such opportunities whenever appropriate—for example, by taking over large numbers of service personnel from their outsourcing customers or collaborating with service partners.

At the same time, across sectors, a growing number of companies prefer to opt for offerings and payments tied to actual use of the product rather than buying products and services. A case in point is operators of rolling stock that increasingly seek to pay for availability or per driven distance. For example, Northern Line in London is Europe's most used underground line with over eight hundred thousand passengers per day. The first parts of the line were in use already in 1890, and one hundred years later it was commonly referred to as "misery line" due to the problems with constant delays. When the old fleet was about to be replaced in 1995, London Underground chose not to buy any new rolling stock; instead, they opted for availability. The requirement was that ninety-six cars should be available every day for a period of twenty years. Global provider of integrated railway systems Alstom seized the opportunity and won the contract. In order to meet the requirements, the company had to build 106 cars and establish a local maintenance organization. If Alstom failed to provide trains in the London Underground, it has to pay penalties according to length of delays and number of passengers held up. Today, such contracts are common practice in the industry.

*Proliferation of competition*

Four types of competitors challenge the traditional business of product firms and prompt them to move into service. In order to respond, managers need to understand the difference between these threats. First, product firms face direct competition from other industry incumbents. If these competitors are product-centric and invest in services in a reactive fashion only, the actual threat may be limited. They pose a much greater threat if they proactively expand their service business to break into competitors' accounts. While such competition may be fierce, the players and usually also the rules of the game are well known.

In this respect, the second form of competition, which is new direct competitors from emerging markets, can be more unpredictable and more difficult to respond to. In many cases, these firms compete through low-cost strategies, which inevitably push product margins down. In other cases, however, they compete through service and innovation. For example, in the telecom sector, China's Huawei (founded in 1988) has achieved remarkable growth and is now neck and neck with the world's largest equipment provider, Ericsson (founded in 1876). The group has expanded rapidly into services and is investing heavily in R&D, having seven R&D centers in Europe alone.[15]

Distributors, consultants, and pure-service players moving up are the third type of competitors that product firms face. This third-party threat can be difficult to respond to, in particular if they control the service market channel and own the day-to-day relationships with the customer. While they may lack many of the strengths of manufacturers (which we discuss in chapter 5), they know the local market conditions, are more nimble, and have the infrastructure in place to grow through services. Being more responsive to changing customer needs, they can move from a position of tactical supplier to a strategic one in the customer's business. For example, when a customer outsources service operations to a third party, the supplier's position in relation to the customer weakens; the ownership of the customer slips away from the supplier to the third party. The supplier ends up being a subcontractor to the third party.[16]

In many industries, however, the most formidable threat comes from disruptive innovators outside the traditional industry boundaries. An executive in a world-leading manufacturing incumbent that we interviewed stressed that her main concern was not the competition from any of the first three types of competitors. Instead, what kept her awake at night was the prospect of Amazon entering—and reshaping—the market by utilizing its data analytics capabilities and Amazon Web Services (AWS) platform. Similarly, as digitization is beginning to have a profound impact on even the most stable businesses, executives in other product industries also highlighted the risks of being overrun by software powerhouses. While many companies share these concerns, the threat is most imminent to those firms that lack service leadership and a clear road map for service growth.

## Internal motivations of the company

Several internal factors push companies to turn toward services as a growth vehicle and source of increased profitability. They can be categorized into three overall factors: exploiting existing product and technology expertise, capturing more value from customer relationships, and opening new market opportunities.

### Exploiting product and technology expertise

By exploiting their engineering and technology expertise, suppliers can provide new services that focus on restoring or improving the functionality of the product. A typical situation is a manufacturer having a high-performing product. Service, such as remote condition monitoring, becomes a strategic weapon to unlock the product's value; without it, the supplier is not able to charge extra for the value added. Similarly, Linde of Germany has successfully utilized its unique knowledge of how to apply industrial gas in the customers' processes to differentiate itself through innovative services, such as extending the durability of groceries or keeping the pH value constant in production plants' waste water. Acetylene, oxygen, hydrogen gas, and other industrial gasses are commonly regarded as commodities, so services are needed in order to be able to charge for the firm's knowledge and differentiate from product competitors, thereby creating a sustainable competitive advantage.

Several executives told us how their companies systematically design products in such a way that competitors are unable to properly service the equipment. They also try to incorporate service components early in the product innovation process in order to design products for the service market. While customers are no longer willing to spend extra money on an overengineered product, they are prepared to pay for hybrid offerings where the product, service, and software elements are seamlessly integrated to tap their full potential. As software costs account for an increasingly large part of the total development costs—in the case of products such as cars, it can be a majority of costs—even products that are typically seen as "dumb pieces of iron" are turning into smart digital devices. Ideally, the ability to analyze and interpret product usage and customer process data from the installed base of equipment can create a virtuous cycle with feedback loops to both product development and service operations, which become enhanced and mutually reinforced. Clearly, the growing digital transformation in many industries opens new avenues for monetizing data and analytics by providing new services and saving costs in delivery.

### Capturing customer relationship value

Service is also an imperative means to create and capture more value from relational assets; it helps to strengthen ties with customers and provides the opportunity to develop closer and longer-lasting customer relationships. By its very nature, service requires more and closer customer interaction, which facilitates connections at different organizational levels and helps the company acquire a better understanding of customers' operations, strategies, and organization (and those of the customers' customers). For example, a study of forty-four national subsidiaries of the multinational equipment manufacturer Atlas Copco showed that labor-intensive services such as maintenance, which imply higher levels of customer proximity, further enhanced product sales.[17] In addition, by the company offering a wider range—products, services, and hybrid offerings—customers have more incentive to pursue closer relationships. Consequently, the opportunities to become a more strategic business partner to customers increase.

To better understand the financial benefits associated with service growth, let us consider the concepts of lifetime value and customer equity:

- *The lifetime value of a customer* represents the net earnings the company makes from the customer throughout the course of the relationship. It can be measured by calculating the difference between annual profit streams and costs of retaining and developing the customer relationship.[18]
- *Customer equity* represents the sum of discounted lifetime values of the company's current and potential customers.[19]

From the company's point of view, services represent a tremendous opportunity to boost the lifetime value of its customer relationships and hence its customer equity. Being closer to clients not only helps to increase customer satisfaction but also to identify new service growth opportunities.

Following the principle that it is easier and more profitable to keep and develop existing customers than it is to acquire new ones, services represent a tremendous opportunity to not only protect existing product sales but also to capture a larger share of the customer's purchases, to amplify the company's presence with the customer, and to access new business opportunities for products. In assuming the responsibility for the management of industrial gas application processes at a customer plant, a leading supplier managed to become the sole supplier, gradually discarding the four other suppliers with whom the customer used to work. The services created extraordinary barriers to entry against competitors and served not only as protection against product competition but also to enable additional product sales. The following statement by the manager responsible for the customer account illustrates our point: "Our experience shows that the more we develop our service businesses with a customer, the more we become indispensable. Over time, the client trusts us, and it's almost as if we were married to him. This is a huge barrier to entry for other providers."

Services represent an excellent opportunity to realize substantial turnover during the entire product lifecycle, including installation, maintenance, repair, audit, retrofitting, and reconditioning. In many cases, there are also opportunities to develop services that are product independent, such as consulting services, and to conduct service on competing brands. In effect, services frequently represent an extraordinary weapon to be able to acquire new customers, which would be difficult to obtain through other means. If a supplier will take a service contract that assumes responsibility for a portfolio of multivendor products, it may slowly replace competitor equipment with its own products. Thus, services become a Trojan horse, as illustrated by this manager who works at a capital goods manufacturer: "If we can't go back to a client because of a product, we can go back for servicing competing brands. Through the quality of our service, we increase our chances of someday taking additional products. Service is a powerful way to develop a relationship with a client."

Third, services permit a business to stabilize, and even increase, cash flows over time. Particularly in industries sensitive to economic fluctuations, services can play a key role as stabilizers; customers who do not invest in new products nevertheless have to service the installed base and might even decide to upgrade it instead of buying new products later on. The truck manufacturer Scania, part of the Volkswagen Group and by many considered the "Rolls-Royce of trucks," is a case in point. During the global financial crisis of 2008–2010, sales plummeted, and the automotive industry was one of the industries most severely struck. While many firms hardly sold any new products during late 2008 and 2009, the service businesses often showed remarkable resistance. In addition, in the truck industry, many haulers went bankrupt or reduced their truck fleet in 2009 due to lower demand. Even so, Scania's service net sales declined by only 3 percent in 2009 and proved a slow but stable growth the coming years. Truck sales, on the other hand, plummeted by 41 percent in 2009 and did not fully recover until 2011 (see figure 1:2). Similar examples can be found in other industries; the service manager of a manufacturer of material-handling equipment told us how the service business of long-term leases had greatly helped to mitigate the decline in product sales during the latest recession.

**Figure 1:2**
**Scania's Truck and Service Sales 2007–2011**

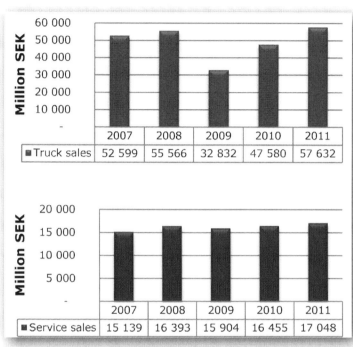

| | 2007 | 2008 | 2009 | 2010 | 2011 |
|---|---|---|---|---|---|
| ■ Truck sales | 52 599 | 55 566 | 32 832 | 47 580 | 57 632 |

| | 2007 | 2008 | 2009 | 2010 | 2011 |
|---|---|---|---|---|---|
| ■ Service sales | 15 139 | 16 393 | 15 904 | 16 455 | 17 048 |

Source: Scania 2007–2011 annual reports

### Opening new market opportunities

Finally, a company can get more value by venturing into entirely new service business models and becoming the architect of new value constellations. This opening of new market opportunities is the internal factor that has the most disruptive effects on the company and the rules of business in the industry. In launching innovative services and hybrid offerings, companies can create a lasting differentiating element that their competitors have a difficult time copying.

An example is British power systems provider Rolls-Royce's archetypal solution TotalCare, begun in 1997 with American Airlines, which transformed the aircraft engine services landscape. It is a sophisticated maintenance service concept based upon predictability and reliability across the lifecycle. Even if competitors like General Electric and Pratt & Whitney soon launched their own versions, Rolls-Royce's business model has proved hard to imitate. With a payment mechanism on a dollar per engine flying hourly basis, risks are transferred back to Rolls-Royce, and reliability becomes a profit driver for both the company and its customers.[20]

A more recent example of a novel value constellation for a pay-as-you-go model is Dutch technology company Philips's Light as a service model.[21] In 2015, the global leader in lighting solutions and Schiphol Group entered into a partnership for the new lighting in the terminal buildings at Amsterdam Airport Schiphol. Philips teamed up with €70 billion electric utility company Engie (formerly Cofely) to take joint responsibility for the performance of the system, which Schiphol pays for based on the light used. Under the new contract, Philips retains ownership of all the equipment, and Engie has round-the-clock presence at the airport to ensure optimal lightning. The model is in line with Schiphol's ambition "to become one of the most sustainable airports in the world," and Philips and Engie will also take responsibility for the reuse and recycling at end of life. As said by Jos Nijhuis, CEO and president of Schiphol Group, "Together we left the beaten path to develop an innovative, out-of-the-box solution."

## KEY QUESTIONS ABOUT THE SERVICE IMPERATIVE

At the end of each chapter, we present ten key questions that managers can ask to assess their companies' strengths and weaknesses in each of our key building blocks of a service-growth strategy. Answering the questions in all twelve chapters allows managers to gain a holistic view of their firms' current situations and lay the foundations of their service-growth strategies. In reviewing the service imperative presented in this chapter and the key drivers for service growth presented in figure 1:1, executives must ask themselves the following key questions:

1. What is our burning platform?
2. Is service a defensive strategy to protect the product business or a proactive weapon to actively tap new growth areas?
3. How is low-cost competition and commoditization affecting our product and service business?

4. How can we increase revenue and profit and stabilize cash flow through service?
5. How are changing customer needs and expectations affecting our business?
6. What are the main threats posed by our direct competitors (industry incumbents and emerging-market companies) and third parties, today and tomorrow?
7. What are the main threats posed by disruptive innovators outside the traditional industry boundaries?
8. How can we harness our engineering and technology expertise to build services around our products?
9. How can service help us to create and capture more value from our customer relationships?
10. How can new service business models provide opportunities for differentiation and potential rewriting of the rules of the business?

# CHAPTER 2

## B2B SERVICES: CHALLENGES AND CATEGORIES

*There are no such things as service industries. There are only industries whose service components are greater or less than those of other industries. Everybody is in service.*
—THEODORE LEVITT

In this chapter, we define more precisely what we mean by "service" and explain why many product-centric B2B companies often find it hard to achieve service growth in their respective markets. We will also see that what is commonly described as "B2B services" actually comprises very heterogeneous activities and offerings that require different resources and skills to succeed in the marketplace. Thus, we also provide a classification framework for business-to-business services. This frame represents the basis for a more thorough understanding of (1) which service(s) a company is already offering, (2) how it can develop new services and combine products and services in novel ways (this is what we refer to as "hybrid offerings"), and (3) which route a firm can take to grow its services portfolio over time. But let's first start by asking what we understand by "service."

## Business Service(s): What Do We Mean?

In a humorous manner, service has been described as "something that can be bought and sold but that cannot be dropped on your foot."[1] Although this definition is short and snappy, it is not really helpful as a guide for how to build the service business. Experts in service management have therefore tried to define service in more rigorous manners. For our topic of services in a business-to-business environment (in short, business services), we can consider that a service consists of leveraging a vendor's specialized knowledge and skills through activities, behaviors, and processes to bring about desired results in business customers' assets, processes, and operations.[2] In other words, B2B services, much like B2B goods, exist above all for the purpose of helping other organizations run their own operations and achieve their own business outcomes. For example, repairing a transformer will allow an industrial customer to keep a production unit running. Likewise, performing an energy-efficiency audit will enable a business customer to save costs in its own processes. This holds true for both goods and services in business markets. Yet the very nature of business services also implies a number of unique challenges for manufacturers moving from a product-centric to a service-led business model. This explains why service-growth strategies represent a culture shift not only in industrial companies but more broadly in all product-oriented companies, be it a manufacturer of industrial goods, a fast-moving consumer goods company, or a supply-chain specialist. We will emphasize the imperative for a culture change in chapter 3.

## Which Hurdles to Overcome for Service Growth?

Why do many product-centric companies struggle with growing their service business? In working with manufacturers, distributors, and professional services companies, we derived six major hurdles that these firms need to overcome (see figure 2:1).

**Figure 2:1**
**Main Hurdles That Product-Centric Firms Must Overcome**
**to Achieve Service Growth**

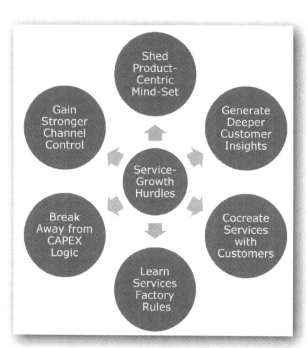

## Hurdle #1: Shed Your Product-Centric Mind-set

From working over many years with companies in diverse markets, we have noticed, time and again, that companies struggling with lifting their services strategy off the ground are those firms that are too inward-looking, production-focused, and overly reliant on differentiation through technology. Product-centric companies spend most of their efforts on marketing and selling what they have. The emphasis on attributes and features is often deeply embedded in the company. As one manager explained, "Deep down in our heart, we are a manufacturing company. We produce stuff. We move boxes. It's our DNA." Many companies we frequently work with are deeply entrenched in capital-intensive industries. Operations are set up for effectiveness and efficiency. The comfort zone of such companies is defined by sourcing supplies, leveraging R&D for product innovation, manufacturing goods, and mastering the supply chain—efficiently and effectively. Product quality control is often pushed to its limits to ensure that every single product leaving the factory is flawless. To no surprise, we have often encountered sales organizations in such companies that excel in "selling features," focusing on technical characteristics and product superiority.

Services typically turn these factors upside down, which explains why so many product companies feel very uncomfortable when it comes to accelerating service growth. First, services are, by definition, intangible. They are hard to specify, produce, market, and sell. It is often much easier to add, change, or eliminate a service element than it is to change a product feature. In almost no time, competitors can step in and differentiate a service by tweaking a service feature or enhancing an element.

Second, in services, the focus of attention shifts decisively toward outcomes achieved. Because customers often find it much harder in a service context to visualize what is actually being sold, they also wrestle with assessing performance and benchmarking one service supplier against another.

In many cases, customers come to rely on the experience that can only be evaluated after a contract is signed and a service is implemented, such as an energy-efficiency audit of a factory. In other situations, customers find it difficult to assess the outcome even after the delivery of the service, as in the case of training senior executives, which requires a customer's trust in an executive education provider's ability to deliver what has been promised. Hence, image and reputation of the institution that sells the training take on important roles in selling such services. In short, we see that the nature of service makes the process of understanding, quantifying, and communicating outcomes achieved and value provided to customers much more difficult.

Trust alone often does not suffice for selling business services. In order to overcome customers' concerns, companies need to persuasively demonstrate a service's value-creation potential. This becomes even more important when approaching key decision makers at different levels of a customer's hierarchy, such as financial directors and senior executives who do not necessarily have detailed knowledge of their firms operating processes. Therefore, Fortum of Finland—a leading North European generator and distributor of electricity and heat—has crafted a compelling service value proposition with these decision makers specifically in mind. The service, Ecotuning, is a year-long overhaul of a power plant's operational economy. Fortum guarantees that the energy efficiency will achieve a savings or revenue gain (e.g., €500,000) during the review period; if not, the company will refund the service cost (e.g., €150,000).

A third challenge in this domain relates to pricing business services. Service pricing's role is to ensure that a vendor captures a fair share of value created. In a product world, customers can test-run equipment, dissect a machine, evaluate costs of individual components, and measure cost savings and/or productivity gains in their processes—with (or without) the help of a supplier. This proves to be much more complicated in a services setting. For example, tool manufacturers today move from selling individual tools to marketing availability and promising performance outcomes of entire tool fleets on construction sites. How should such an offer be priced? What is a fair price both from a customer and a supplier perspective? What levels of risks are involved on both sides? Should the price for such a service be cost-based or value-based? Should it be subscription-based or grounded in a pay-as-you-go model? The change from selling individual tools at a fixed price to selling an available stock of ready-to-use tools makes assessment, communication, and determination of value through price particularly precarious. While companies often navigate in safer waters when it comes to pricing goods, setting prices for business services often prove to be way more challenging.

## Hurdle #2: Generate Deeper Customer Insights

"We don't know which services really matter to our customers." This is a sentence often heard in companies with very limited services sales and basic service offerings. From analyzing service portfolios and working with companies to help them increase their service revenues over time, we found that lack of customer insights and involvement in service development, design, and delivery count among the main roadblocks to service growth. Many goods-centric companies tend to underestimate the need for generating unique customer data and insights to fuel service innovation and growth. The way such "inside-out" focused firms use, for example, segmentation illustrates well a lack of customer intimacy. Many firms today still prefer segmenting markets by product characteristics, or by industry applications, rather than using value-based segmentation or customers' willingness to pay for deeper insights. Likewise, many firms don't differentiate at all between product- and service-segmentation schemes. Finally, they typically underinvest in services market research. In one company we worked with, service sales only took off once it had recruited a marketing director, in addition to its sales vice president. As services sales gained traction, the manufacturer created the role of a services marketing manager, under the wing of the marketing director, which allowed the company to better understand customers' services needs and grow its portfolio of services offerings.

## Hurdle #3: Cocreate Services with Customers

Business services typically not only require deep customer insights, but they also rely on active customer involvement or even cocreation during the service-design and delivery process. Many services provided in a business environment cannot be sourced off the shelf; they require customer actions. Active customer involvement is most visible when customers and suppliers jointly develop, integrate, and roll out complex services such as customer solutions. For example, when tire manufacturer Michelin provides management of professional tires on a fleet of thousands of trucks and trailers, client and vendor must closely cooperate to bring the service to life. Both parties establish a dedicated team, composed of members from both the supplier and the customer organizations, to define the content and monitor the execution of a fleet management offering. Key performance indicators need to be defined and agreed upon; drivers must be trained and incentivized to operate trucks in the most efficient and effective way. In short, goals and activities of both parties must be aligned to bring such a complex service contract to fruition.

Most business services imply some level of customer participation. Even a straightforward service, such as routine machine maintenance, includes regular meetings and might involve regular interactions with customer staff on an operational level. Even though many processes may be automated or performed without direct human interaction, thanks to digitization, customer and supplier interact with each other's equipment, facilities, and systems throughout the service production process.

While interaction enables stronger relationships and deeper customer insights, active involvement of customers may also pose challenges; it can create uncertainty for the provider as the customer is more difficult to control than internal employees. Inadequate knowledge and skills, lack of motivation, or poor task execution by customers may hurt productivity and curtail service quality and value derived. It therefore becomes important to develop user-friendly products and systems, train customers to perform effectively, and provide customer support.[3]

## Hurdle #4: Learn the Rules of a Service Factory

Increased customer involvement and cocreation lead to another hurdle. Letting customers participate in the process typically does not resonate well with the need for standardization of products and processes, economies of scale, productivity, quality control, and cost containment— the buzzwords in every manufacturing-oriented, product-centric firm. Before any product leaves the factory floor, it must pass through multiple quality checks and controls. In this manufacturing logic, customers are generally not involved—neither in producing nor controlling the quality and cost of a service.

In services, there is also a need for a factory logic, but service-factory thinking works differently. Customers' active roles in service processes may become a disturbing factor for smooth operations. Design and deployment of services—often locally and close to the customer—make it more difficult to standardize and control the quality of operations. Frequently, there is a tradeoff between customer satisfaction (that is, giving customers all they want) and service productivity (such as ensuring that service delivery costs won't go through the roof). Compared to products, there is a larger risk that things go wrong in the service production and delivery processes; service quality may differ between local markets, from one frontline service technician to the other, due to customers' staff and behaviors, and even from one time of day to another. As the CEO of PetSmart put it, "I assure you, as you move up the trust chain, the penalty for disappointing people on a service is more severe than the penalty for disappointing people on a product."[4] Clearly, many product-centric companies feel very uncomfortable with the idea of having to hire hundreds, if not thousands, of service employees who create services for (and with) customers.

Business services also require standardization of processes and quality and cost control. But the service factory looks and feels different than the production plant that manufacturers are generally familiar with. Successful services firms reduce variability of services by also adopting standardized procedures, implementing rigorous management of service quality, training employees, and automating tasks previously performed by employees. They ensure that employees are trained in service recovery procedures in case things go wrong.[5] In short, they take a production approach to services. Yet the way it is done differs from a manufacturing culture. Consider the example of Thales Group, a world leader in critical information systems in aeronautics, space, security, and defense. The company not only sells a complex portfolio of products and systems, but it also experiences strong growth in services and customer solutions. For example, Thales's in-flight entertainment solutions increasingly appeal to international airlines and their customers. Commercial success in this growing market requires outstanding products and an ability to adapt systems to the needs of each individual airline. But the company found that product excellence did not suffice. To guarantee outcomes obtained (such as keeping video screens up and running on every single flight) rather than quality products installed, it needed to put in place a demanding global service delivery system. In the early stages of deployment, this proved more costly than anticipated. To ensure that each airline was satisfied and to maintain profit margins of solutions deployed, Thales had to learn how to strike the right balance between customization of airline offerings and standardization of the entire service delivery process.

Finally, in business services, customers are often active contributors to quality achieved. The way customer staff behaves in the service production and delivery process greatly affects service quality and delivery costs. For example, the way a worker uses a tool on a construction site can make or break the profitability of a tool management contract. Keep in mind that customer roles in services not only include user, buyer, and payer of a service but also a designer and quality controller of a service provided.

## Hurdle #5: Break Away from a CAPEX Logic

Today, many business customers still want to own a forklift truck or purchase ball bearings. In the oil and gas industry, the rule of the game still is that customers buy steel pipes and manage their own inventories. Likewise, mining companies have been used for decades to source mining equipment. Hence, professional buyers in the mining industries have been used forever to send out tenders and pitch equipment manufacturers against each other. In short, many companies' prevailing sourcing logic is still deeply embedded in a capital expenditure (CAPEX) mind-set; a firm invests in or upgrades physical assets such as industrial buildings, equipment, or consumables.

However, from a rational business point of view, owning assets often makes no sense. The very nature of B2B means that professional buyers only source goods for the sake of running a process or achieving an outcome in their own operations. If that process or outcome can be achieved in a different manner, customers will stop buying the product. Customers can obtain benefits and outcomes without investing in goods, for example by gaining the right to use an equipment, hire an expert, or obtain access to facilities and networks only when needed. Enabling customers to rent or lease—in the form of access or usage fees—instead of buying the product thereby allows new market opportunities.[6] For example, Vallourec, the seamless steel tube manufacturer we worked with on service growth for capturing more value in business markets, began to explore selling new commercial offers built around renting steel tubes and managing inventories on behalf of customers. Likewise, one earth-moving machine manufacturer we interviewed started to sell "tons of iron ore excavated" rather than number of machines sold. In healthcare, General Electric was among the first to promote leasing of MRI scanners rather than investing in expensive equipment. Today, leasing medical devices has become commonplace.

Such shifts reflect the transition from the above-mentioned CAPEX logic to an emphasis on operational expenditure (OPEX). Operational expenditures are those expenditures that are required for the day-to-day functioning of the business. Hence, when a customer switches from buying an industrial printer to a full-service contract, paying for printing labels in a food-processing plant, it effectively moves its perspective from a CAPEX to an OPEX expenditure, thus freeing up capital for investments needed elsewhere, increasing flexibility, and oftentimes reducing costs. This is an offer that Markem-Imaje, one of the companies we worked with, successfully promoted to industrial customers.

Seizing these market opportunities is seldom plain sailing. As we will see in chapter 10, this logic requires a different sales approach. Selling services instead of products means that the company has to approach different decision makers in the customer organization and understand the operational processes and costs of a customer in depth. This shift may even lead to selling fewer products. For example, in one case we studied, Caterpillar, a global leader in earth-moving products, ended up selling fewer earth-moving machines than initially planned. The customer specified a certain amount of required machines in the tender it sent to potential suppliers. While all competitors diligently responded to the tender specifications, Caterpillar proposed to sell a solution based on volumes of iron ore moved. Ultimately, Caterpillar won the customer's business by effectively demonstrating that it could get the job done with fewer machines than the customer had planned for. The potential to cannibalize existing product business is likely to meet with fierce resistance internally—hence, the need for management to anticipate possible conflicts and proactively steer the change process (see chapter 6).

## Hurdle #6: Gain Stronger Channel Control

Industrial companies often rely on channel partners for distribution and after-sales services of goods sold. Yet when moving beyond their traditional product core, firms often find that their current channel structures obstruct service revenue growth. Thus, firms are often challenged to rethink their distribution channels. In the process, they typically tighten the control of what happens in the channel (such as stronger control and coordination), or they directly invest in the channel (in that they shorten the channel by buying out distributors or developing their own distribution outlets).

Why are control and channel length important factors? Industrial services cannot be put on a shelf. In addition, they mostly are performed locally, such as an on-site repair of an offset printing press. Finally, demand typically greatly varies over time—a permanent headache for service organizations.

Against this backdrop, two specific hurdles are worth mentioning in a channel context. First, in many industries, large-sized distributors already take on a key role in serving customers once a supplier's equipment or component rolls out the factory door. Empire Southwest, for example, ranks among the top Caterpillar dealers in the world. The company has more than sixteen hundred employees in a territory that includes the state of Arizona, southeastern California, and portions of northern Mexico.[7] Services are at the very heart of Empire Southwest's business model. The distributor heavily relies on selling services and customer solutions as a significant part of its business. Likewise, Avnet serves as one of the world's largest global distributors of electronic components, computer and IT solutions, and embedded technology and services. With revenues of $27.9 billion in 2015, this supply-chain specialist connects eight hundred suppliers with more than a hundred thousand customers annually, shipping more than thirty thousand line items per day.[8]

Beyond sheer size of channel intermediaries, a second hurdle refers to the number of intermediaries in the overall channel. It is not uncommon to see multiple actors intervene between a manufacturer and a final business customer. Wholesalers, agents, distributors, and dealers all form a long channel. Each intermediary performs a multitude of services. This inevitably raises questions over the division of roles between intermediaries and suppliers. Distributors often consider services as an additional revenue source, jealously protecting the relationship with their customers (and their margins). For example, in the cable industry, a host of small- and medium-sized distributors perform a multitude of services from bulk breaking, cable cutting, and subassembling cable bundles to delivery of entire subsystems. Global cable manufacturer Nexans found it hard to break into distributors' natural home turf when growing its services revenues. Another concern refers to the resources and skills of channel intermediaries themselves. Distributors can be overly product-centric themselves, lacking both competence and commitment to accompanying a manufacturer on its move into services.

Lack of skills can become particularly harmful in the domain of demanding service offerings based on data and analytics, such as remote monitoring of sophisticated equipment and systems. In such situations, companies may even find themselves obliged to bypass distributors and perform these complex services themselves. For example, German Linde Material Handling, a global leader of material-handling equipment selling prestigious brands such as Fenwick and Linde, initially pursued two very different channel strategies in two European countries. Over more than ten years, Fenwick had continuously invested in strongly controlling its distribution channel. As a result, it acquired selected distributors and created its own in-house distribution network. In Germany, on the other hand, the group took a different trajectory. In this country with a strong industrial culture, Linde concentrated itself on the design, production, and sale of forklifts and warehouse trucks, granting a much bigger role to distributors in selling value-added service. Over time, the breadth and depth of the service portfolio and share of services in overall sales appeared to be greatly superior in France compared to Germany. This can largely be explained by these strategic channel choices. We will return to this point in chapter 12.

In summary, the major hurdles we discussed in this chapter should not draw an artificial divide with products on one side and services on the other. In reality, the border between the worlds is much thinner than one might believe, which goes back to Theodore Levitt's (1972) claim that "everybody is in service."[9] In addition, firms seldom provide single products and services only. Instead, they combine both into innovative, integrated offerings. In reality, companies provide a host of very different offerings that all fall under the denomination of industrial services. Hence, there is a need for clarifying the similarities and differences among these activities.

## B2B Services: Four Main Categories

Managers often mistakenly view B2B services as a homogeneous set of offerings and activities. Yet they greatly vary in terms of underlying characteristics, key success factors required, and resources and competencies needed before a supplier should even think of launching such offerings in the market. When discussing service-led growth, we therefore need to understand which types of services a firm can develop and how it should grow these services over time in a systematic manner. To provide a more granular discussion of how to understand service and what service infusion options the firm has at hand, we need a classification framework. Our proposed classification of B2B services, which has been used by companies we worked with for analyzing and growing their services portfolio, is based on two distinct dimensions:

- **Who is the service recipient?** Is the service oriented toward the supplier's product—focusing on restoring or improving the functionality of the product through services (such as repair and maintenance), or is the service directed at the customer's activities and processes (such as tire management for a logistics company or managing a payroll process)?
- **What is the nature of the value proposition?** A service provider can fundamentally make very different promises. Is the vendor's value proposition grounded in the promise to *perform a deed* (input-based)? Or, in contrast, does the company promise to achieve a level of performance (output-based)? When services are sold on an input basis, such as express delivery of components, customers are generally invoiced for time and material, whereas the revenue models of output-based services revolve around availability or results.

In combining these two dimensions, we derive four categories of offerings that differ fundamentally in the key resources and capabilities needed for a successful market rollout. All four categories imply very different combinations of goods and services—that is, hybrid market offerings. When designing a service-growth strategy, companies not only need to think through the success factors needed in each category. They also must decide which of these types they want to develop and draw a road map visualizing how they want to grow in these categories over time (see figure 2:2).

Figure 2:2
The B2B Service Classification Framework

| | Service Oriented toward the Supplier's Good | Service Oriented toward the Customer's Process |
|---|---|---|
| **Promise to Achieve Performance ("Outputs")** | **2. Asset Efficiency Services (AES)**<br>Services to achieve productivity gains from assets invested by customers<br><br>Examples:<br>- Remote monitoring of a high-voltage circuit breaker<br>- On-site preventative maintenance on a ball bearing<br>- Online software retrofitting of a banknote printing system<br>- Uptime guarantee on a pump in a nuclear power plant | **4. Process Delegation Services (PDS)**<br>Services to perform processes on behalf of the customers<br><br>Examples:<br>- Tire fleet management for a global logistics and supply chain expert<br>- Operating of paint shop in a car manufacturing plant<br>- Total gas and chemicals supply sourcing for a semiconductor plant<br>- Fly-by-the-hour agreement for commercial jet engines |
| **Promise to Perform a Deed ("Inputs")** | **1. Product Lifecycle Services (PLS)**<br>Services to facilitate access to and proper functioning of a product throughout the lifecycle<br><br>Examples:<br>- Delivery of industrial cables<br>- Calibration of a gas chromatograph<br>- Inspection of an ATM<br>- Installation of a power transformer<br>- Regrooving of a truck tire | **3. Process Support Services (PSS)**<br>Services to assist customers in improving their own business processes<br><br>Examples:<br>- Diagnostics of a welding process<br>- Energy-efficiency audit of a store<br>- Warehouse material flow assessment<br>- Training on new safety regulations<br>- Consulting to achieve cost reductions |

**Nature of the Value Proposition** (vertical axis label)

**Service Recipient** (horizontal axis label)

Source: Adapted from Ulaga and Reinartz (2011), p. 17

## Product Lifecycle Services (PLS)

In order to sell products to business customers, most companies have to offer at least a basic set of core services. Thus, by definition, any manufacturer can be considered to be in the service business without necessarily having the ambition to use services as a vehicle for growth or source of profitability. Product lifecycle services (PLS) refer to the range of services that facilitate the customer's access to the manufacturer's goods and ensure its proper functioning during all stages of its lifecycle, whether before, during, or after its sale, such as the delivery of industrial cables to a customer's construction site, installation of a high-voltage circuit breaker, inspection of an ATM, or recycling of a power transformer. These services are directly attached to goods, so the value proposition derives from the most generic definition of service: a promise to perform a deed on behalf of the customer. For example, if a coolant pump at a nuclear power plant breaks down, the equipment manufacturer promises to repair the defective pump within a contractually agreed-upon time frame.

Customers often perceive PLS as "must haves" and, therefore, may express low willingness to pay for such services. What is more, they may find it hard to differentiate a PLS of one supplier from the same service provided by a competitor. But PLS play a key role beyond merely enabling product sales. They are critical in establishing the vendor's reputation as a competent service provider. PLS build trust—a prerequisite for expanding into adjacent, value-added service categories. Thus, these characteristics have important implications for pricing PLS. Suppliers are often tempted to give away PLS for free to secure equipment sales or simply invoice customers for time and material, according to a "break it, fix it" logic. To escape tedious pricing discussions with customers around PLS, firms resort to bundling goods and services, thus hiding the service component within an "all-inclusive" offer. These are nonoptimal ways of addressing PLS. Whenever possible, managers should differentiate their offer by providing different levels of a PLS. Or vendors can outsmart competitors by providing the same level of a PLS at a lower cost than competition. This can be achieved by standardizing PLS more effectively and efficiently. Leveraging innovative technologies and tools, such as remote diagnostics, can help here.

How can firms grow beyond these fundamental services? One path of development is to evolve toward services that aim at helping customers gain more return on investments in assets made. While PLS facilitate customers' access to a product and ensure its proper functioning, this second category of services includes all offerings to assist the client in improving asset productivity.

## Asset Efficiency Services (AES)

How to differentiate from competition and grow beyond generic PLS? One way to venture into new service offerings is to change the customer promise. For example, instead of promising a customer to repair a machine once it breaks down, a manufacturer can now guarantee machine uptime. Asset efficiency services (AES) are services a supplier provides to help customers achieve productivity gains from investments made into assets. These services are still designed around a specific product sold; however, the value proposition now focuses on achieving a specified level of performance or outcome gained in using that product. AES include such services as predictive maintenance of ball bearings, on-site condition monitoring of an offset printing press, or remote monitoring of an industrial transformer.

Similar to PLS, AES are still attached to a supplier's product. For example, Siemens, a manufacturer of MRI scanners, proposes AES for its own medical equipment. Yet AES differ from PLS in at least two ways. First, when venturing into AES, firms fundamentally change their value proposition. With PLS, a vendor promises to perform a deed (e.g., "We fix the in-flight entertainment system in your aircraft when it breaks"). But with AES, the customer promise goes one step further, and the supplier commits to performance outcomes achieved (e.g., "We guarantee availability of 99.5 percent of video screens up and running in an aircraft"). This difference has important consequences in terms of resources and competencies needed to design, sell, and deploy such services (see chapter 5). For example, to sell AES successfully, companies must be able to collect unique customer usage data and develop distinctive risk mitigation skills. Second, unlike PLS, AES are typically not considered "must haves." They rather represent a source of differentiation. For example, power utilities increasingly view high-voltage circuit breakers as plain commodity products. Hence, by adding a remote monitoring service, a supplier can find a way to enhance its core offering (that is, the "naked" product) and set itself apart from competition by selling a value-added service. Customers generally understand that AES reach beyond enabling an equipment's basic functioning. They acknowledge more easily that AES are sold separately from a vendor's core offering. Customers therefore often express a higher willingness to pay for AES under the condition that a supplier can persuasively communicate the benefits of productivity gains in a proactive manner. There are two important concepts to be considered with regards to proactivity. *Proactive prevention* refers to "a supplier proactively initiating efforts to detect problems that may be imminent for a customer and taking action to avert them." *Proactive education*, in turn, refers to "a supplier initiating effort to educate customers on how they can derive greater utility from its products."[10] Many AES draw on these proactive supplier behaviors. When customers understand benefits gained from AES, suppliers are in a much better position for price negotiations. To no surprise, firms thus often shift from cost-based to value-based pricing techniques in their move from PLS to AES.

## Product Support Services (PSS)

The two previous categories focused on services attached to a supplier's product. But firms can also develop their overall portfolio by growing into services directly geared toward their customers' processes. We thus define process support services (PSS) as the range of services a company provides to assist customers in improving their own business processes. PSS focus on the customer's processes, not the manufacturer's product, and include services such as auditing the welding process in a customer's automotive plant or performing an energy-efficiency audit, designed to improve electricity consumption in a customer's retail store. For example, Schneider Electric of France, a global specialist in energy management, can provide expertise in the field of energy management in commercial buildings. By capturing and analyzing data from instruments installed in the customer's premises that measure energy consumption, the company has a distinct competitive advantage over third parties or power utilities when commercializing such consulting services.

Although firms may prefer to provide PSS in conjunction with their own products, suppliers often develop PSS regardless of the underlying equipment. For example, a forklift truck manufacturer may offer warehouse optimization and logistics consulting to a customer without selling its own material-handling equipment to that client. Thus, in PSS, the value proposition focuses on leveraging the supplier's unique resources and distinctive competencies to help customers optimize their own processes or specific elements thereof. In other words, suppliers commit to perform specific, process-oriented deeds to assist customers in what they have to do. However, they will not take responsibility for outcomes achieved from customer processes, nor will they conduct the processes on their behalf. For instance, when analyzing welding processes in a customer's automotive plant, a supplier of industrial gases can ask its global welding expert (a unique resource) to use his or her process application skills (a distinctive competency) to assess the customer's process and make recommendations for improving the quality of welded products and for reducing production costs. However, the automotive customer still remains solely in charge of performing the welding process and whether to implement suggested process changes or not.

PSS are typically tailored to customer-specific contexts and needs. These offerings have a strong potential to differentiate a supplier in the market. For example, while industrial gasses (such as azote, hydrogen, or oxygen) may be considered as pure commodities, global supplier Air Liquide combines its unique expertise of industrial gasses with deep knowledge of customers to innovate process steps (such as using gasses for packaging frozen pizzas in a food-processing plant). This effectively sets the firm apart from most competitors. In such situations, customers' willingness to pay for services tends to be high. In general, PSS are priced similar to professional services: vendors typically bill customers according to the time and resources mobilized to provide the service, much like per diem rates in a consulting firm or training days charged in an educational context. Success fees for this category of industrial services exist, but they are still rare.

## Process Delegation Services (PDS)

Finally, across markets, firms are increasingly interested in venturing into a fourth category of offerings. We define process delegation services (PDS) as combinations of goods and activities that a supplier integrates in order to perform processes on behalf of customers. These types of offerings are typically referred to as customer solutions. Solutions can be small in scope, such as printing labels in a food-processing plant.

But they can also refer to complex end-to-end processes, such as those involved in signing a fly-by-the-hour agreement for commercial jet engines. Examples of PDS are fleet management of professional tires on behalf of a trucking company, total gas-supply management for a semiconductor plant, or document management for an industrial company. PDS are directed at a customer's process. But unlike input-based PSS, in which customers remain in control, suppliers go one step further in PDS. The value proposition is focused on the promise to achieve process performance (a process outcome). Suppliers that offer PDS take charge of and control the processes together with, or on behalf of, their customers. Thus, this category captures the most complex type of combinations of goods and services. Not surprisingly then, true PDS remain limited in many markets and often are only provided by the market leaders.

Overall, we consider six defining aspects of PDS (see figure 2:3). First, suppliers typically integrate goods and service elements into complex hybrid PDS offerings. Second, PDS are highly customized to address customers' specific requirements. Third, agreements in this category require a high level of customer involvement, ranging from information sharing to active cocreation, adaptation, and joint implementation of the PDS agreement. Fourth, and as a consequence, the interests of both parties are strongly aligned in PDS. For example, in Michelin's fleet management solution, the customer's truck drivers must be trained and incentivized to avoid burning rubber on the road, which would reduce contract profitability from the supplier's perspective.

Fifth, in PDS agreements, customers require that a supplier assumes some level (or all) of the process outcome risk. Risk transfer represents one of the main motivations for customers to enter into such complex agreements. Sixth, in line with the notion of risk transfer, PDS frequently involve complex gain-sharing agreements. Firms have to develop, in cooperation with their customers, entirely new sets of key performance indicators that serve as the basis for pricing PDS. To succeed in PDS, companies must master these key factors and develop the resources and skills needed. Thus, many companies today still hesitate to grow into this area as they feel that they are not yet ready to make the move.

In chapter 5, we will return to these four service categories and discuss how the framework presented here can be used to develop the

Figure 2:3
**Key Characteristics of Process Delegation Services (Solutions)**

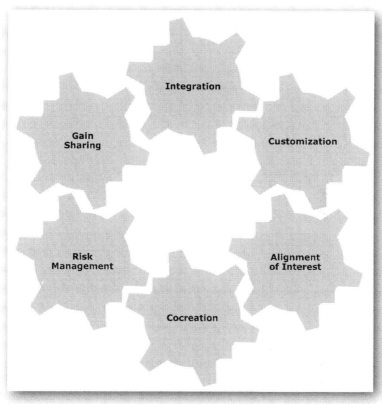

Source: Adapted from Ulaga and Reinartz (2011)

firm's service portfolio, analyze the resources and capabilities needed to succeed in each category, and define a road map for service growth.

## KEY QUESTIONS ABOUT HURDLES TO SERVICE GROWTH AND SERVICES ALREADY PROVIDED BY YOUR COMPANY

Managers must be cognizant of barriers to service growth inside their organizations. They must further understand which types of services their companies already offer to customers. In reviewing both internal hurdles to service growth and the nature of services already provided by their firm, managers must ask themselves the following fundamental questions:

1. To what extent is our company still dominated by a product-centric mind-set?
2. How deep are our insights of customers' business models, operations, and key performance indicators?
3. To what extent do we involve customers on our service development, design, and implementation processes? Do we cocreate services with customers?
4. Do we know what it takes to operate a lean service factory?
5. Are we still locked in a CAPEX logic?
6. Is our current channel structure helping or hurting service growth?
7. Do we give many product lifecycle services (PLS) away for free? Are they very profitable in our business?
8. Do asset efficiency services (AES) already represent a significant portion of our service business?
9. How important are process support services (PSS) today in our overall service revenues and profits?
10. Do we see opportunities for developing process delegation services (PDS)—that is, true customer solutions?

# CHAPTER 3

## BUILDING A TRUE SERVICE CULTURE: KEY MILESTONES

*In the old days, we had a bicycle shop mentality.*
*We sat and waited for customers to come*
*to us for placing an order*
*when they experienced a problem or needed a spare part.*
*We had to change this and become more*
*sales and services driven.*[1]
—OLIVER RIEMENSCHNEIDER, PRESIDENT OF ABB TURBOCHARGING

In the previous chapter, we defined what we mean by service. We also discussed the major roadblocks companies face when embarking on the road to service growth. Without a sound understanding of these roadblocks, their origin, and how to overcome them, service-growth strategies are doomed to fail. We finally saw that the notion of service actually covers a broad set of very different activities. Hence, we introduce a framework to understand fundamental similarities and differences across four categories of B2B services. In this chapter, we will turn to a challenging task for many product-centric companies: how to nurture a service culture. In working with many companies, we have seen over the years that a strong service culture serves as a powerful enabler of successful service growth.

First, we define what we mean by service culture and highlight the differences between product-centric and service-centric firms. Next, we identify four critical milestones on the transformation journey from a product-centric to a truly service-oriented company. Finally, we summarize our key ideas about instilling a service culture and igniting service growth by reviewing what we call the *seven deadly sins of service-myopic firms*, a synthesis of our experience gained in working over many years to navigate the cultural transition and build a service-centric organization.

## What Is a Service Culture in a B2B Firm?

Steering the service transition requires a major cultural shift, and companies therefore need to understand how a service culture deviates from a product-centric culture. A strong organizational culture guides employees' behavior, enables them to act in a certain, consistent manner, and facilitates the assimilation of new employees into the prevailing culture.

In our context, corporate culture can make or break a firm's ambition for achieving service growth. Service businesses are people businesses. Customer interactions are key. Attitudes and behaviors of frontline employees profoundly affect a company's top- and bottom-line results. Therefore, companies moving into services beyond their traditional product core must address a paradox: while a strong manufacturing expertise and product heritage often represent a sound base for developing value-added services, the very same organizational culture may also prove to become a company's barrier to change. Before we further elaborate on this apparent conflict, let us clarify what we mean by the notions of organizational culture and service culture:

- *Organizational culture* is a pattern of shared values and beliefs that give the members of an organization meaning and provide them with the rules for behavior in the organization.[2]
- *Service culture* is a culture where an appreciation for good service exists and where giving good service to internal as well as ultimate, external customers is considered by everyone a natural way of life and one of the most important values.[3]

Corporate culture is a result of the firm's organizational past. An organization with strong shared values often has three common characteristics:

- The shared values are a clear guidance for task performance.
- Managers devote much of their time to developing and reinforcing the shared values.
- The shared values are deeply anchored among the employees.[4]

Product firms usually have strong cultures based on a proud engineering heritage. The shared product-centric values and beliefs serve the firms well when striving for manufacturing excellence and product leadership. In situations where the environment has changed and service growth is required for long-term competitive advantage, however, such culture may inhibit the changes needed to adapt and prosper. Established engineering-driven firms often are unwilling to deviate from their prevailing product-centric practices, norms, and values until they are faced with a burning platform. Managers may also be reluctant to abandon investments made in manufacturing assets, or they may refuse to steer R&D efforts away from products to accelerate service innovation. Furthermore, strong shared values may become a problem for the following reasons:

- The shared values may have become *obsolete* and are therefore not consistent with current strategies and service ambitions.
- Strong shared values may lead to *resistance to change*, which makes it difficult for the organization to respond to external challenges and seize service-related market opportunities.
- New employees are formed by existing values, and in situations where the culture needs to be changed, differently thinking newcomers are easily *swallowed* by the existing culture.[5]

## Service Culture Transcends Delivering Service

The true meaning of a service culture reaches beyond a company's commitment to providing service. Service culture touches upon the very values, beliefs, and norms that permeate the organization. Simply adding ancillary service offerings to the core product portfolio does not change the manufacturing mind-set of a firm. Unless the firm can attract service-minded people and nurture a service culture, a service transformation initiative will most likely fail. Just think about pure-service firms with whom you have had a bad experience, either as consumer or in your profession. Just because the firm provides service, it does not mean that service quality and service excellence are the guiding norms. In fact, many service firms have a product-centric mind-set with no genuine interest in the customers after the sale. Nevertheless, as former chairperson and CEO of PetSmart, Philip L. Francis, pointed out, offering service implies moving up the trust chain, which means that the penalties for failing become much higher. Because customers are merciless with suppliers that cause them problems by failing to deliver service, any service initiative needs to go hand in hand with the development of a service culture.

## Service-Centric Firms Are Different

In table 3:1, we contrast key characteristics of product-centric firms with those of service-centric ones. Service-centric firms are inherently customer-oriented, which means that the basic philosophy is to serve customers rather than sell products. As illustrated, such service-centricity is fundamentally different from a traditional, product-centric culture. Therefore, it is no surprise that the instilling service-centric values and norms can meet with internal resistance in firms in which product centricity prevails.

While a service culture is needed for successful service growth, managers should not throw the baby out with the bathwater. To master a service-growth strategy, companies must build on their product heritage and culture and learn how to integrate the virtues of a service culture. It is management's responsibility to implement the needed cultural change. Instilling a service culture does not have to be a radical change. If the company is doing well, it is critical to maintain carefully nurtured values that brought success and integrate these values with new ones. Consider the example of aircraft engine manufacturer Rolls-Royce. A focus on cost control and manufacturing efficiency improvements is deeply rooted in the company's DNA. Rolls-Royce realized that its world-class products actually became problematic for the traditional after-sales services model. Its engines required too little service in comparison with competition, which affected revenues negatively. Yet its relentless

Table 3:1
**Key Differences between Product-Centric and Service-Centric Companies**

|  | **Product-Centric Firm** | **Service-Centric Firm** |
|---|---|---|
| Overall Goal | Move Boxes | Serve Customers |
| Source of Differentiation | Superior Product Features; Product Quality, Standardized Manufacturing Processes | Superior Customer Experience, Service Quality; Standardized Service Processes |
| Value Creation Perspective | Value Stacking: Value creation is sequential and unidirectional. Value Chain Logic. | Value Cocreation: Value is created in collaboration with customers. Value Constellation Logic. |
| Buyer-Seller Interaction | Transaction-Oriented: Sales focuses on closing deals. | Relationship-Oriented: Sales focuses on growing the pie. |
| Mental Model | Divergent Thinking: *How many possible uses can we find for this product?* | Convergent Thinking: *What combination of offerings is best for this customer?* |
| Organizational Focus and Structures | Internally Focused— Built around Products: Product profit centers, product managers, product sales teams. Sales and marketing "own" the customer. | Externally Focused— Built around Customers: Market/segment profit centers, customer account managers, customer teams. Everybody "owns" the customer. |
| Performance Metrics | Portfolio of Products: Product innovation, product profitability, market share by product/brand | Portfolio of Customers: Share of wallet, customer satisfaction and loyalty, customer equity/lifetime value |
| Strategic Assets | Emphasis on Tangibles: Equipment, inventories, factories, etc. | Emphasis on Intangibles: People, brands, and intellectual property |

Source: Adapted from Bowen et al. (1989); Galbraith
(2002) p. 196; Shah et al. (2006), p. 115

emphasis on product quality and costs also opened entire new opportunities for service growth. Rolls-Royce recognized that its jet engines could serve as a platform for process-delegation services. The supplier leveraged its product leadership position to venture into new output-based power-by-the-hour service agreements with commercial airlines.

As seen in table 3:1, service culture is firmly related to concepts such as customer-centricity, customer intimacy, and customer orientation. Yet it transcends these notions and requires additional expertise and skills. Service culture emphasizes factors such as service quality and proactivity. Many companies still look at customers only through the lenses of existing products, aiming at trying to sell customers more of what they already make rather than focusing on helping customers in getting their jobs done. For instance, at one point in time, financial services company American Express was criticized for treating customer-centricity as equivalent to analyzing customers' purchase behavior in order to offer the "next best [credit card] product" and using customers' demographic information to determine when to offer "special Membership Rewards on [life event] purchases from merchants in its network."[6] In contrast, a service-centric view would extend thinking beyond selling what the company produces by encouraging questions such as "How do customers judge value in making purchases?" (a job for which a credit card is hired) and "What unique know-how does the company possess that might help customers make better purchases?"[7] Indeed, in financial services, too many companies today still think in terms of pushing financial products rather than pursuing the goal of truly serving customers.

Service-centricity involves changing mentality and approach to service activities, from a reactive taking of orders, where the sales force and service organization is waiting for the customers to call, to proactive service management, striving to educate, predict, and act before problems occur. As we discussed in the previous chapter, the importance of acting in a proactive manner is especially evident when going from product life-cycle services to asset efficiency services. Proactive prevention and proactive education are two service concepts related directly to the notion of providing performance.

Accordingly, such change is a deliberate move away from a fire-fighting after-sale service culture and a mentality of "overtime heroes" to a service culture embraced by the entire organization. In a fire-fighting-service culture, employees are, for example, sent from the United States to South America to urgently deliver a critical component needed for a gas turbine just because the contractual agreement has not been well managed. Likewise, a technician may need to rush on dark and snowy roads to a customer's factory on Christmas Eve to connect a new gas cylinder to the customer's system. In these cases, employees witness exemplary service-oriented behavior. Yet these examples also illustrate the lack of an organizational service culture—a proactive climate in which such critical incidents are avoided in the first place. SKF, a leading global technology expert for bearings, seals, mechatronics, services, and lubrication systems, is an outstanding example of a company that has shifted from a product-centric fire-fighting culture to a service culture that spans the entire organization (see exhibit 2).

## Exhibit 2
### SKF: From a Product-Centric to a Service-Centric Culture

SKF Group is a leader in the $76 billion global market for bearings, seals, mechatronics, services, and lubrication systems. Services include technical support, maintenance services, customer training, condition monitoring, and remote diagnostics. SKF was founded in Gothenburg, Sweden, in 1907 on Sven Wingqvist's patent of the world's first self-aligning ball bearing. Although SKF is the global leader in bearings, it does not want to be perceived as a product-centric manufacturer. Instead, the company puts great emphasis on a service-centric approach aimed at enabling superior customer value through its offerings, which is increasingly provided through advanced services and customer solutions. For SKF, ball bearings are not just products—they are the "brains of the rotating machinery." Enabled by self-powered, wireless sensors, they transmit real-life operating data to boost performance, reduce mission-critical downtime, and prevent accidents.

Over the last fifteen years, SKF has moved from a culture of firefighting and reactive maintenance by overtime heroes to a service culture. This implies a change from a product to a process perspective for service improvements; rather than letting breakdowns and failure avoidance be key drivers for the service operations, uptime and growth are in focus.

"Service infusion provides a key opportunity to leverage our knowledge engineering expertise through services and solutions to work more strategically with our clients, helping them to become more profitable by delivering superior customer value. Thereby, we can strengthen our competitiveness and increase our margins. It is a win-win arrangement" (business-development manager).

To drive the service transition, SKF has developed several success stories of value selling and examples of failure with traditional technical selling to get the attention of the sales personnel. Selling services requires another approach: more service-centric, customer focused, and proactive. During the internal sales training, trainers may show a real-world case in which the salesperson lost the business based on price despite doing a correct technical sale. Furthermore, SKF's "area value champions" spend a week with individual salespeople, conducting joint sales calls and customer visits and building personal relationships. Together, they will use SKF's Documented Solutions Program (DSP) software that calculates the expected value of SKF's hybrid packages. As part of the partner relationship with SKF, the customer has access to the software and can view cost reductions in over 250 areas, including energy, inventory, warranty costs, manpower, machine life, reliability, and quality. Between 2003 and 2015, SKF could show customers documented cost savings of SEK 35 billion.

In addition, SKF now provides over forty different iPad apps that allow managers to monitor the condition, speed, and reliability of up to eight thousand types of smart objects. As of 2015, more than half a million machines are connected to the SKF cloud, which is further driving service infusion.

*Sources:* Nordin et al. (2015); Sinfield et al. (2015); SKF

In many cases, service-centric firms may become more knowledgeable than customers themselves about processes and operations, which represented a basis for providing new offerings such as asset efficiency services. Service-focused employees are able to gain deeper knowledge of a customer's business, recover service failures faster, tackle unforeseen changes quicker, and suggest new and better ways of solving problems. Companies with a strong service culture are well positioned to create more value for customers through productivity enhancements and cost reductions. Consider the following quote from an executive of a tire manufacturer:

> To successfully sell fleet management solutions, our company had to gain deep knowledge in correctly assessing the risks involved in taking responsibility of individual customers' tire fleets, learning how to spread tire management risks across multiple trucking companies, and proposing solution contracts in such a way that we were able to meet customers' expectations while maintaining profit margins for individual contracts. Imagine the culture shock that these changes involved: deep down in our DNA, we still are a manufacturer. But we had to acquire actuarial expertise, we had to bring in people with entirely different skills and mind-sets and learn how to evaluate and take risk.[8]

## Building a Service Culture in B2B: Four Steps

Managers must take a step back and evaluate their company's organizational culture in light of their service-growth ambitions. Does your current culture enable or hinder service growth? What is needed for embracing a service-centric culture? What are critical milestones on the journey? Figure 3:1 describes our road map of four stages that product-centric B2B companies typically go through when moving toward a true service culture. Navigating away from a product-centered culture is not a straight path forward. The journey is particularly challenging for service-myopic firms deeply entrenched in a manufacturing mind-set. It requires top management's attention and commitment to change. Let's review the four stages.

Figure 3:1
Four Steps to Building a Service Culture and Growth

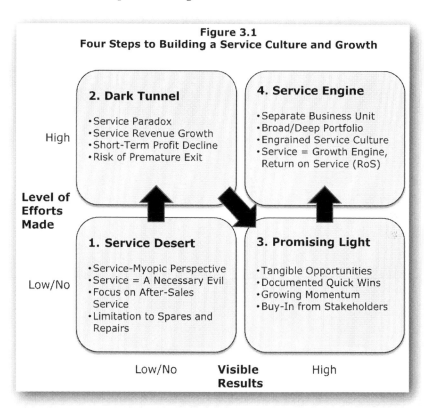

**Figure 3.1**
**Four Steps to Building a Service Culture and Growth**

Service Desert. Many service-myopic firms find themselves stuck in what we call the *service desert*. Every company is, to some degree, a service company even though the notion of service may not be front and center in everyone's mind. For example, ASML is a worldwide manufacturer of lithography machines and software for semiconductor manufacturers. The company estimates that a well-maintained lithography system can have a useful life measured in decades. According to ASML, 90 percent of all systems shipped since the company's inception in 1984 are still in use. After use for many years in a semiconductor manufacturer's fab, a lithography system will find its second life with other manufacturers, for example, companies that produce other equipments such as accelerometers, gyroscopes, silicon microphones, radio-frequency chips, thin-film heads for hard disk drives, or LEDs, among others. This opens up opportunities for providing a host of lifecycle services, refurbishment, and enhancements for cost reductions in high-volume manufacturing contexts.[9]

Unlike ASML, many companies don't "think service" and therefore don't realize the many opportunities that value-added services and solutions can provide. These firms still consider services wrapped around goods as a necessary evil—activities they must provide just to enable product sales. Interestingly, managers in goods-centric firms often think of services as "must haves" just to enable product sales. This is why the notion of after-sales services (or ASS—not the nicest acronym for describing services) still prevails in many firms when relating to service. Yet when describing services as occurring after the sale, this clearly translates the underlying mind-set: services just follow what "really" matters—that is, a product sale. More often than not, service thus often refers to costly activities the company rather would like to get away with or delegate to an intermediary. Beyond spares and repairs (which often are recognized as profit havens), remaining services activities are considered as profit drains. Make the test yourself inside your company: Ask an executive in a traditional goods-centric firm to name a sales figure and percentage of revenues generated through services in his or her company. Then ask him or her to deduct those services sales that are directly flowing from any product sale (such as spare parts). Chances are that percentages mentioned will fall into the single digits. We have made this exercise over and over; when you ask managers in product-centric B2B firms to just focus on counting services beyond mere product lifecycle services, overall services revenues are low. For example, in one manufacturing company we worked with, management proudly announced services sales of 20 percent of total group sales of $3.5 billion. When we subtracted easy services—that is, services revenues naturally flowing from product sales without any particular effort—the real figure appeared to be 4 percent at the most. Once top management realized the potential of the company's vastly untapped service-growth opportunities, it immediately jumpstarted its strategic service-growth initiative.

**Dark Tunnel.** When firms start to step out the service desert, they are at risk of getting stuck in what we call the *dark tunnel*. In this stage, the company starts to ramp up investments in service-specific infrastructures, new service offers, and people. For example, a firm may acquire smart technologies to venture into asset efficiency services (AES). Likewise, it may hire consultative salespeople to grow its process support services (PSS). Yet results may not become visible. These firms face the service paradox, which means that they have to swallow the bitter pill of suffering short-term losses and sluggish service growth despite substantial investments and commitments made.

The time lag between investing in resources and having to wait for the rewards of service growth is a nagging problem; studies have shown that companies generally experience declining margins with growing revenues up to a threshold before the benefits of investments in service infrastructure and people kick in.[10] Managers must realize that they need to build up a critical mass of service revenues first before reaping the benefits of a service-growth strategy. Decision makers may become frustrated when launching new offerings and hiring additional salespeople, and other up-front investments won't immediately turn into additional revenues and profits. In the course of working with firms on service growth, we have seen multiple situations where an excessive focus on short-term goals led managers to sacrifice long-term service growth. In such context, which selected individuals might have a service-centric mind-set, it still remains very difficult for a companywide service culture to emerge.

***Promising Light.*** Overcoming the service paradox, companies start seeing the first glimpse of what we call the *promising light.* Some firms might at first not even experience the dark tunnel of the service paradox. They may actually learn that with reasonable levels of efforts made, they already achieve initial promising results. This is what we call "quick wins." Ideally, companies must identify and seize profitable service-growth opportunities as early as possible in their service journeys. Two aspects are important in this context. First, quick wins must translate into tangible revenues. Second, quick wins must persuasively demonstrate that the company could turn a profit. Finally, these low-hanging fruit must be harvested fast. Time is important to create momentum and bring along change. Quick wins come in many ways. For example, a manager may decide to turn around a service from free to fee—in other words, start invoicing a service that was hitherto provided free of charge.

A company may also want to launch a new service for which customers have expressed interest for a while. In all those instances, building those early successes fast will contribute to a "yes, we can" attitude inside the company. This is a very fertile ground for growing a companywide service culture by showcasing best-practice behaviors and outcomes.

**Bright Landscape.** Finally, the *bright landscape* is the final destination on the service transition journey. In this stage, companies allocate significant resources to infrastructures and people dedicated to serving customers. The overall service business has become a unique profit center in its own right and serves as a growth engine of the firm.[11] Service revenues flow from a broad and deep mix of service offerings that reach way beyond must-have services. Return on service (RoS) is visible throughout the organization. In such companies, the vast majority of stakeholders have espoused a service-centric mind-set.

To master the service-growth journey and successfully manage a cultural shift, we also need to know who will actively support the initiative inside your organization or who will outright work against it. Understanding individual stakeholders' goals and motivations is what we will discuss in the next section.

## Service Growth: How to Drive Adoption

Mastering service growth requires the support of everyone in the organization. All levels, from top management to frontline service technicians, must get involved. Implementing a service strategy requires strong support from employees at all levels of the organization. If the support of one single element in the chain is not strong enough, chances of falling back into a product-centric approach to services are very high. Service-centric thinking has to permeate the organization at all levels. Pushing a service strategy down from the top will inevitably face strong resistance. Likewise, bottom-up service growth initiatives alone won't suffice. Top management commitment and visionary leadership need to go hand in hand with grassroots efforts to make the transformation stick.

When working with companies on service growth, we have seen many times that management typically overestimates speed of adoption. Much like any other strategic initiative, service infusion follows the well-known

S-curve pattern (see figure 3:2). Executives need to know whom they can rely on for successfully moving forward with their service-growth strategy.

**Figure 3:2**
**Adoption of Service Growth over Time**

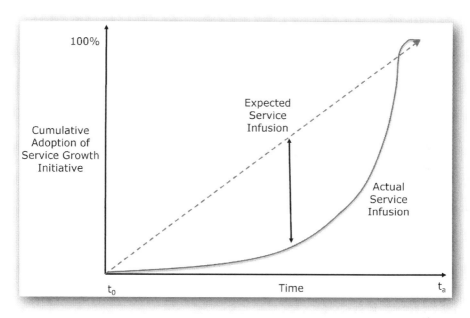

People inside the company hold very different beliefs about service-growth, which may range from unconditional support to outside resistance. Their attitudes and behaviors will not only affect overall success or failure but also influence the speed of adoption of such a strategic initiative; therefore it is paramount to understand where individuals position themselves vis-à-vis the company's service strategy. In figure 3:3, we provide a framework identifying nine fundamental positions stakeholders inside a firm generally adopt toward service growth. Understanding the positions your key decision makers have adopted in your situation is key to successfully driving adoption of your initiative.

Our framework distinguishes among three hierarchical levels: top management, middle management, and frontline or field organization employees. Next, we distinguish three archetypal views on service growth: internal stakeholders can be actively against, neutral, or strongly supportive of your service-growth strategy. Understanding the internal political landscape represents the basis for influencing key stakeholders and fostering a service culture on all levels of the organization.

**Figure 3:3**
**Nine Stakeholder Positions toward Service Growth**

| | | Actively Against | | Strongly Supportive |
|---|---|---|---|---|
| **Top Management** | | **Board-Level Detractor**<br>Views service as an outright danger to profitability. Service is not part of the DNA | **Board-Level Bystander**<br>Can swing in different directions on board decisions regarding service growth | **Service Evangelist**<br>Views service as a panacea, provides unconditional support |
| **Middle Management** | | **Outright Obstructor**<br>Uses position to work against service, places products over service when possible | **Half-Hearted Follower**<br>Practices a hands-off approach. Follows directions without much conviction, doesn't follow-up on service goals | **Service Enthusiast**<br>Spends all his/her energy convincing top management and motivating troops |
| **Frontline Employees** | | **Diehard Resistor**<br>Views service as a necessary evil, is willing to give away service for free to secure sale, doesn't see revenue/cost impact | **Indifferent Employee**<br>Is willing to give service a try, will drop initiatives that do not show immediate success | **Service Promoter**<br>Promotes service out of intrinsic motivation—"does it all the time," is part of how he/she operates, serves as example for others |

Hierarchical Level in Organization

Attitude toward Service-Growth Strategy

## Board-Level Engagement

Starting at the board level, top management support is a critical condition for a cultural shift. In every company, you need a service champion at the top who carries and personifies the service-growth strategy. One of the firms we worked with wanted to grow services revenues from a very low level to $1 billion over a period of five years. To achieve its ambitious goal, it created a board member position of vice president of strategy and service to communicate throughout the organization that service growth was a top priority to the group. *Service evangelists* are executives who show unconditional support for service infusion. Such proponents are crucial for instilling service growth and a service culture. Yet there is also a risk: service should not be seen as a panacea. Similar to executives who decide to push ahead with disastrous mergers and acquisitions or boards that pursue new business ventures in uncharted territories with devastating results, many service initiatives fail because managers rush ahead with superficial understanding of the complexities involved, underestimating internal resistance, time, and effort needed to grow a service culture and service revenues. If a service initiative fails, especially if the firm is in the *service desert* or *dark tunnel* discussed in figure 3:1, their unconditional support may backfire on its proponents and any future attempt to instill a change. *Board-level bystanders*, the second category at the top management level, have no strong opinion about service infusion. They can lean either way when it comes to board decisions about service growth. Bystanders are therefore critical for building internal support and forming guiding coalitions to push service-growth initiatives ahead. Finally, senior executives working actively against service infusion are best described as *board-level detractors*. These key decision makers view services as an outright danger to their firm's overall profitability and as a threat to the company's core product business. Detractors typically view services as falling outside their company's DNA. Any initiative to change the strategic direction of the firm by moving toward a service-savvy business model should therefore be fought down.

## Middle-Management Commitment

Likewise, when moving to middle management, the next hierarchical level, executives need to rely on *service enthusiasts*. These managers are essential for both convincing their immediate superiors to support bottom-up service initiatives and motivating the local troops to sell and deliver services. Experienced and enthusiastic service managers generally are an indispensable but scarce resource. Hence, their resources and skills must be employed wisely, and every effort must be made to retain them. A second category at this organizational level is *halfhearted followers*. Practicing a hands-off approach toward services, their stance also proves problematic, although for somewhat different reasons. Managers in this group don't take pride in pursuing service goals. They handle service because "somebody has to do it" and follow directions without much conviction. It is not rare to see that they won't follow up on service-growth goals, especially in situations when they seem to conflict with other objectives. A halfhearted manager is not the kind of person you want to assign as service manager. Finally, there is a third group of managers at the middle-management level. *Outright obstructors* are middle managers working actively against service infusion. These managers use their position to oppose service initiatives and whenever possible place products over service; service initiatives placed under the wing of such managers are doomed to fail. If middle-management obstructors have strong internal leverage, service initiatives should be managed far away from their spheres of influence.

## Frontline Buy-In

At the frontline, not surprisingly, strongly supportive natural *service promoters* are often found in field organizations. This category readily adopts new approaches and tools that foster service growth. A service technician who spots an opportunity for selling a new or different service, relaying the information to a salesperson, is a perfect example in this category. Likewise, a salesperson experimenting with new ways of presenting a service offer to a customer, thus turning a free service into a for-pay service can be considered a natural service promoter. A second category, *indifferent frontline employees*, is generally willing to give service a try. However, they are equally ready to drop initiatives that do not show immediate success. Managers, therefore, should put effort into motivating these employees, which includes using the natural-born service promoters to serve as examples. Finally, *diehard resistors* consider service as a daily nuisance, a necessary evil in the process of moving boxes. They see no harm in giving services away for free if that gets the job of selling a product done. Diehard resistors generally don't see, nor do they devote much attention to, the revenue and cost implications of their actions. With the growing digitization of service-delivery processes, this last category also easily rejects deployment tools such as smartphones or tablets—a nagging human resource problem in many field service organizations.

A thorough understanding of all nine categories is key to managing internal resistance and driving change for service growth. We will return to this framework when discussing visionary leadership in chapter 6. Next, however, we will wrap up this chapter on service culture and growth by summarizing what we call the seven deadly sins. These are attitudes and behaviors we have seen time and again in service-myopic firms.

## The Seven Deadly Sins of Service-Myopic Firms

Service-myopic firms hold on to values, beliefs, and behaviors that stand in the way of service growth. These can best be summarized in the following seven deadly sins that executives must address:

1. **View Service as a Necessary Evil.** Don't fool yourself. When services are considered as an after-sales activity, when managers think of service as an aftermarket domain, the message is loud and clear: services take a backseat in corporate strategy and growth ambitions. How to address this first deadly sin? Clearly, executives must demonstrate the revenue and profit potential of services built around products. In many industries, the potential revenues flowing from product lifecycle, asset efficiency, process support, and process-delegation services exceed by far the revenues of boxes sold. Service(s) must become a top strategic priority; the goals for service growth must be communicated relentlessly—both internally and externally.

2. ***Delegate Services Away to Dealers.*** It can make perfect sense to delegate some types of services to dealers, but such strategic decisions must not be based only on shortsighted cost savings, internal capacity constraints, and lack of service capabilities. Such moves generally weaken the firm's market position vis-à-vis both dealers and customers; eventually the firm may lose its customer interface altogether. How to address this challenge? If services represent a strategic priority, then companies must also take control of the channel and coordinate its activities. Truly service-centric firms actively work with their channel partners.

Rather than simply trying to eliminate middlemen, companies must develop a clear channel strategy, identify and select strategic channel partners, and jointly implement a win-win action plan for service growth.

3. *Give Services Away for Free.* When companies consider that giving services away for free is an acceptable everyday practice, they commit a third deadly sin. If services are merely regarded as activities that support product sales, it becomes very tempting to give them away to land a deal without charging customers for service provided. Of course, there are situations and good reasons when a company may want to provide a service free of charge. Yet free services often send the wrong signal both to customers and the company's own staff. Customers will get used to free services and will ask for more next time. Companies' own staff will consider free services as no big deal. As long as it doesn't hurt to give away a free service, why not? Customers will love it, and a technician or salesperson can shine before the client. How to tackle this issue? First, customers must see the value provided by service, and staff must realize how much money actually goes down the drain by not charging for a service. Second, free services must come in return for a pain. Customers must give up something else in return for obtaining a free service (such as conceding higher purchasing volumes or taking off a costly service element). Likewise, employees must feel a pain, too, before giving away a free service (like a hit to a salary bonus paid). In short, managers must raise the bar.

4. *Treat Services Just Like Products.* Service-myopic companies take a cookie-cutter approach to services. Managers apply the same recipes and use the same processes—just like those tried and tested products. As we have seen in chapter 2, services have their unique challenges and characteristics. How to cope with this sin? Managers must acknowledge that services require their own processes, such as innovation, pricing, or sales. They may require structures and people specifically dedicated to services, such as R&D organizations and teams or service-specific salespeople. Finally, they also require their own resources. For example, too

often, R&D for products and services compete for the same scarce resources with services taking a backseat. Managers must devote proper attention to services and processes, resources, and structures specifically to services.

5. ***Adopt a Laissez-Faire Approach to Service.*** We have met with situations where top management saw very well the potential of services as the company's next growth engine. But then executives delegated away the task of crafting and implementing a service strategy to middle management. This was not because top management wasn't convinced of potential benefits. Rather, they considered services as a functional issue to be addressed solely at the level of VP of operations and/or services. What to do in such a situation? The last thing needed when managing the transition to a service-centric business model is a hands-off approach. Driving a service-growth strategy requires a strong service champion at the top, service enthusiasts in middle management, and strong guidance at the frontline. Such a strategic initiative cuts across business units and inevitably leads to overlap between activities and conflict between units and people. For example, services revenues may cannibalize product revenues, and services salespeople may pursue different goals than product salespeople. Inevitably, many issues raised will require an arbitrator to step in—and this arbitrator can only come from the top.

6. ***Define Business as Value Stacking.*** For decades, managers have been taught that all businesses are linked in a value chain. The idea that value is being created in a value chain is firmly grounded in traditional industrial economics. Suppliers of raw material provide input for manufacturers of components, ingredient suppliers pass value down to machine manufacturers, and so forth. At the end of the chain is a consumer. To no surprise, the verb "to consume" stems from the Latin roots "consumere," which means "to eat, devour, or swallow." Hence, the idea that value is created, on one side, in a value chain and gobbled up, on the other side, by a consumer. Such a perspective on value creation is counterproductive to service growth. How to address this sin? Executives must espouse the principle that value is cocreated

with customers, adopt novel ways of gaining customer insights, crowd-source service innovation ideas, and cocreate services with customers, not only rely on dreaming up the next big service ideas from within their organizations.

7. ***All Talk, No Walk.*** Finally, a last sin committed by service-myopic firms relates to the gap between stated goals and real-life actions. Far too often, the service initiative remains mostly empty rhetoric for investors, customers, and other external stakeholders. Executives make only halfhearted attempts; there is no real will to change the corporate culture. We have seen business unit leaders or CEOs of country organizations paying only lip service to service initiatives launched by corporate headquarters. How to address this challenge? Companies truly committed to moving away from a service-myopic view make it unequivocally clear that there is no way to opt out. One of the worst management mistakes we have seen is that executives turned back the wheel as soon as they met with the slightest headwinds. If you are convinced that service growth is the way to go, then stick to it. Make it clear that bailing out is not an option. If worse comes to worst, this may also imply stating an example and dismissing an outright resistor to get the message across—loud and clear.

Managers should take a step back and critically review whether they find evidence of one or several of these signs of service myopia. If too many light bulbs go on, then this is a clear sign that the company's culture requires a serious overhaul before embarking on a service-growth journey.

## KEY QUESTIONS ABOUT YOUR SERVICE CULTURE

Here are a number of key questions executives should answer regarding their firm's cultural readiness for service growth.

1. What is the percentage of service revenues compared to total revenues in your firm? Subtract all easy services sales that naturally

flow from product sales (spares and repairs). What percentage is left?

2. Where is your company today on the four-stage route to a service culture? Is your firm product-centric, service-centric, or in between?

3. Which roadblocks could slow down the adoption of your service growth initiative? Do you know your friends and foes, supporters and opponents?

4. Do you view service as a necessary evil?

5. Does your company delegate services away to dealers?

6. Is giving services away for free a common practice in your company?

7. Do managers in your firm treat services just like products?

8. Has top management delegated service strategy and growth to middle management?

9. Do decision makers in your company view value creation as value stacking—that is, something that happens inside your company?

10. Do executives in your firm only provide lip service to service growth?

# CHAPTER 4

## SERVICE STRATEGY: IS IT ALIGNED WITH CORPORATE GOALS?

*Grow your service business—it's the wave of the future.*
*The [service] market is bigger than we ever dreamt.*
*However, one thing remains absolutely certain:*
*We will continue to expand and manufacture [products].*
*Without products, you're dead.*
*—JACK WELCH*

Having focused on the foundational components of our road map in the first section of the book, we now move to the strategic part. In the next three chapters, we will investigate the core components of service-growth strategies. These issues inevitably push managers to ask a number of fundamental strategic questions related to the very mission and positioning of the firm. This chapter should provide guidance for any executive wishing to develop and implement a service strategy. Service strategy touches on the way firms define their business. Because of the magnitude of change required, we will see that the road is bumpy, strewn with obstacles. Executives must know how to take the temperature of the firm at all times, to be able to evaluate and judge whether the organization is ready to embark on the transformation, to recognize the resistance to change found in the firm, to manage arguments against service initiatives, and to find the right transformation path. The process must be structured and methodical; nothing should be left to chance. We discuss what executives must consider before defining and implementing a real strategic plan to achieve the objective.

## Service Transition or Service Infusion?

Business leaders must constantly question the relevance of their current business model. Will it allow the integration of a service business? Should it be changed? If so, how? Should it change dramatically? Or should we instead make incremental changes? These questions and many others must be debated and resolved before setting a service strategy and venturing into the deployment of a service portfolio.

Service-led growth in manufacturing firms is frequently discussed in terms of a product-service transition. An increased emphasis on, and importance of, services can be rudimentally illustrated as a move from a product firm to a service firm. As firms move along the product-service spectrum in figure 4:1, the relative importance of services increases. Executives need to know why and how they want to expand their service business, what their target position is, and when not to go further. They need to ask themselves three questions:

- What position should the organization occupy on the change line?
- How should change take place: gradually or in leaps?
- What are the most challenging aspects of change?

**Figure 4:1**
**The Product-Service Spectrum**

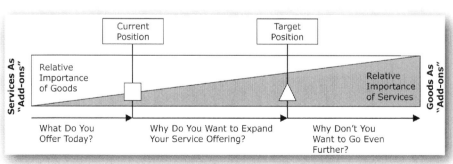

Source: Adapted from Oliva and Kallenberg (2003), p. 162

At one extreme, services are regarded as add-ons or even a necessary evil; firms only sell products, supplemented with the minimum of service elements required to sell the products, such as free customer service and support. At the other extreme, no products are sold separately—they are purely seen as vehicles for service provision. For these firms and their customers, products and hardware always comes second; what matters is the utility value generated by the offerings. For firms with in-house manufacturing, it means that whenever competitor products are cheaper (and equally good) or better suited for a customer-specific service, they should be used instead,[1] something that is not really possible if the firm is product-centric.

In reality, however, few manufacturers can be placed on either of the two extremes. Even if many firms do not work with services in a systematic manner or struggle to grow through services, there are often at least some services they sell and thereby charge for. For example, many firms analyze their customers' operations before an eventual product sale (which is a service) and charge for this activity if the customer decides to buy a competitor's product instead, whereas the service is included in the product price if the customer decides to fulfill the product purchase. Similarly, few firms can be regarded as pure-service providers because it would imply that the products always come second and that there is little or no value in protecting the traditional product business. One exception would be IBM, which has deliberately made a service transition, combining organic growth with service-related acquisitions and product-related sales (see exhibit 3).

## Exhibit 3
## IBM's Service Transition

IBM is one of the firms most frequently used success stories of a strategic move toward services. The firm has outsourced its manufacturing operations, which previously was its core business, and expanded its service and software business though major acquisitions. For example, in 2005, IBM sold its PC business to Lenovo of China for $1.75 billion, and in 2014, the low-end server unit was sold to Lenovo for $2.3 billion. Even if services have always been an integral part of the firm's business, IBM was still a product-centric firm twenty-five years ago. As often is the case, external factors in terms of increased competition from companies like Sun Microsystems and Compaq, technology diffusion, and commoditization forced the firm to reconsider its product-centric business model. For the former undisputed heavyweight champion (in 1985, it accounted for a staggering 6.4 percent of the Standard & Poor's 500 stock index), the mass layoffs that followed caused a morale crisis. Investors doubted whether IBM would be able to reinvent itself.

Standing on its burning product platform, IBM came to the insight that the future of the IT business was not computers *per se*. In spite of strong internal resistance, the firm made a strategic turnaround starting in the early 1990s under the leadership of CEO Lou Gerstner. In a painstaking process, it shifted its focus from manufacturing and computer sales to business customers to information-and-communication-technology services and solutions. The service transition was based on a radical shift in viewing strategy: instead of being about how to beat the competition in the first place, it was now about understanding the needs of the customers and supporting their businesses with value-added solutions, one customer at a time.

The serious top-management commitment to the service strategy was essential for its success. Major milestones include the following:

- 1991: The formation of the specialized service unit Integrated System Solution Corporation (the precursor to IBM Global Services) and the IBM Consulting Group
- 1993: The first comprehensive service strategy for the whole firm
- 1996: The establishment of IBM Global Services by combing IBM service businesses with the IBM Consulting Group
- 2000: The addition of hosted storage and storage management to their portfolio of services delivered via network
- 2002: The consultancy business of PricewaterhouseCoopers acquired for $4 billion
- 2008: The business-intelligence company Cognos acquired for $5 billion

- 2014: The IBM Watson Group, with headquarters in New York's Silicon Alley, is created, focusing on cloud-delivered services.

Today, IBM, with its 378,000 employees and fast-growing service units, is a world-leading supplier of business and ICT-based services. The revenues for Global Services were $4.5 billion in 2000; fifteen years later, the revenues were over $49 billion. Now the next massive disruption has begun as IBM is transforming into a cognitive-solutions and cloud-platform company that leverages as a service-business model.

*Sources: Financial Times*; Fischer et al. (2012); IBM; *New York Times*; Spohrer (2017)

Even if firms across industries have outsourced manufacturing of components and subsystems, few leaders in other industries than the IT sector, such as General Electric or Siemens, would follow IBM's route and essentially turn away from manufacturing. Rather than a *service transition*, service-led growth is more often a matter of *service infusion*—that is, extending the firm's offering rather than moving away from product to service sales. BT Industries (today, Toyota Material Handling Europe) is an example of a firm that has successfully pursued service infusion initiatives through organic growth, including building a substantial and profitable rental business (see exhibit 4). Without losing focus on its product business, it invests significantly in an ever-growing service business and combines products and services into innovative hybrid offerings. Despite the stepwise expansion, service infusion has implied a major strategic shift, which has required top management support on both central and local levels.

**Exhibit 4**
**BT Industries' Service Expansion**

The warehouse truck supplier BT Industries of Sweden is a good example of a company that has successfully expanded its service business organically, in a stepwise manner, while at the same time maintaining a strong product core. The firm was founded in 1946, and the first service centers were established in 1954. The firm began to build its own international sales and service organization in the 1960s through an acquisition in the United Kingdom and the establishment of subsidiaries in continental Europe. BT Industries was the world's largest manufacturer of warehouse trucks when Toyota Industries acquired it in 2000, whose materials handling division held the number-one position for counterbalanced trucks. Five years later, Toyota initiated the long-term work of integrating the two companies into what became Toyota Material Handling Group. Whereas one of Toyota's core competences was its Toyota Production System, BT Industries differentiated itself by having a well-established service organization and worked actively to develop its service portfolio and improve service deployment.

Over the years, BT has developed its service business in parallel with successful product expansion and extension such as the acquisition of the Raymond brand in the United States. A key driver for service infusion has been new customer demands driven by such things as outsourcing of material-handling services. Two senior executives gave their views on the incremental service infusion process in the firm: "Our history has not been a series of dramatic changes at all; it's been a series of minor adjustments along the way. We change something or introduce something to our portfolio or new method of approach every year" (senior director). "It's quite a mature industry and many of our customers, whether we like it or not, view our products as commodities. It's quite difficult to differentiate the hardware. We have to innovate by using software or 'soft products.' And it's a mature market; innovations that we make are small and incremental, rather than huge steps" (rental director).

BT's first major rental customers in Sweden were paper mills in the 1960s. Over the years, the rental concept has developed gradually in terms of the number of different offerings and service market share, although the core idea of rental with maintenance included has remained consistent. Being able to achieve synergies between the product and service business, these hybrid offerings are generally more profitable than not only product sales but also service contracts. Both long- and short-term rental markets have grown significantly over the last decade, and in several of the most competitive markets, more than half of all new trucks entail rental agreements. Customers generally lease a materials handling solution with trucks, financing, maintenance, spare parts, and driver training for a fixed monthly fee, thereby having a stipulated and clear cost for the materials handling activities. More recently, Toyota Material Handling Europe is also selling advanced fleet management services that can advantageously be combined with its rental options. The strong commitment to be a leader in service is embedded into the company's business strategy, and half of its employees are engaged in service.

*Source:* Kowalkowski et al. (2012)

As the IBM and BT Industries cases show, service growth can be more or less disruptive: it can span from a stepwise expansion through organic growth to a radical transformation through acquisitions and sales. However, regardless of which service trajectory the company pursues, it needs a clear service strategy and strong top management commitment to navigate the journey.

### The key role of senior management

Building on service as a vehicle for growth does not represent a minor change to the company, such as a product line extension. This is a real *strategic shift* for many companies that affect the very foundation of the firm. Consequently, such a change must be driven at the highest level of the company; the role of senior management is essential for a success-ful breakthrough in services—as well as decisions when not to invest in services.

Schneider Electric, a global specialist in energy management and automation, is a case in point. The Fortune Global 500 Company, which is considered a bellwether of European industry, has successfully pursued its move into service. Since it pursued an aggressive growth strategy in 2004, organic service growth has persistently outgrown the rest of the company. Back then, Schneider Electric reviewed all its activities to identify new growth areas. After a period focused on cost reduction and outsourcing noncore activities, the group designated hybrid offerings, services, and innovation as key platforms for growth for the years to come. For this purpose, a vice president of strategy and deployment of services was named to anchor sustainable resources in the daily activities of executives and group managers. The message such an appointment signals is clear and unambiguous. Revenues from services and hybrid offerings now amount to 43 percent of total revenue.[2] The Schneider Electric case highlights the fact that when expanding its business scope, the company is often obliged to redefine its mission and its strategic positioning in the market. This is what we will discuss next.

## Redefining the Mission and Positioning of the Firm

As long as services are simply viewed as activities augmenting the product sales, strategy and organization do not need to be fundamentally revised and relatively minor changes may suffice. But when it comes to the development of a proactive service-growth strategy and a wide-scale transformation, executives need to redefine the fundamentals of the firm's mission and positioning.

### Review the mission of the firm

Why is a company's mission statement so important when it comes to service growth? Peter Drucker, by many revered as the father of modern management, already affirmed in 1973 that the most important cause for business frustration and failure comes from inadequate thought of the company's mission. In many cases, the mission statement does not point at a service mind-set. To put it differently, service is not coded into the DNA of the organization. Far too often, firms define their mission based on the products manufactured and sold. For proof, just check the websites of many industrial firms. The information for customers, investors, and other stakeholders generally exhibits a strong product orientation.

The business purpose and the very essence of a firm should be found in its mission statement. It must be clearly defined and can usually be determined through a few questions: Who are we? What are our core capabilities? Who are our customers? What do they value in our offerings? How should we advance over time? Despite their apparent simplicity, these questions are among the most difficult that any manager must eventually answer. In other words, the mission statement captures, in summary, the main responses to the questions that arise for the organization's future. We can define the mission statement as follows:

- The firm's *mission statement* is the definition of the purpose of the organization and the ambition of what it seeks to achieve to ensure its survival and long-term growth.

Defining the core purpose of the firm through its products may prove to be a key obstacle to the development of and true commitment to a service-growth strategy. By reviewing the firm's mission statement, top management can lay the foundation for a necessary strategic and cultural shift in the organization. A redefined mission sends out a strong signal internally and to customers and other stakeholders about the service transition path the firm is pursuing. We can say that the firm's mission statement represents the litmus test of its commitment to service.

For a long time, BASF, the world's leading chemical company, saw its mission as to "help our customers to be more successful through intelligent system solutions and high-quality products. Our portfolio ranges from chemicals, plastics, performance products, agricultural products and fine chemicals to crude oil and natural gas."[3] The company's move into service and solution partnerships was reflected in its revised mission statement: "We offer intelligent solutions based on innovative products and tailor-made services. We create opportunities for success through trusted and reliable partnerships."[4] For instance, the company decided to move from being a paint supplier to a solution partner to its automotive customers, going from selling paint at a price per gallon to price per painted car.

Redefining the mission of the company provides large slates of new opportunities to grow beyond the traditional activities of the company; however, executives need to beware of paying lip service to their service initiatives. In recent years, an increasing number of firms have redefined their missions from product manufacturers to service or solution providers, supported by statements such as "we don't sell pumps; we sell cost-effective fluid handling," and "we don't sell trucks; we sell transportation solutions." Nevertheless, many of these firms derive only a minor part of their revenues and profits from services, only scratching the surface of the service business with no real long-term commitment or strategic focus. Thus, redefining the firm's mission is only the first step to consider; executives must also reconsider the positioning of the firm.

## Review the competitive positioning of the firm

Senior management must thoroughly review the position it wishes to adopt in the market. What customer needs will the service address? What business model should we choose? How should we position ourselves against the competition? What value proposition will address each customer segment? These fundamental choices have ramifications on the definition of the portfolio of offerings and services deployment in the field.

In the first chapter, we observed the accelerated product commoditization across industries. This trend, considered irreversible by some, has been described as the "commodity magnet."[5] In many industries, successful firms usually position themselves as suppliers of specialty products that are differentiated by superior technical characteristics to those of their competitors. In such a situation, the firm creates a competitive advantage through a product leadership strategy. This differentiation alone justifies a higher price. For example, ATM manufacturers have traditionally been accustomed to drive negotiations with their bank customers on an argument based on the technical characteristics of equipment (e.g., the number of tickets distributed per second). The primary contact on the client side was mostly limited to IT management, which proved to be disadvantageous when manufacturers wanted to enter the service market. Services required more profound customer knowledge and access to other decision makers in the customer organization.

A firm in a product leadership position does not usually need to consider service as a strategic posture in the short term. As long as it manages to keep ahead of its lower-cost rivals and attract new customers on the basis of technological superiority of its products, it had better stay focused and concentrate on its core business. It was the case for many years for suppliers of ATMs and other interactive kiosks; there was simply no need to develop any type of innovative services and hybrid offerings for their bank customers unless the market demanded it. Today, however, the competitive position has eroded in terms of product differentiation.

The need to change value proposition becomes even more evident as customers' concerns shift from better products to the improvement of customers' processes and outcomes. In industries such as healthcare, overall productivity and efficiency take priority over technical, product-related issues. Optimization of workflow, integration of equipment in all the processes of the hospital, and healthcare data management outweigh the classic product attributes. Such changes also mean that new decision makers in the customer's organization influence the buying decision. Suppliers need to identify these decision makers and understand their priorities. In the case of ATMs, suppliers must negotiate with the agency director or the marketing manager of the bank, seeking to integrate the equipment as part of the bank's overall customer relationship management efforts.

One way or the other, the downward spiral pushing companies toward commoditization is inevitable. Figure 4:2 below illustrates how this commodity magnet pushes firms from a specialty product position—differentiated by superior technical characteristics—to a commodity position. The result is a movement along the power axis, from the upper left quadrant to the lower right quadrant. Unless they have not done it already, product-centric firms have to face the challenge of repositioning themselves in relation to this development.

Figure 4:2
Beating the Commodity Magnet:
What Market Position Should Be Adopted?

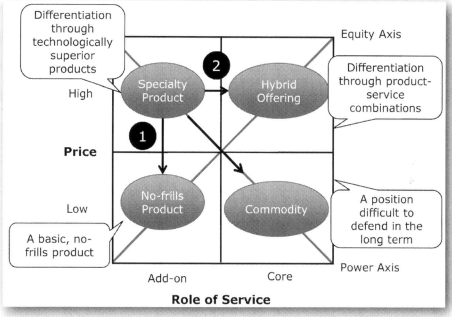

Source: Adapted from Rangan and Bowman (1992), p. 17

How can the commodity magnet be avoided, or, at least, how can it be dealt with? To beat it, the firm essentially has two action strategies to consider. The first option is to adopt a low-cost position of a company called No-frills Product, which results in migration to the lower left quadrant of figure 4:2 (trajectory 1). In this case, services are reduced to a minimum, costs are compressed, and prices are adjusted downward, in line with the expectations of certain market segments. The business model of no-frills airlines, such as Ryanair or easyJet, illustrates this market positioning. The same logic is at work in many B2B markets. In the gas industry, local or regional players like Westfalen of Germany or Sol of Italy, attack the market leaders, such as Air Liquide or Linde Gas, with a range of basic products at competitive prices, all accompanied by a reduced set of services. Note that "low cost" does not necessarily mean "low margin"; in Europe, Ryanair and easyJet consistently enjoy higher operating margins than incumbent operators like Lufthansa and Air France-KLM.

To make this strategic shift, the company must then transform its business model and reconfigure its market channels, permanently focusing on costs and charging for any auxiliary services. However, established firms often consider such change way too radical or challenging. For example, in an attempt to manage the commodity magnet and stay profitable, many incumbent airlines sign codeshare agreements with low-cost operators or manage their own low-cost airlines, such as the case with Lufthansa and low-cost airline Germanwings.

In other cases, customers are willing to pay more for the value added. In such cases, the best strategy is to move toward the top right, "Hybrid Offering" quadrant in figure 4:2 (trajectory 2). Companies going in this direction seek to differentiate themselves from competitors by their ability to segment the market ever more perceptively and provide superior customer value through innovative hybrid offerings rather than separate products and services only. In some cases, the trajectory from specialty products to hybrid offerings can be coupled with a strong desire to refocus on developing partnerships with a more limited range of clients. The hybrid offering strategy is pursued by many of the companies that we have worked with. The service framework presented in chapter 2 is useful when crafting a strategy for how to tap hybrid offering growth areas, something we will discuss in the next chapter.

There are also cases where a company undertakes a dual approach to competitive advantage—that of both low cost and differentiation through hybrid offerings. Michigan-based Dow Corning perfectly illustrates this point. In the early 2000s, this world leader in silicones faced increasingly tough price competition, mainly from emerging markets. Furthermore, just as experienced customers in the computer industry two decades earlier, many experienced silicone application users no longer needed technical services. Consequently, Dow Corning saw its markets burst: on one side, a growing number of customers seeking to source bulk silicone at market-driven prices without value-added services, and on the other hand, many customers continued to seek support from Dow Corning to enhance performance and be more sustainable.

To meet these opposing forces, in 2002 it created a standardized, no-frills offering under the Xiameter brand to distinguish it from the established Dow Corning brand. Built around a reduced range of commodity products, with a dedicated sales force and a low-cost, online-only distribution channel, Xiameter became a blockbuster success and a case study example of how incumbents can create growth through business model innovation.[6] Today, Dow Corning operates two radically different business models in parallel with fully differentiated products and services offerings. In doing so, the group has advanced both its turnover and profitability.

## Major Pain Points for Service Growth: A Manager's Perspective

What are the main issues executives wrestle with when it comes to service-growth strategies? Over three years, we conducted a detailed study of 250 European manufacturing companies to understand the key factors of success or failure from a manager's perspective (see exhibit 5). All companies were among the leaders in their respective markets. They were strongly committed to service-led growth, admittedly with varying success.

---

**Exhibit 5**
**Study of the Service Strategy of 250 Industrial Firms**

To better understand the issues faced by companies in managing the shift from a product-centric to a service-savvy business model, we conducted a three-year study of 250 manufacturers. The primary aim was to understand the practices they do, the factors influencing success or failures, and the outcomes achieved in terms of service growth. To this end, we adopted a two-step approach. First, we interviewed key decision makers within twenty-two selected corporations. Each company was among the market leaders and for a number of years had made sustained efforts to grow beyond their historical product core, with varying degrees of success. The companies came from very different sectors: cable manufacturing, medical equipment, motors and electronic equipment for aerospace, material handling, industrial paints, offset presses, production materials and energy distribution, specialty chemicals, and ball bearings. Participants in these qualitative interviews occupied key positions related to the service business, such as service director, sales director, business development manager, and head of strategy, including several executive board members. In a second step, we conducted a survey of 250 European manufacturers. This step aimed to deepen the insights gained in the first phase and to provide quantitative validation of the initial results.

Two key lessons can be learned from the study. First, it shows that companies greatly vary in terms of profit and revenue outcomes when pursuing the same goal of service growth. While some have successfully leveraged services into a real growth engine and profit generator, others struggle to profit. Second, our results underscore the critical role of senior management's commitment; it makes or breaks the service-growth strategy. Let us take a closer look at each lesson.

### Difficulty in Charging Customers for Service

A substantial portion of companies face low customer willingness to pay and find it very hard to charge for the services provided. While many of the firms are satisfied with their service performance, our survey shows that one company out of four reported having trouble actually charging customers for the services provided (see figure 4:3 a and b). Many firms reported that it was particularly difficult charging for services previously provided for free. For example, a sales manager told us that until a few years ago his company still employed an entire floor of technicians at the company headquarters to provide technical drawings to customer demand without charging for this service. In our sample, the list of services provided free of charge ranged from basic technical assistance or software installation to connecting industrial gas cylinders or invoicing for battery charges on forklift trucks.

Figure 4:3
**Study of the Service Strategy of 250 Industrial Firms**

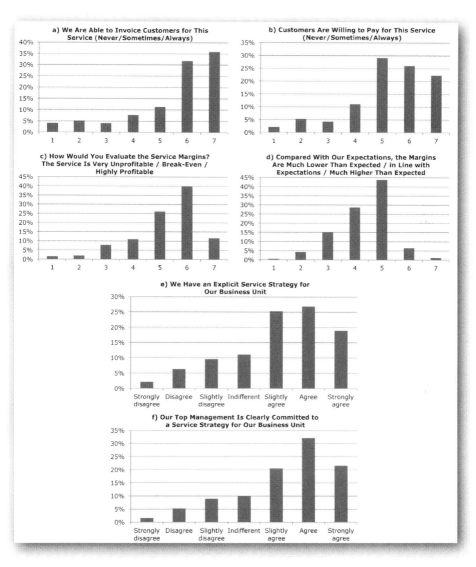

The companies also expressed their dissatisfaction with the margins achieved from service activities. Among the companies we studied, one in five did not make profits from service (see figure 4:3 c). Moreover, for half of the 250 companies in our sample, the margins were below initial expectations by those who made the original business plan (see figure 4:3 d).

Our results show a strong correlation between top management support and successful implementation of service-growth strategies. Conversely, companies that lacked such support voiced strong dissatisfaction with their financial results. Our analysis confirms what may appear as obvious to many and yet is a root cause behind the majority of failures: if management only pays lip service to service growth or erratically changes direction, a firm's service ambitions cannot be met.

The experiences of one of the managers we interviewed illustrate the consequences of frequent changes in senior management commitment:

> *At first, our mandate was to focus on services to counter competition from low cost countries. Rather than selling a "naked" product and allowing competition to beat us on any proposal, we realized the need to comprehensively address the customer's problem. Basically, buying our products was not an end in itself; our customers were looking at increasing the performance of their machines. Consequently, the newly formed service business experienced strong growth. Once the economic crisis hit us, however, the attention of our leaders turned away to focus on other goals: reducing costs and achieving short-term results. The effect was almost immediate. Middle managers did not know where to turn, and service activities instantly suffered.*

One in three managers in our sample clearly explained that their firms had not explicitly defined a service strategy (see figure 4:3 e). Moreover, one in four businesses did not benefit from sufficiently strong support of senior management (see figure 4:3 f). These are also the least successful companies in terms of service revenue and profits. Collectively, the figures underline the crucial role of senior management in defining the service strategy and communicating it to the employees.

### The time factor

We have seen that embarking on the service journey requires the company to reconsider both its mission and its market position. Such a transformation cannot happen overnight. It requires the establishment of a structured plan and long-term commitment. To know how to stay on course, ensure profitable service growth beyond a certain threshold, and understand the contextual factors supportive of service growth are all key elements that managers should take into account.

Typically, a company must recognize the time factor and reach a critical mass in services, without which it cannot expect to receive significant financial benefits. One of our studies, which included 513 German mechanical engineering firms, shows that a wide-scale transformation often takes time to pay off: service strategies generally lead to lower profitability levels before firms can realize profit growth and compensate for initial losses.[7] A study of 477 US-based companies from different industries during 1990–2005 confirms our findings and demonstrates that the impact of service sales on the market value of a company is moderate below a critical mass of 20 to 30 percent of total firm sales. However, beyond this level, the positive effect increases rapidly[8] (see figure 4:4).

Figure 4:4
Firm Value across Different Service Ratios

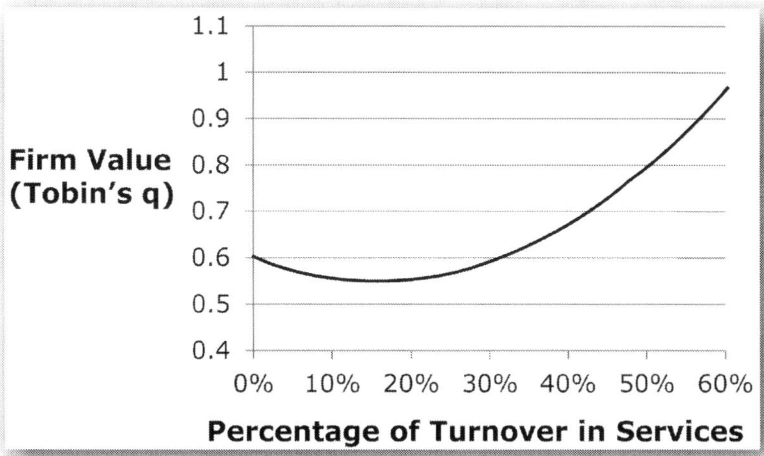

Source: Adapted from Fang et al. (2008), p. 11

The effect of revenue generated by services on the firm value depends on a number of contextual factors related to the company and the industry in which it operates. The more the services are related to the core competencies of the company, the more the service strategy can translate itself into a positive effect on the firm value. Moving too far away from the core competencies of the firm is never a good thing; without clear synergies between the product and service businesses, shareholder value is unlikely to increase. Similarly, as we discussed in chapter 1, firms operating in saturated product markets have more interest to invest in services than those with strong product revenue growth. Finally, the turbulence of the industry also matters: the more stable the market environment, the less investment in services seems profitable in the long run.

## KEY QUESTIONS ABOUT SERVICE STRATEGY

In reviewing the strategic issues in this chapter, it is clear that managers must ask themselves several fundamental questions:

1. Do we have a service strategy in place, and how well are our people aligned with it?
2. What are our ambitions and goals with the service business?
3. Is service included in our mission statement? If not, how can we incorporate a service mind-set?
4. What are the biggest roadblocks on the path to service growth?
5. How can we organically grow the service business?
6. What are the prospects of igniting service growth through acquisitions and/or sales of product units?
7. Does the current business model allow the integration of a service business? If not, how do we change it or develop a distinct service business model?
8. What competitive repositioning is needed in order to beat the commodity magnet?
9. Are our service margins in line with or above expectations? If not, what is needed to achieve our profit targets?
10. Do we have the long-term commitment it takes to pursue the service strategy?

A logical next step is to take the pulse of the organization to determine if it is fit for service. This is the subject of the next chapter.

## CHAPTER 5

# RESOURCES AND CAPABILITIES: ARE YOU FIT FOR SERVICE?

*We were expert at managing factories*
*and developing technologies.*
*But the [service] business model is different.*
*The economics are entirely different.*
*In services you don't make a product and then sell it.*
*You sell a capability. You sell knowledge.*
—LOUIS V. GERSTNER, JR.[1]

In the previous chapters, we have seen that top management plays a decisive role in defining and implementing a companywide service-growth strategy. Senior executives must be prepared to meet with strong internal resistance to change and know how to navigate the transformation journey from a goods-centric to a service-savvy business model. Additionally, we identified key challenges that managers face in that transition. But before launching at full speed into crafting and implementing such a strategy, it is worth asking whether your company is actually ready for such a significant change. Are you fit for service? To answer this question, executives must take the pulse of the organization.

This chapter provides guidance for examining whether a company has laid out the strong foundations for successfully mastering service growth. Does your company command the key resources and capabilities needed for a successful breakthrough in services? For example, a manufacturer may lack specific strategic resources or skills that the company must first secure before it can venture into the services space. For example, an aircraft manufacturer may first have to hire salespeople experienced in consultative selling before attempting to sell fuel-efficiency solutions to commercial airlines. Likewise, contrary to pure-service players, they may also possess unique assets and skills, which they can leverage for commercializing innovative service offerings. For example, by analyzing data flowing from thousands of its medical devices installed in hospitals nationwide, a manufacturer may start offering patient flow benchmarking and optimization consulting services to its customers.

To understand whether a company is ready for making the leap, we first develop a framework that identifies the unique resources that product companies need to secure and protect from competition. We then discuss how firms must leverage these specific resources for developing distinctive competencies needed for service growth. Third, we show how these unique resources and distinctive competencies translate into competitive advantage. Finally, based on our framework, we introduce a scorecard that executives can use for conducting a fit-for-service assessment. This analysis identifies your company's strengths and weaknesses, opportunities and threats, before launching head on into a service-growth initiative. From studying hundreds of companies, we derived these main building blocks as a common core across industries and markets. It is up to each company to complement these core resources and competencies with industry-specific ones to gain a thorough 360-degree view of which specific success factors are required for achieving successful service growth in your company.

## Critical Resources and Capabilities for Service Growth

By comparing the successes and failures of more than 250 European manufacturing companies, we identified strategic resources and capabilities that every company must secure for succeeding its service-growth strategy. Our framework in figure 5:1 shows how these unique resources can be leveraged for building distinctive capabilities, which, in turn, translate into competitive advantage—in the form of differentiation and/or cost leadership.

**Figure 5:1**
**Unique Resources and Distinctive Capabilities**
**for Successful B2B Service Growth**

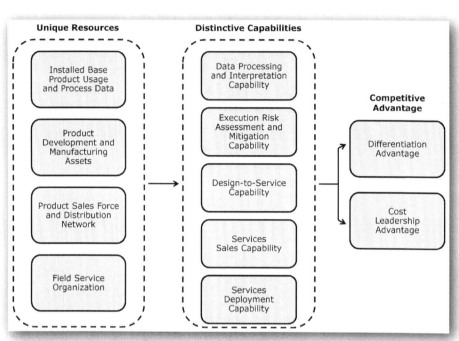

Source: Adapted from Ulaga and Reinartz (2011), p. 10

## Unique Resources Available to Manufacturing Firms

To understand strengths and weaknesses, managers can start on the left side of our framework and examine first the unique resources that the company controls. Resources are productive assets that the company may already own. When lacking selected strategic assets needed for service growth, a firm may want to first develop these resources internally, acquire them from the outside, or secure access through its business network. A wide range of services can be developed from the existing resources held by product firms. There is no one-size-fits-all solution, yet here are a number of manufacturer-specific resources that are critical prerequisites in many industries for accelerating service revenues and profits.

***Installed Base Product Usage and Process Data.*** The installed base of products sold represents probably the most strategic asset held by manufacturing firms today. We have seen in chapter 1 illustrations of ratios between the numbers of new products annually sold and equipment already installed. For example, for every new industrial transformer sold, there typically are already seventeen transformers in place. Throughout the lifecycle, manufacturers collect valuable data on equipment usage in their installed bases of products. Thus, manufacturers of printing presses possess a complete record of systems sold in the past, their customer locations, and usage conditions. By servicing its installed base through maintenance and repair agreements, a company thus systematically collects product usage and customer process data. Smart technologies increasingly allow for remotely capturing data, 24-7 and in real time. Vendors thus control a powerful resource in terms of product usage and process data in the installed base. Consider the quote of one executive we worked with: "Today, our forklift trucks are equipped with a multitude of data sensors. We remotely monitor operations on a real-time basis, 24-7. This allows us to collect data on how many hours the forklift truck runs per day, how many hours of downtime the equipment endures etc. We consolidate all that data in an online database."

When used strategically, access to data provides a significant advantage over both direct competitors and third parties such as pure-service players. A manufacturer in building technologies had this to say: "In energy efficiency services, we're not afraid of those consultants. Let them chase after customers with their PowerPoint presentations. We'll always beat them because when it comes down to comparing them versus us, customers understand that we are in the pole position. We build those electricity meters, we install them, we run them and we have all the historic data of how electricity flows in that building. That's unique."

Many B2B customers do not collect product usage or process data, nor do they systematically analyze data themselves. Even if they do, suppliers potentially have the advantage of collecting data from multiple sources and across multiple customers and usage situations, which allows them to benchmark, drill for deeper insights, and build the foundations for a host of new data and analytics services. Against this backdrop, it is absolutely paramount that companies understand that data represents a strategic asset they must acquire, grow, and—jealously—protect to gain competitive advantage. Giving data away for free or letting others freely access your data, undermine your opportunity of securing a unique asset and selling services that others can't. Valuing the benefits of data as a strategic asset, companies today design next-generation products in such a way that neither competitors nor pure-service players can properly provide service or collect data on their equipment, further protecting access to this unique resource.

***Product Development and Manufacturing Assets.*** Product companies control unique resources linked to R&D, design, and production processes. These resources may be tangible (such as components, machines, or tools) or intangible (like patented technologies and production licenses). When other competitors, or pure-service players, lack such assets, suppliers can develop unique competitive advantages through differentiation and cost leadership.

For example, tire manufacturer Michelin developed a new tire casing that allowed customers to regroove and retread its tires more often than its competitors could. By extracting four lives over the entire lifecycle of a Michelin tire, customers' trucks thus could effectively roll tens of thousands of miles more with its tires than with any other competitive product. By achieving substantial productivity gains, Michelin was able to lower trucking companies' total cost of ownership. What is more, this product innovation also put the manufacturer in a position to develop a new fleet management offer. With a superior technical product in hand, the tire manufacturer was able to take greater risks and sign novel performance-based contracts. Logistics companies paid according to the number of miles traveled rather than by number of tires sold and maintained. The unique and distinctive solution contracts were only made possible once Michelin had a unique asset (a technically superior tire) in hand. Neither competitors nor third-party service providers could deliver the same outcomes at the same costs.

***Product Sales Force and Distribution Network.*** Manufacturers typically rely on direct sales organizations or work through channel intermediaries for reaching business customers. Privileged access through direct and indirect sales organizations represents another unique resource that B2B companies can leverage to their advantage when growing services revenues and profits.

However, covering sales territories with a dense network and leveraging close customer relationships won't guarantee success alone. From our experience of working with companies on service growth for many years, we experienced multiple situations where a company's strong sales force and well-established channel structure did not sufficiently support service growth. For example, one equipment manufacturer we worked with generated 90 percent of its sales through a network of more than two thousand exclusive and independent distributors in North America, with an average sales force of four to eight sales reps in each dealership. Yet the manufacturer's service revenues stagnated at well below 20 percent of overall sales. Management realized that its dealer network was not strategically aligned with its service growth ambitions. Clearly, the company had a unique asset in hand. But it was not leveraged to its full potential for achieving the company's strategic goals. Likewise, Syngenta, a Swiss-based global producer of agrochemicals and seeds, found it harder than initially expected to grow services and customer solutions targeted at farmers. Its indirect channel structure required entirely rethinking how to go to market with innovative service offerings. In turn, the supplier's US-based competitor, international seed company DuPont-Pioneer, found that its strong direct channel control greatly contributed to leveraging this strategic asset for services growth.

*Field Service Organization.* A significant portion of manufacturers' revenues and profits stems from field services and spare parts sales. For example, studies have shown that manufacturing firms often derive substantial revenues and often twice as many or more profits from services revenues compared to goods-related sales.[2] For example, at ABB Turbocharging, headquartered in Switzerland and part of ABB's Process Automation Division, one-third of revenues are generated from new business such as selling new turbochargers, and two thirds of overall revenues are derived from its service business, with the latter providing virtually all the EBITDA[3]. ABB Turbocharging had an operational EBITDA above ABB's average and a solid historical performance with both revenue and EBITDA compound annual growth rate (CAGR) in the high single digits over the last two decades. In such a context, field organizations represent a strategic asset to the firm.

While most manufacturers invest in field organizations to deliver and install goods and service their installed bases, they often fail to maximize their potential. Field-service networks represent not only a key resource for effectively providing product lifecycle services but also an opportunity for venturing into new and more complex services such as asset efficiency or consulting services. Yet field-service organizations often quickly become a strategic bottleneck due to scarce human resources. Consider this quote from one executive: "We find it extremely hard to recruit and keep good service technicians. There's a blatant shortage of high-quality people, especially as our equipment isn't the most attractive in the eyes of well-trained service employees in other industries. We try to hire them away with attractive salaries, but it hasn't been easy."

Frontline service technicians are key to profitable service growth. They are first in line to spot opportunities for placing new or different service offerings. They also are well placed when it comes to serving customers more cost efficiently. Thus, service technicians represent a strategic asset that a firm must strategically acquire, nurture, and protect from competition in order to grow service revenues and profits.

The four unique resources highlighted above represent strategic assets that manufacturers must secure. With an understanding of their companies' strengths and weaknesses, executives can then develop strategies to transform these unique resources into distinctive service-growth capabilities.

## Distinct Capabilities Available to Manufacturing Firms

In order to achieve competitive advantage, acquiring unique resources is not enough. Companies must translate these assets into distinctive service capabilities. In working with many firms, we have identified five key capabilities that product firms must develop for successfully mastering service growth.

***Service-Related Data Processing and Interpretation Capability.*** Having access to customers' strategic product usage and process data derived from an installed base is only a first step. Manufacturers still must determine how to translate these data into a source of new revenues and/or identify opportunities for providing existing services at lower costs.

For example, one industrial equipment manufacturer installs dozens of electricity meters in commercial buildings to monitor customers' energy consumption. Using the data collected, the manufacturer is able to analyze energy consumption as a basis for gaining unique insights for optimizing facility management. Over the years, the company has successfully leveraged insights gained from data collected and analyzed to develop novel value propositions and package innovative offerings in energy-efficiency consulting. These new commercial offers immediately resonated with customers. For example, having tested the vendor's offer in several of its retail store locations and achieved substantial cost savings, one major retail account immediately asked the supplier to roll out its energy-efficiency consulting services across all of its store locations worldwide. Not only did this additional business become a new source of revenue generation for the firm but the vendor also gained a competitive edge over pure-service providers, consulting firms, or even power utilities. As it turned out, the only factor slowing down the speed of adoption of this new service was the supplier's ability to hire enough people—fast.

Similarly, over many years, bearings manufacturer SKF developed a unique expertise in collecting and analyzing data flowing from customer machines 24-7. By developing skills based on condition monitoring and vibration analysis, the company provides customers with recommendations for improving machine uptime. Interestingly, in many instances, the bearings manufacturer may over time become more knowledgeable about specific factory processes than customers themselves, which represented a basis for providing a host of new offerings related to asset-efficiency services.

These types of skills reach far beyond generic notions such as customer orientation or customer satisfaction.[4] Advanced data processing and interpretation capabilities allow vendors to gain truly novel and unique insights into how they can leverage customer data for achieving customer benefits in terms of productivity enhancements and cost reductions. Which key performance metrics truly matter to customers? Which levers can we activate to make a lasting impact on customers' revenues and costs? The following quote from one of the executives we worked with illustrates the key challenge for suppliers to understand how to gain and use insights for adding value to a customer's bottom line:

> *We sell ATM machines for customers in retail banking. To develop our solution offerings, we went beyond the usual interviews or customer satisfaction surveys. Instead, we took a deep dive into the economics of retail banking and studied how the data we have on consumers' usage of ATM machines could be leveraged for improving cash management in retail banking operations. Moving cash in and out of a branch costs a bank a tremendous amount of money. So we wanted to understand how we can help them save costs in their operations. At the same time, we knew these guys look for new ways to differentiate themselves. In that industry, the ATM is a key touch point for managing customer relationships. So we wanted to know how we can help the bank's marketing people to improve consumers' interactions with their bank...It's not that we have to become experts in how to run a bank. But we need to know how we can add value to their bottom line. The questions are: "Do we understand their business model?" and "Can we help them?"*

This example illustrates the extent to which vendors must gain better insights about what customers really need, and data analytics skills are critical in this space.

*Execution Risk Assessment and Mitigation Capability.* Risk can be defined as "uncertainty or variance in outcomes (especially losses) of some significance."[5] In the context of business services, execution risk refers to uncertainty about whether contractually agreed-upon service outcomes will be achieved. The ability to assess and mitigate execution risk is critical in order to strike a balance between designing innovative yet competitively priced service offerings on the one hand and meeting internal profit targets on the other. Companies often fail in correctly anticipating the nature and volumes of future resources needed to meet contractually agreed-upon performance commitments (such as 96 percent fleet availability). Thus, manufacturers often face the risk of committing to outcomes that they cannot achieve or promising results that can only be achieved by adding substantial unforeseen resources.

Execution risk can be mitigated in different ways. One generally used approach is to build price buffers into agreements in order to safeguard contract profitability. For example, one company we worked with had a habit of systematically raising prices whenever customers asked for contractual performance commitments. However, this approach can fail when the company effectively prices itself out of the market. By setting prices so high that they will surely cover all unforeseen risks, there ultimately may be no customer left willing to follow suit. A second approach to risk mitigation relies on pooling risk across multiple accounts. Here, risk is spread across a broader base. This approach, widely practiced in disciplines such as inventory management with random demand or financial portfolio theory,[6] is also often used when crafting performance-based services contracts. The following quote from an executive in a manufacturer's business unit selling customer solutions illustrates the key role of a critical size of accounts needed to pool execution risks across a sufficiently large customer base: "We quickly learned that to roll out our solution offer, we couldn't just sell a few performance-based contracts here and there. We had to achieve a critical mass to spread out risk across many customers. One customer can't handle downtime risks alone. But, if we group them, and if we bundle that risk, then it becomes manageable. To me, there's no surprise that it's only the leaders in many industries that go after those complex performance-based agreements. You need to have a critical size. A small 'boutique' player just can't handle that kind of risk."

A third way of effectively evaluating and mitigating service-execution risk is based on in-depth analyses and understanding of archival contract performance data. Time and a willingness to accept a steep learning curve are required to develop these skills similar to those of actuaries in an insurance company. However, once acquired, strong execution-risk assessment and mitigation capabilities can represent a powerful source of differentiation from competitors. For example, one capital goods manufacturer we worked with developed from scratch a dedicated risk management department by hiring away actuaries and experts from other industries. This department defined and implemented principles and tools for service contracts that were crafted, sold, and implemented by the company's business development and salespeople. Sourcing these new skills from outside and growing these competencies organically from within reached far beyond the company's traditional skill sets. At the same time, no other competitor had developed such skills yet, effectively providing the supplier with a competitive edge.

*Design-to-Service Capability.* Another challenge companies frequently face is how to develop a system and culture that incorporate the opportunity for providing a service down the road already as *early* as possible in a firm's innovation process. We discussed hurdles linked to companies' product-centric cultures already in chapter 2. By overly focusing on product innovation processes, managers too often miss out on opportunities for unlocking service revenue and profit potentials. Product and service innovation must interact synergistically for value creation rather than in a merely additive manner, as the following quote illustrates:

> *One of the main problems we face is that our teams don't think "service" when it comes to innovation. Our R&D efforts are geared toward products. Take our most recent product launch. Our product development folks focused their attention on improving product features. This product beats competition on any possible technical criterion that you can think of. Problem is customers are not willing to pay for an overengineered product. When we sought for other ways of squeezing value out of this technological beauty, we found that we could change the business model and sell an outcome instead of selling features. Did we plan this from the outset? Did we build service capabilities in the product from the beginning? No! Were we happy when we learned that we could do so much more with the product down the road? Yes! To be honest, we were lucky. We didn't take a systematic approach, but we should "think service" from scratch whenever we design a product.*

As this quote shows, by prioritizing the service component throughout the product innovation process, manufacturers can gain a competitive advantage in two directions. First, it allows the firm to go to market with innovative new hybrid offerings—that is, it enables effective differentiation. For example, design-to-service capabilities today enable manufacturers of jet engines to sign performance-based contracts with airlines, which they would never have accepted years ago. Today, many jet engines are already engineered from the outset in such a way that suppliers are in a position to make more engaging fly-by-the-hour agreements tomorrow.

Second, design-to-service capabilities also allow manufacturers to identify opportunities for cost reductions in new offerings. For example, by retrofitting its offset printing presses, one manufacturer enabled its service technicians to remotely perform first-level maintenance, thus reducing the number of costly on-site interventions. In this particular case, pure-service players face disadvantages in both domains because they lack access to the offering's underlying physical product features and cannot influence technical design decisions. Again, holding these assets is not enough. The company must proactively grow its design-to-service skills. In our experience, too many product-based companies have not realized the challenges and opportunities involved in this particular domain.

*Service Sales Capability.* Beyond improving service-design processes, companies still need to master critical service sales skills. When selling complex services, such as asset efficiency services, process support, or delegation services, salespeople typically must rely on a very different approach and mind-set than when selling goods for several reasons. For example, service requirements are identified in close cooperation with customers, or even codeveloped, rather than initiated by customers. Demanding services are also characterized by more complex and longer sales processes. Salespeople must have a capacity to move beyond their comfort zone and access different decision makers in a customer organization, often higher in the hierarchy, as the following quote illustrates: "You need to develop the right argument for the right person. Don't talk to a warehouse manager if you want to sell consultancy for productivity…The higher the contact person in the customer organization, the easier it is to talk about value-added services. The higher you go in a customer's management, the more vision they have on a problem."

However, even though a salesperson may already have a foot in the door, building the specific sales capabilities needed to value-added services beyond standard product lifecycle services often still represents a formidable challenge. As a sales manager explained, "We need a new kind of salesperson. The salespeople we have are often too narrow-minded and product oriented. In particular, the sales representatives at our resellers are typically very reactive. We are trying to educate them, but it is not easy."

Beyond hiring and leading a service-savvy sales force, the most successful companies we work with rely on specific documentation and communication tools for demonstrating value to customers. Companies further train frontline employees to facilitate or even perform service sales. Recall that field technicians can not only make or break a sale. They observe customer operations firsthand. Field technicians can identify new sales opportunities. They see areas for improvement or cost reduction in service delivery.

Finally, as many manufacturers also rely on channel intermediaries for indirect sales, firms must ensure that their own service sales initiatives are also aligned with the sales goals and activities of their distribution network. The critical assets and capabilities mentioned in this chapter are of such importance that we decided to dedicate a specific chapter to this topic (see chapter 10).

*Service Deployment Capability.* In chapter 2, we have seen that product-centric companies must learn how to play by the rules of a service factory. How to strike the balance between giving customers what they need and ensuring that service delivery costs won't eat up service margins? To answer this question, firms must develop an ability and willingness to take a production-line approach to service operations—a prerequisite for efficient execution.[7] This allows companies to learn how to standardize back-office service processes while achieving front-office customization at the same time.

Three subsets of capabilities are of particular importance in this domain: companies must learn how to achieve repeatability and economies of scale of services, modularity of service elements, and proactive management of service delivery costs. First, in terms of economies of scale, Toyota Material Handling is highly successful with its service deployment processes. With a majority of service revenues in major European markets coming from long-term service contracts, the firm is able to plan its service activities well ahead and maximize service technician productivity.

Second, regarding modularity, one firm we worked with built a set of six preconfigured service bundles for its industrial customers. The bundles differed from each other in terms of individual service elements included and service quality levels provided within specific service elements. For example, while the basic service bundle did not include emergency repair, other packages offered same-day or next-day emergency repair. Customers were free to choose from an options menu. While the supplier thus communicates its ability to cater to individual customer needs, customers' choices had to fall within six predefined service boxes. As a consequence, customer satisfaction rose dramatically, while service delivery costs decreased. Finally, managers must also find other ways to minimize delivery costs. Smart technologies can facilitate first-level maintenance and reduce the need to deploy costly field technicians. For instance, one company we worked with invested in training its customers to perform troubleshooting and simple maintenance tasks themselves. Another company transferred standardized service tasks to its distributor network to take advantage of dealers' lower cost structures and achieve cost savings. Furthermore, switching from reactive order taking to proactive service management can save substantial unplanned costs. Firms can incentivize customers to schedule routine maintenance during slow periods for making better use of idle capacities in field service organizations.

One final remark: although standardizing back-office service operations and achieving greater levels of productivity can minimize service delivery costs, these efforts should by no means come at the expense of providing individual customers with the specific benefits and problem solving they seek. An excessive focus on cost reduction can actually reduce service revenue generation.[8] In chapter 9, we will return to this key imperative.

## Building Your Services Portfolio: A Roadmap

With a clear understanding of the critical resources and capabilities required, a company can now decide how to build its service portfolio over time. Let's return to the four main types of industrial services discussed in our framework presented in chapter 2. The framework is built on two fundamental dimensions. The first dimension distinguishes between services oriented toward the supplier's product (such as repairing a machine) and services directed at the customer's activities and processes (like managing a payroll process). This dimension refers to the question "who is the service recipient?" The second dimension relates to the nature of the customer promise made by a service. Is the value proposition based on the promise to perform a deed (input-based)? Or, on the contrary, does the company promise to achieve a level of performance (output-based)? Based on these dimensions, we identified four fundamental categories of services: product lifecycle services (PLS), asset efficiency services (AES), process support services (PSS), and process delegation services (PDS).

Each of the four service categories requires its own combination of strategic resources and capabilities for achieving profitable service growth. What is more, to succeed in certain categories, companies must first master the key success factors of others. In short, with these resources and capabilities in mind, a company can now think about how to strategically build a growth trajectory for its services portfolio over time. Figure 5:2 describes three growth trajectories companies typically take when expanding their portfolio of service offerings. A fourth route to service growth is also shown in figure 5:2. However, over the many years we have worked with companies on service growth, we have never seen a company successfully follow this fourth avenue. Let's look at the trajectories in detail.

***Product Lifecycle Services (PLS)*** represent a natural starting point on the road map for growing a company's services portfolio. As we have seen in chapter 2, even a deeply product-centric firm can be considered, to some extent, as being a services company insofar as it must ensure provision of a set of fundamental services. For example, if a packaging machine manufacturer were unable to provide maintenance and repair of equipment installed, either by itself or through a third party, its industrial customers would not even consider the supplier for purchase. PLS have their own keys to success. In this first category, suppliers can dramatically improve their competitive position in different ways. For example, by providing the same must-have service like any other competitor but at a lower cost, a vendor may achieve (or maintain) better margins where others can't. Likewise, a vendor may understand better than competition how customers perceive value in a specific PLS or in specific quality levels thereof. In such a situation, the supplier may be

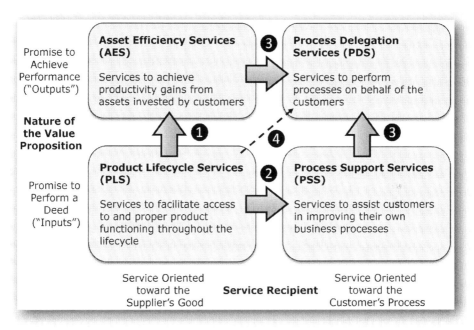

**Figure 5:2**
**Service-Growth Trajectories:**
**The Roadmap for Building a Service Portfolio**

able to charge more for more. It may also be able to simply turn a service around from free to fee—start invoicing a service hitherto provided free of charge. In each of the cases described above, the company achieves either more revenues or better margins than competition. Hence, when building a services portfolio, a firm must first make the most of its fundamental PLS for two reasons. First, PLS often represent a low-hanging fruit that companies can pick first before moving into more complex services. Second, PLS often play a critical role for building trust vis-à-vis business customers. Before sourcing more complex and risky services from a supplier, customers often want to first test a vendor with a more straightforward service. Hence, suppliers must first strive for excellence in PLS before moving into adjacent areas.

*Asset Efficiency Services (AES).* How to grow the services beyond PLS? A first growth trajectory described in figure 5:2 is the vertical move from PLS to AES. As companies grow their portfolio, many firms naturally venture into AES by shifting the promise of the service provided. While remaining in a secure comfort zone by staying close to their own product, suppliers now commit to helping customers achieve productivity gains from assets invested. For example, by remotely monitoring the functioning of a high-voltage circuit breaker in a power utility's plant, a vendor can now provide better levels of preemptive maintenance and guarantee equipment uptime. Services built around asset efficiency require that vendors invest in a host of new resources and build distinctive competencies often not held before. In the above-mentioned example, the manufacturer must equip its product with sensors, collect data 24-7, or develop software in-house or partner with another firm—in short, secure data and develop analytics skills. Thus, AES represent a first attractive growth trajectory pursued by many firms today to secure service revenue growth.

*Process Support Services (PSS).* A second growth trajectory described in figure 5:2 is the horizontal move from PLS to PSS. This category of services aims at a different direction. Here, companies grow their portfolio by getting more deeply involved in customers' processes. In the case of PSS, a supplier will not take on a process and perform it for its customer. But it will apply its knowledge and skills to assist the customer in performing that process better. Typical examples in this category are auditing, consulting, or training services. To grow a supplier's portfolio in this direction, the company must again secure and combine distinctive resources and capabilities. For example, a vendor may hire industry experts to gain deeper understanding of customers' applications. It may allocate specific resources and grow its capabilities not held before. For example, a semiconductor manufacturer we worked with spent significant amounts of time into understanding consumer shopping behavior in fashion retail stores. At first sight, this might appear as far-fetched from the firm's core business of manufacturing integrated circuits. But the investment also allowed the company to better assist fashion retail store chains in monitoring inventories, understanding and responding faster to consumer trends, and improving their customers' experience. Much like AES, PSS today also greatly benefit from enhanced data and analytics resources and skills.

*Process Delegation Services (PDS).* The moves from AES and PSS into process-delegation services are described in figure 5:2 as a third growth trajectory for a company's services portfolio. PDS are targeted at a customer's entire process. They also shift the value proposition. Instead of assisting a customer in performing a process, in this category of most complex services, the vendor performs the process and takes on responsibility for performance achieved. For example, a coatings manufacturer may take charge of an automotive manufacturer's paint shop and get paid by the number of flawlessly painted cars leaving the plant. Likewise, a jet engine manufacturer may take on aircraft maintenance for a low-cost airline based on a fly-by-the-hour agreement. Compared to the first three categories of business services, fewer firms venture into PDS, also commonly described as customer solutions. As shown in figure 5:2, these complex service offerings require committing resources and building up capabilities in both directions. Thus, to no surprise, companies often can only provide PDS once they have established a solid position in each of the three other service categories. There are two reasons companies typically foray into PDS only at this point. First, the specific resources and capabilities already developed for AES and PSS can now be leveraged for growing PDS. Second, from a customer perspective, sourcing a solution often implies to making substantial commitments and signing multiyear contractual agreements. Hence, PDS require a customer's trust in a vendor's ability to keep promises made. Here again, a proven track record of success in AES and PSS serves a basis for customers' willingness to work with a supplier in this fourth category of industrial services.

The nature of PDS and the amount and complexity of resources and capabilities needed in this category also explain why we have never seen the fourth trajectory in figure 5:2—the direct move from PLS to PDS—actually successfully made by a company. In several instances, we have worked with manufacturers that were tempted to make the immediate switch to a solutions provider out of the position of a traditional product-centric firm. In all cases, the companies pulled back after realizing the amount of resources and capabilities needed and the magnitude of short-term change such a drastic move would have required.

## The "Fit-for-Service" Diagnostic
The matrix described in figure 5:2 allows executives to assess the current status of their company's service portfolio. Is the firm still only active in

product lifecycle services? Have first attempts been made to grow into adjacent areas? Can we draw on existing resources needed for growing into a promising new service category? Do we control the required capabilities? Once managers know the current state of their service portfolio and which trajectory they want to pursue, they then can assess whether their company is actually ready to grow in this particular direction. To diagnose their companies' strengths and weaknesses, we have developed a straightforward tool described in figure 5:3, the fit-for-service assessment.

How can you apply this tool in your context? First, your assessment must be linked to a specific industry. If your company operates across industries and markets, the diagnostic should be made for each business unit separately. Second, our tool asks decision makers to identify all areas of critical competencies required for service growth. The five critical domains discussed in this chapter may serve as a starting point. These generic domains hold across many industries. Nonetheless, your particular industry and business unit may require additional industry-specific competencies for a more fine-grained assessment. Third, evaluate the extent to which you control the competencies needed in each domain. For example, in the hypothetical example of figure 5:3, a manager considers that his or her firm needs to improve its data processing and interpretation skills before it can move into Asset Efficiency Services (AES). Critical skills need to be improved in this domain. Hence, he or she rates this area four on a nine-point scale. The underlying reasons for each evaluation should be made explicit. For example, in the assessment described in figure 5:3, the manager explains that his or her company already collects quite a substantial amount of data, but data analysis and interpretation skills are lacking. Fourth, by analyzing all relevant capability areas and summating individual results into an overall score, decision makers thus establish an overall fit-for-service indicator for their company and identify specific problem areas.

We have conducted many service-growth assessment exercises with companies over the past years. From this experience, we found that such a diagnostics tool allows a company to bring key stakeholders from different departments inside the company together, encourage them to share and compare different viewpoints, and facilitate a discussion among all parties involved to clarify critical bottlenecks and milestones for designing and implementing a service-growth strategy.

**Figure 5:3**
**Fit-for-Service Assessment:**
**Is Your Company Ready for Service Growth?**

Business Unit _____**Example BU "XYZ"**_____

To achieve service growth, which skills and resources are needed in your business unit? To which extent does your BU already dispose of these assets and capabilities to further grow services? First, complete this table individually, and then discuss it as a team. Here's an example:

| Strategic Capabilities Required for Service Growth | We lack critical skills and resources in this area — Score: 1–3 | We need to improve specific skills and resources ☺ Score: 4–6 | We have a good command of skills and resources required ☺ Score: 7–9 | Your Score For This Category |
|---|---|---|---|---|
| Data Processing and Interpretation Skills | | Example: We retrieve an incredible amount of data from our installed base, but we need to do a better job in analyzing it. | | Example: " 4 " |
| Execution Risk Assessment and Mitigation Skills | | | Example: We hired experts with actuary skills who know how to correctly assess risk and commit to performance outcomes. | Example: " 9 " |
| Service Sales Skills | Example: We still have a product-centric sales force lacking the training, incentives, and tools to promote services. | | | Example: " 2 " |
| Design-to-Service Skills | Example: Our R&D and innovation processes are still goods-centric. We don't design offers with a service logic. | | | Example: " 1 " |
| Service Industrialization and Deployment Skills | | | Example: We've done a great job in standardizing service elements for cost savings. | Example: " 8 " |

Your Overall Score: " 24 " (out of 45)

## KEY QUESTIONS ABOUT RESOURCES AND CAPABILITIES: IS YOUR COMPANY FIT FOR SERVICE?

In reviewing the key resources and competencies needed for service growth and laying out a road map for their companies' service portfolio growth, executives must ask themselves the following key questions:

1. What is the current status of our service portfolio? In which direction should our portfolio grow beyond product lifecycle services?
2. Do we collect product usage data on our installed base? Do we control access to data? Is it proprietary?
3. Do we have unique product features and/or assets from which we can derive new and unique services tomorrow?
4. Do our distributors understand our service goals? Are our interests aligned? Can our dealers actively contribute to accelerating service growth?
5. Do we take full advantage of our field engineers and frontline service technicians for growing service revenues and profits?
6. Do we have the analytics know-how and skills needed for selling data-enabled advanced services?
7. Have we built execution risk assessment and mitigation capabilities?
8. Is service innovation deeply engrained in our R&D processes? When developing new products, do we "think service" from the beginning?
9. Can our salespeople sell value-added services? Do they have the skills and profiles needed for selling services? Are salespeople motivated to grow services sales?
10. Do we take a production-line approach to service? Have we built a services factory? Do we strike the right balance between customizing services and standardizing delivery processes?

## CHAPTER 6

## VISION AND LEADERSHIP: ARE YOU READY FOR CHANGE?

*Who says elephants can't dance?*
—LOUIS V. GERSTNER, JR.

S
ervice-led growth is essentially about leading change. Just adding services to the portfolio or adjusting current routines and practices is simply not enough. Once managers have set a service strategy, aligned it with the vision and mission of the firm, and reviewed its internal service-related resources and capabilities, vision and leadership are required in order to drive the change. To first show how critical change management in this space is, we will review frequently mentioned arguments against service-driven change initiatives. In order to drive the internal change process, managers need to convincingly respond to these objections. We will then depart from Dr. John Kotter's seminal-process model for change management and discuss service-specific traits for each step of the process.

### Why Is Change Management Needed?

Embarking on the transformation journey from product to service is about change; it is a profound change that needs to go down to the DNA of the firm, calling for a redefined strategy and mission and requiring a major cultural shift. Halfhearted initiatives or reliance on lower-level service enthusiasts will not be enough. Frequently, we found that the strongest resistance for change does not come from the outside but from channel partners or even the organization itself. As a global product manager who had been working for years with a worldwide service initiative said in frustration, "You would not believe the resistance we are meeting—it's a hell of a bell." In this change process, active top management dedication is needed. However, not every executive and manager is capable of driving the change. The leaders in charge need to be both visionaries and change agents in order to transform the organization and institutionalize the new business model.

When energy management and automation company Schneider Electric appointed a vice president of strategy and deployment of services, it signaled a clear message internally that service growth was a top priority of the firm. Such service champion at the highest level of the company is essential as there are frequently many *internal opponents to change*. The arguments typically presented against a service strategy in a product-based business—technology, engineering, or capital goods firm—include the following:

- *"With services, our profitability goes down the drain."* Revenues and margins from the sale of products are quite comfortable, and promising growth prospects are attractive enough. Building on services requires substantial resources that are needed to support investments in the core product business. If we invest in service growth instead of the product business—which is well known and which our shareholders also understand—we may jeopardize the overall profitability of the firm and destroy firm value. This would incur the wrath of shareholders and other investors.

- *"Selling services burns too much of our time and is irritating."* After investing heavily in human resources, hiring, training, and managing people, the development of services can still amount to unsatisfactory results. This argument is even more frequently put forth as many manufacturers are accustomed to managing stable, profitable, and predictable business models. They operate in a well-defined product market, have a well-functioning distribution network, and know their customers' product needs and channel partners' product sales and distribution skills. Why should they put this business model at risk by entering the service business, which is a very different animal of which they have little knowledge and no incentive to focus on? In addition, they may lose strategic focus if they try to implement another business model and logic. Since the service business is seen as an intruder competing for valuable resources rather than a sibling to the product business, the concern is that the needed synergies between the two will not be possible to achieve.

- *"Services cannibalize our product sales."* This is one of the most common arguments frequently raised by sales teams. Why should we knock ourselves out to sell a contract for remote monitoring of several thousand dollars when the offset press we sell is worth several million? Moreover, without an appropriate marketing approach, customers often do not understand why they should pay for a service associated with already expensive equipment, especially when this service had previously been free. According to its opponents, selling services becomes an obstacle to—and may even cannibalize—the product sales. A service business model, under which a firm sells the use of a product rather than the product itself, evidently reduces the need for products by increasing the utilization rate. Similarly, services such as fleet optimization enable customers to operate more effectively with fewer machines.

  What these opponents also turn a blind eye to is the inevitable fact that a single firm is not able to stop innovation and a turbulent business climate. If competitors are willing to disrupt their own product business when needed to offer the best customer-specific solutions, any company pigheadedly clinging on to its service-myopic views runs the risk of becoming irrelevant altogether.

- *"Selling services is not our responsibility."* In companies endowed with a strong product culture, the argument that services do not fall within the scope of the company's activities is frequently heard. A common concern is that service strategies will create internal confusion, tension, and even conflict. The culture shock factor is significant, and changing the business model often requires not only the integration of new skills but also changing business practices and behavior.

For example, since its inception in 1889, Michelin was defined as a tire manufacturer. Therefore, the implementation of its Fleet Management Solutions has not progressed without creating an internal stir. The change has required new skills such as expertise in risk-sharing agreements related to fleet management and in the processing of invoices from service partners. The necessary profiles for such expertise have proven to be very different from the traditional competences and skills of Michelin. Despite the solution's unique differentiation advantage, opponents of the service strategy never miss an opportunity to criticize and question the motivations driving this transformation, claiming that it can even be dangerous for the company to deviate from its traditional position as a tire manufacturer.[1]

In fact, the last argument highlights the fact that when expanding its business scope from product to service, the company is often obliged to give meticulous attention to the change process. Given the internal resistance and organizational inertia expected, especially in industry incumbents, each step of the process has to be carefully planned and executed in order for change to stick. This is what we will discuss next.

## How to Transform Your Organization

In order to make the necessary changes to enable service-led growth, companies can apply leadership and change guru John Kotter's eight-step model,[2] which is the most influential model for making fundamental changes in how business is conducted. We will go through each step and take a look at service-specific traits for each step of the process. To ensure lasting success of their strategic service initiative, leaders should give meticulous attention to each phase. Critical mistakes in any step of the process can have a detrimental effect, slowing momentum and even revoking the gains achieved so far.

The process will require both leadership and stamina. While some firms can reap benefits of the service initiative early on, other service transformations are associated with potential short-term negative effects. In such cases, resistance is often fierce, and leaders need to have the persistence to drive change beyond the inflection point. Remember that we said in chapter 4 that most firms will not be able reap the benefits immediately. Service revenue has a positive effect on shareholder value but generally only after the firm reaches a critical mass of 20 to 30 percent service revenue of total firm sales.[3] Consequently, leaders need to both devote attention to detail and adopt measures to reach the inflection point quicker.

The eight steps to transform your organization and enable a shift from a product-centric to a service-savvy business model are summarized in table 6:1. While the real-life service transformation may not necessarily follow a linear eight-step path, it is vital to pay careful attention to all of them and not declare victory until the service transformation is anchored in the corporate culture of the firm. Quick changes in today's marketplaces may require rapid adjustments irrespective of the long-term service strategy and vision. What is important in such cases is to not lose track of the overall objectives. During the latest global financial crisis, companies in many industries faced near-death experiences. Among those who came back, some decided to turn back to their core product business and no longer expand to adjacent service spaces. Others, however, came back more determined than ever to accomplish the service transformation they have already envisioned.

## Step 1—Establish a sense of urgency

An abiding sense of urgency around the big opportunity in sight is the bedrock upon which the entire change process is built. Urgency starts at the top of the organization, and a critical part is to have a clear view of what the target for the strategic renewal is. If it is the entire company, the CEO has a natural key role in establishing the sense of urgency and initiates the change process. However, many change initiatives do not need to—and should not—concern the entire company, especially not if it is a large, multinational enterprise. Instead, change is often needed

Table 6:1
Leading Change for Service Growth: Kotter's Eight Steps Applied

| Step | Key Ideas | Application to Service Change | Service-Specific Pitfalls to Avoid |
|---|---|---|---|
| **1. Create a Sense of Urgency** | Identify and discuss burning platform or, if this is not the case, work on the idea of lost opportunity. | Establish a sense of urgency also among product units and general management. | A majority of people still think that there are fat margins in the product business. The sense of urgency is only felt by the service department. |
| **2. Form a Powerful Guiding Coalition** | Build and maintain a group with enough power to lead the change effort. Encourage the group to work together as a team. | Identify those who are strongly supportive and actively against service growth. Depending on service strategy, different coalition members may be needed. | Support is ensured only among those who already believe in service. The dealers' management teams are not on board. |
| **3. Formulate a Vision** | Create a vision to help direct the change effort. Develop strategies for achieving that vision. | Ensure the product business does not feel threatened. | The vision appeals only to the service department. OR The vision is too vague and wishy-washy, and does not embody a service mind-set. |
| **4. Communicate the Vision and the Strategy for Buy-In** | Use every vehicle possible to communicate the new vision and strategies. Teach new behaviors by the example of the guiding coalition. | Bystanders, who can swing in both directions, need to be convinced. | Company leaders fail to show that they support the service strategy. All talk, no walk in terms of service. |
| **5. Empower Others to Act On the Vision** | Get rid of obstacles to change. Change systems and structures that seriously undermine the vision. Encourage risk taking and nontraditional ideas, activities, and actions. | Introduce service-oriented performance criteria. Ensure you are fit for service. | The mental barriers of a service transition to individuals are underestimated. Resistance from board-level detractors and middle-management obstructers is not tackled. |
| **6. Create Short-Term Wins** | Plan for visible performance improvements. Create those improvements. Recognize and reward employees involved in the improvements. | Show benefits of the service initiative to convince those who doubt and boost morale. | Lack of short-term service goals easy to quantify. Inability to identify and communicate service performance improvements. |
| **7. Do Not Let Up** | Consolidate improvements. Use increased credibility to change systems, structures, and policies that do not fit the vision. Reinvigorate the process with new projects and change agents. | Replace product-centric practices that are inconsistent with the service business model. Hire, promote, and develop service-centric employees. | Service promoters are overconfident and declare victory too soon. Lack of human resources: the service business is (still) not seen as a promising career path. |
| **8. Make Change Stick** | Institutionalize strategic changes in the corporate culture. Articulate the connections between the new behaviors and corporate success. Develop the means to ensure leadership development and succession. | New leaders should also personalize the service culture. | Requirements for promotion remain the same; product-centric behavior is rewarded. Leadership succession decisions are made by boards of directors who do not understand the service transformation in any detail. |

at the division or business unit level. If so, the managing director of the unit is key.

Ideally, the service transformation should be initiated in times of good business results, when the company has more resources and time to help make both the short-term and long-term changes needed. On the other hand, if there is no burning platform, the change leader will have a much harder time convincing people that change is needed. We have seen many examples of complacent companies in cozy positions with stable product sales. The more stable the position is perceived to be, the less they can be convinced to also develop services because it often has such a disruptive effect on the business. Therefore, top managers need to have an honest discussion about the competitive position of the company and what challenges that lie ahead in terms of shrinking product margins, declining market share, disruptive innovation, competition from a new breed of savvy emerging-market competitors, and other strategic issues. In these situations, outsiders such as customers, consultants, and analysts may need to be brought in to deliver the bad news and pump up the necessary urgency rate.

If the company is not in the midst of a severe crisis, standing on a burning platform, the change leader can instead create urgency around a strong desire to seize an exciting and strategically rational opportunity. For instance, there may be a window of opportunity for becoming a service outsourcing partner to large customers. Unless the company seizes the opportunity, rivals such as system integrators will take the currently uncontested market space and become middlemen between the company and its most important clients. Once the space is occupied, any future service maneuver will be much more challenging. In order to establish urgency and build momentum, change leaders need to proactively focus on both the challenges and service opportunities ahead.

A well-known attempt to galvanize the troops is CEO Stephen Elop's "burning platform" memo to the employees of Nokia in 2011, which back then was the world's biggest mobile phone manufacturer.[4] The CEO started the memo by telling the story of a man who was working on an oil platform. When the worker woke up from a loud explosion, he found himself surrounded by flames. He had mere seconds to react: whether to stay on and be consumed by the flames or plunge into the icy waters. He decided to jump and was eventually saved; the burning platform had caused a radical change in his behavior. CEO Elop then linked the story to the situation the company was facing: "I have learned that we are standing on a burning platform. And we have more than one explosion—we have multiple points of scorching heat that are fueling a blazing fire around us. For example, there is intense heat coming from our competitors, more rapidly than we ever expected." What is worse, "We poured gasoline on our own burning platform" through a series of severe misses.[5] Such a dramatic letter clearly gets the attention of managers and employees. However, while bad business results or, in the case of Nokia, a life-threatening crisis catches people's attention and creates awareness, it also gives less room for maneuver. For Nokia, decline was rapid, and the sense of urgency came too late; competitors vigorously poured flames on the company from all angles—Apple now owned the high-end range, and Android was quickly expanding to the low end after winning the midrange. Once the company plunged into the freezing waters, it was unable to build another stable platform.

When is the sense of urgency high enough? Based on his experience with change management initiatives, Kotter (1995) argues that it is when about 75 percent of the organizational unit's management is truly convicted that the current situation is unsustainable and that change is needed. For service growth, the creation of a dedicated service unit is often a means to achieve strong support within an organization. However, with such a decision, there is a risk of only ensuring high urgency rate among service managers and employees. In order to drive change, general managers and other parts of the organization also need to be involved. If a company wants to move to a service-savvy business model with world-class hybrid offerings, all parts of the organization need to be onboard.

## Step 2—Form a powerful guiding coalition

In order for the initiative to succeed, the change leader needs to create a powerful enough guiding coalition with a shared commitment. This team may initially consist of a few members only, but once it is established, it needs to grow in order to drive the change process successfully through the next phases. Depending on the size of the organization, the size of the coalition will evidently vary; while five to ten members may be sufficient on a smaller firm, the twenty to fifty range may be needed before progress can be made in big companies. Regardless of the size of the coalition needed, each of the hierarchy's departments and levels should be represented, and the members should have equal status. The coalition should be powerful in terms of titles, reputation, expertise, experience, and relationships. If relevant, it may also include representatives from a key customer or an influential union leader. When selecting members, Kotter (2012) recommends that companies create a guiding coalition made up of volunteers selected by filling out applications. Activities such as off-site retreats can help the team to develop the shared commitment needed. The coalition may well work outside the normal hierarchy; otherwise, it may not be able to instill change fast enough.

While it is crucial that the chairman, CEO, or division general manager take active part, it is wise not to include the entire top management team. The reason is simple: some people just won't buy in. As we have discussed in chapter 3, board-level detractors regard service as an outright threat to the business and will actively resist any large-scale service initiative. What is crucial is therefore not to have everyone on board from day one (or even the first years) but to have a critical mass of the right people needed to produce change and make it stick. If the company is reliant on a dealer network for its sales and service provision, the directors of the dealers should also be on board; otherwise, the coalition will never have the local leverage needed. Similarly, the change leader must avoid the temptation to ensure support only among those who work with services and have seen the light already.

When building the coalition, the change leader needs to diagnose the resistance. Failure in this phase usually comes from underestimating the difficulties of driving change, especially as it requires a cultural revolution for product-centric firms. Stakeholder mapping can be used to assess systematically who might resist the service-growth initiative and for what reasons. Because of the different cultural standpoints within a product firm, we come back to the discussion in chapter 3 around figure 3:3, which provides a tool for analyzing how different employees in the firm see service. The figure can serve as a template and be adapted to company-specific conditions to help understand how services are seen on an individual level among the different employee groups—top management, middle management, and field organization employees—and how to influence key stakeholders. In this step, focus should be on building a powerful coalition among those strongly supportive of the service strategy on all levels of the organization (see figure 6:1).

**Figure 6:1**
**Using Stakeholder Mapping to**
**Build a Coalition and Galvanize the Troops**

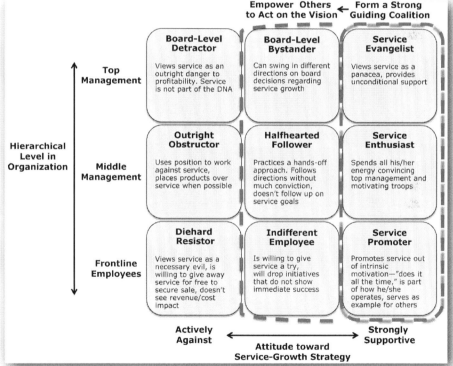

## Step 3—Formulate a vision

The vision should focus on taking advantage of the market opportunity or burning platform. It should be a picture of the future that is easy to communicate and have clear, pragmatic goals that appeal not only to employees but also to customers and shareholders. At the same time, a sound vision should be emotionally appealing; it needs to inspire change. The first version, or even the second or third, of the vision might not be clear enough, but after the vision-creation team has worked on it for some months, it usually becomes unambiguous and straightforward.

When formulating the vision, the team needs to address fundamental issues about how the business should be conducted, which is related to the strategic issues we discussed in chapter 4. For example, should the firm transform from a product to a service firm, or should it actively leverage its product and service resources and capabilities to move into hybrid offerings? While the strategy for achieving the new vision may be complicated, the vision should take no more than five minutes to communicate.

The guiding coalition has to be prepared to handle negative responses, especially from those in the product business who may feel threatened by the change. Uncertainty, insecurity, powerlessness, hopelessness, and a wish not to lose something of value are common emotional reactions, especially if the company may soon be consumed by burning flames. Unless the concerns are addressed, these feelings lead to paralyzed or even antagonistic employees. Therefore, the vision and strategy for achieving it should instill positive feelings such as optimism, trust, openness, and a strong determination to seize the opportunity. Any form of fear-inducing language should be avoided like death: the vision should inspire hope, not generate fear.

The director of the service research unit of a Fortune Global 500 company that we have worked with was very clear on this matter. Internal politics mattered a lot, and the service transformation was a very sensitive issue among many product units. Instead of talking about becoming a service or solution provider, managers used the term "product-service system." This was a deliberate choice of words: it starts with product, which may be interpreted as if the hardware is still what matters most. While the example may seem trivial, it illustrates that the change leader and guiding coalition need to have an instinctive feel and a thorough understanding of the entire organization to avoid creating unnecessary stir.

## Step 4—Communicate the vision and the strategy for buy-in

Credibly communicating the vision and the strategy is absolutely essential in order to attract and grow the internal supporters needed. Change leaders and enthusiastic members of the guiding coalition should use available communication channels to send the message to colleagues. Done right, communications such as meetings, speeches, newsletters, postings, and discussions on intranets and social media will generate buy-in from employees who begin to share a commitment to the vision and strategy.

A former division of ITT Corporation dedicated an entire issue of the company magazine, including the CEO column, to the opportunities of service growth through new technologies and innovative hybrid offerings. When Volvo Group launched a vision for their service growth, the company set up tangible targets that would be easy to communicate, such as 50 percent of revenues coming from "soft products" within seven years. Similarly, in its Vision 2020 strategy, aerospace and defense corporation Airbus (formerly EADS) stated that services should be worth €20 billion by 2020.

The buy-in is particularly challenging if it involves painful sacrifices for employees, such as job losses due to back-office automation and other service productivity improvements. Because the service business in many product-centric firms has been neglected over the years, there is generally major improvement potential, which tends to go hand in hand with job cuts. The fact that a successful service transformation can lead to significant job creation in many years to come is no comfort for those who no longer are needed. The negative feelings among employee groups therefore have to be managed in a sensible manner.

An example of how not to communicate is Stephen Elop's 2014 "Hello there" memo. Elop, who served as CEO of Nokia from 2011 to 2014, wrote it when he became Microsoft's vice president when the software powerhouse acquired the bleeding handset maker. The memo was aimed at the employees previously working for Nokia. After a long harangue of management jargon and abstract nouns about the need for strategic renewal, the memo eventually comes to the point: "We plan that this would result in an estimated reduction of 12,500…employees."[6] *Financial Times* journalist Lucy Kellaway scolded the memo, saying, "This memo deserves to become a set text for all executives interested in communication. It adds value by showcasing the delivery of business piffle that is perfectly aligned with current high-end management guff. It is a case study in how not to write, how not to think, and how not to lead a business."[7]

While much effort needs to be spent on the right form of communication—the problem is seldom too much communication but rather too little—the service initiative can easily fail if leading managers behave in ways that are at odds with the vision. If visible managers are unable to "walk the talk," one of the seven deadly sins committed by service-myopic firms (chapter 3), the belief in communication will decrease, and cynicism among the troops will grow. Leading managers need to symbolize the cultural shift through their behavior. For example, a middle manager can purposefully implement new work practices—from reactive taking of orders to proactive service management and problem solving—and act accordingly. Since many employees are initially lukewarm to service initiatives, they may swing in both directions, becoming either strongly supportive of the new vision or working actively against it. Therefore, members of the guiding coalition—the top-level service evangelists, middle-management service enthusiasts, and frontline service promoters—all need to communicate in both words and deeds to convince these bystanders (see figure 6:1). Without their support, the service initiative is unlikely to sustain.

## Step 5—Empower others to act on the vision

Once employees on all hierarchical levels have bought in to the vision and strategy, it is time to remove the major obstacles that hinder the employees to act on the vision. In some cases, the obstacles are in people's heads. Even individuals who understand and commit themselves to the new vision may struggle to overcome this mental barrier. Many times, however, the barriers are real, such as inadequate processes, organizational structure, or training. Perhaps the most difficult obstacles to remove are top managers who refuse to change. A board-level detractor could feel personally threatened by the new initiative and therefore try to undermine or obstruct the overall effort. If such a person is a key barrier, the issue becomes delicate, and he or she needs to be treated in a sensible manner, especially if the manager will continue to have a strategic role in the company.

A salesperson who has comfortably sold products throughout a long career may lack confidence to assertively sell new services. Through adequate training and support from successful peers in the sales team, the mental barrier may be removed. In other cases, a sales company manager may hesitate to help grow service sales because of an undersized service infrastructure and lack of skilled service technicians. Building up the local service business would require new employees such as technicians. Before being able to provide leadership and trying to implement the new service strategy, the strict headcount restrictions imposed by the headquarters would therefore need to be removed. Unless the company will have the delivery infrastructure needed, the service strategy will backfire if the company actively sells service but is then unable to fulfill what it promised.

Product-oriented performance metrics is another major obstacle that impedes the employees' incentives to develop the service business. Therefore, service-oriented and cross-functional metrics need to be in place in order to encourage employees to act on the vision. As discussed in the previous chapter, managers must take the pulse of the organization to ensure that it has the key resources and capabilities needed; it has to be fit for service.

## Step 6—Create short-term wins

In order not to lose momentum, short-term wins are critical, and they should be celebrated when met. In chapter 3, we refer to these gains as the first glimpses of promising light (figure 3:1). Managers should therefore vigorously look for performance improvements, establish yearly goals in their planning and systems, and reward the achievements made. The guiding coalition should have no status or territory to protect that may hinder the short-term wins to materialize. Unless short-term wins materialize, skeptics will erect new barriers. If the company is unable to start reaping early harvest within twelve to twenty-four months, bystanders may shift from positive to negative, and even members of the guiding coalition may start to raise doubts about the initiative.

A shift from a product-centric to a service-centric culture is a major change that takes time in large organizations. The long-term time horizon of several years may lead to dropped urgency levels and complacency. Good short-term goals must therefore be obvious, unambiguous, and clearly linked to the vision and strategy.[8] Examples of measures include service quality, operating profit per service unit, response time of service technicians, and downtime of customer equipment on preventive service plans. If the aim is to have 50 percent of revenues coming from services within seven years, annual targets are needed as well to keep track of performance and celebrate when achieved. A well-documented pilot project is one way to show progress. A typical short-term win, which is easy to measure and communicate, is to showcase that the company can turn around a free service to a profitable fee service.

Focus on short-term wins also helps continuous monitoring and analysis of the vision and service strategy. If the vision or strategy needs clarification, calibration, or larger revision, ongoing analysis of the change process and service performance will facilitate the modifications needed.

## Step 7—Do not let up

Managers must not be tempted to declare victory too soon. As long as the change has momentum, the cultural and political resistance is usually held back, only to arise once it halts. According to Kotter (1995), it can take five to ten years for change to sink into a big company's culture. In the meantime, the transformation is still vulnerable. The gains made can still be reversed and tradition creep back in. Great attention should therefore be paid to human resources and making sure that the right people are put in the right jobs. Recruitment, promotion, and development are key ingredients to keep up the change once major obstacles have been removed and glimpses of short-term wins seen. A critical mass of managers and employees should now be strongly supportive.

Managers in charge of the service initiative should be aware that both service resistors and service promoters could be the ones causing the change process to halt too early. A typical example would be a project where an external consultant works with the company to devise a service strategy. When the project is completed after two years, the consultant leaves, and the service promoters in the guiding coalition, thrilled by short-term signs of progress, declare a premature victory that kills momentum. For instance, early on in the development of its solutions business, Xerox hired a team of external consultants. Management hoped they would be able to swiftly convert existing business to solutions selling. To no surprise, the effort failed; the skills and mind-set required for the solutions business were simply too different.[9] The Xerox case is by no means unique though; most firms struggle with the challenge of aligning the management of their human resources with their service strategy.

A major headache for one company we have worked with was the high employee rotation rate. While people stayed within the firm, middle managers and specialists would normally change position every two to three years. Such behavior made it more difficult to anchor the change, especially since there was a constant shortage of experienced service employees such as service-pricing expertise. While the headquarters were struggling to keep momentum, individual sales companies were more successful. In one case, the leader in charge had been managing director for seventeen years and was well respected both within the sales company and at the headquarters. He had a clear service vision in mind and worked proactively to seize new service opportunities, sometimes long before headquarters had identified them. He worked tirelessly to motivate his troops and achieve the service goals set, even when employees and customers initially were skeptical or even actively against the change.

## Step 8—Make change stick

To make change stick, it needs to seep into the bloodstream of the organization. New behaviors need to become rooted in the shared values among employees who provide them with norms for conduct. In practice, it means that the service transformation is anchored in the corporate culture through a shared appreciation for giving good service.

Two factors are particularly critical in order to institutionalize the change. First, people need to see how the service strategy and its new behaviors and attitudes have boosted performance. A typical pitfall is when executives bury service in a general bucket; instead, companies have to show the performance of their service businesses. The improvements need to be clearly communicated in order for employees to see the connections between the change and the improved results. Second, when a new generation of top management is appointed, they, too, need to personify the service culture. The wrong successor in charge of the company may undermine even a decade-long service transformation. The new executive might not even have to be an active resistor; it may be enough with someone lukewarm to the service initiative to make the renewal halt.

Xerox is a case in point regarding a successful succession. In 2009, when the company appointed a successor to acclaimed CEO Anne Mulcahy, they named Ursula Burns. Mulcahy, who was named CEO in 2001, had taken the company through a successful transformation from a burning product platform on the verge of bankruptcy to a lucrative service business. Burns also personified the change, having worked closely together with Mulcahy for almost a decade in a relationship that both executives describe as a true partnership.[10] She was named a senior vice president in 2000 and was told by Mulcahy that her help was needed on the turnaround team that would form the core of the guiding coalition. When she succeeded Mulcahy as CEO nine years later, in July 2009, Mulcahy remained as chairwoman until May 2010. Between 2009 and 2015, Burns followed in the footsteps of Mulcahy by continuing the wide-scale service transformation.

## KEY QUESTIONS ABOUT VISIONARY LEADERSHIP AND CHANGE MANAGEMENT

In reviewing the eight steps to transform the organization, it is clear that leaders must ask themselves several fundamental questions:

1.  What are the strongest arguments against service growth within the organization?

2. What is the single biggest opportunity around which we can create a sense of urgency?

3. How do we establish and maintain a great enough sense of urgency and motivation throughout the organization and change process?

4. Do we know who the service promoters, bystanders, and resistors are and how to approach them?

5. Does the guiding coalition include members from all levels and relevant departments, including dealers, who share the commitment?

6. How do we create a service vision and strategy clear and easy to communicate?

7. What are the major structural and mental obstacles that have to be removed?

8. What are the visible, significant, short-term wins we need to achieve?

9. How can we hire, promote, and develop service-savvy managers and employees?

10. Has the service transformation become anchored in the DNA of the firm? Has it changed the corporate culture?

Having reviewed the key questions on vision and leadership and structured the development of a change management process, managers need to turn to implementation issues. These will be discussed in the next section of the book, starting with the key issue of what to sell: your service portfolio and pricing activities.

# CHAPTER 7

## CAPTURING MORE VALUE: PRICING SERVICES FOR PROFITS

*Price is only ever an issue in the absence*
*of—quantified—value.*
—TODD SNELGROVE, VICE PRESIDENT OF
VALUE, SKF NORTH AMERICA

The first two parts of our book lay out the foundations of a service-growth initiative and introduce the strategic questions a firm needs to address when formulating its service-growth strategy. Management must have a clear strategy and vision, secure critical resources and capabilities, share its vision, and demonstrate strong leadership when steering this transformation journey. In the following three chapters, we now turn to the challenges managers face when implementing their service-growth strategy. When growing a services portfolio, setting prices becomes a particularly challenging issue. Hence, in this chapter, we first focus on how the company can capture (more) value through value propositions and pricing. In chapter 8, we discuss how managers can embed service innovation in their structures and processes to make it a day-to-day practice. Finally, chapter 9 investigates how to turn the idea of a service factory into action.

### Making Most of Existing Services

Many firms launch new services that are not adopted in the market. Others give services away for free, even though customers would be willing to pay for them. In all those instances, firms miss out on opportunities of capturing more value from the service-growth strategy they deploy. In this chapter, we discuss how executives can better capitalize on existing and new services and craft compelling value propositions that truly resonate with customer needs. We first examine how companies can make the most of existing services. We then review which pricing approaches firms can use for different types of service and how to handle risk. Finally, we discuss how to craft competitive value propositions that take into account both customer-perceived value and price points adopted relative to competition.

Launching new services is fraught with multiple challenges and potential risks. Hence, before venturing headfirst into generating revenues from new services, managers are well advised to take a step back and consider whether their company already exploits the true value potential of services already provided but not at all (or not sufficiently) billed to customers. In our experience, we found that turning existing services from free to fee—starting to invoice services hitherto provided free of charge or selectively invoicing more—represents low-hanging fruit that companies should pick first.

For example, consider product lifecycle services (PLS) introduced in chapter 2. Many must-have services, such as providing technical drawings and prototyping, delivery and installation, inspection and maintenance, and training on product usage and regulatory changes, are often considered essential for enabling a product sale. However, from working with companies over many years and researching pricing practices for business services, we have learned that companies too often are unable to fully capture the value their services create for customers.[1]

Few customers will insist on paying for a service when given an opportunity to receive it for free. Many suppliers often mistakenly make the assumption that nothing can be done as competition provides the same service for free. Likewise, it is often assumed that customers don't perceive much value in a given service, hence the need to provide it free of charge. Even worse, many activities performed may not even be considered as a service provided. Against this backdrop, vendors should permanently check their assumptions. Recognizing that they already are, in fact, a service provider and that they need to act accordingly is already a major step forward. At this stage, an obvious question comes to mind: how can we better capitalize on our existing service offerings? To address this fundamental issue, we suggest that managers answer the following three questions:

## Step 1—How Do We Sell Services Today?

A critical first step is to take stock of services already provided, independent of whether they are invoiced or not. Taking a snapshot of the service portfolio as it currently exists is key. Building a catalog of services already performed is a tedious but always revealing task. From having conducted such assessments with several companies, we have learned that establishing an inventory of existing services carries many benefits.

A *first benefit* refers to generating awareness among your own employees. Building a service catalog allows everyone to actually see the breadth and depth of service activities already provided. Employees often are surprised to realize the extent to which their company already supports customers. Often neither employees nor customers are fully aware of these activities. When an activity is not documented as a service in its own right, when it is nowhere codified in an IT system, it becomes an invisible service.

A *second benefit* flowing from the first is that once a service becomes visible, it can be defined and measured. What exactly do we mean by performing this service? What are its key service elements? What does not fall within the scope of this service? How often do we actually perform this service? What does it cost us to deliver the service? While companies often pay meticulous attention to systematically measure and benchmark how well their products are performing, this is not always the case with service activities. The very same firm that knows the costs of each nut and bolt may be unable to tell the costs and profitability of its services. Identifying, codifying, and understanding the cost of providing a service all contribute a lot to raising internal awareness, communicating a burning platform in case a service reveals itself as a significant profit drain and preparing employees for a change, if needed.

Finally, taking stock of services already performed allows managers to reveal differences across units or territories. Definitions of the same service may vary considerably from one business unit or country to another. For example, in one of our workshops, we asked the participants from different geographical units of a cable manufacturer to describe established practices of making cable drums available when shipping cable to customers in their respective countries. To the surprise of all participants, the exercise revealed half a dozen different practices of invoicing for cable drums, all the way from free of charge to asking for a consignment fee. Clearly, country representatives had not realized the extent to which practices varied across subsidiaries.

## Step 2—Can We Leverage Best Practices from within Our Company?

Once the company has made a systematic inventory of its services, it can search for opportunities to improve existing pricing practices. Even small decisions regarding existing service elements, prices, or even simply price presentation formats can have a great impact. For example, in one study we conducted among five hundred purchasing managers in machine manufacturing industries, we found that customers' willingness to pay can change by as much as 5 percent simply by altering the price presentation format. In particular, this willingness increased when individualized service bundles were offered to customers, identifying each service element and price rather than all-inclusive packages with a single price. Giving decision makers more choices and putting a price tag on each individual service element led managers in our study to agree to pay more. Yet these findings are in stark contrast to the commonly adopted practice of packaging all services into a single price.[2] Insights for making those changes can come from outside. Yet before asking for external consultants or venturing into unknown waters, we found that there is often a tremendous potential for learning from internal best practices. This transfer of knowledge can be made between business units or geographic entities within the same group. The company should pick this low-hanging fruit first.

For example, in one of the companies we worked with, global supplier of industrial and medical gases Air Liquide, one division had accumulated extensive experience in developing and providing a full-fledged solution offer for inventory management. Air Liquide's Total Gas and Chemical Management (TGCM) ensures an efficient, safe, and reliable supply chain for delivering hundreds of specialty gases and chemicals on-site for global semiconductor manufacturers.[3] This offer was greatly appreciated by customers who considered supply of raw materials to be a complex, cost-intensive activity that they did not perform well and which exposed them to considerable risk of production downtime. Customers generally did not wish to assume risk in this area and therefore naturally turned to their supplier for help. The experience accumulated over time in its electronics division allowed Air Liquide's industrial merchants' division, serving industrial customers, to successfully transform its supply-chain services offer and launch a similar service.

## Step 3—How Should Existing Services Evolve over Time?

After taking stock of all service activities already performed and having identified best practices inside the organization, the company can then decide how these offerings should evolve over time. Figure 7:1 presents three fundamental choices that managers must make for a given service:

**Figure 7:1**
**Evolving Existing Services over Time: Three Main Decisions**

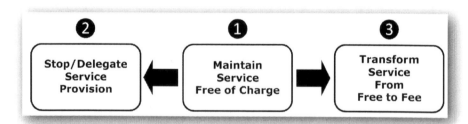

**Maintain the Service Free of Charge.** A first obvious choice is to continue providing a service free of charge. Not every service must be systematically invoiced to customers. There are good reasons why a company may want to stick to this practice. The key issue, though, is that these reasons must be clearly laid out and openly discussed. In some cases, increased competition and product commoditization may cause the company to maintain the status quo and provide a free service to defend its competitive position. Yet this decision must be carefully considered. Whenever we work with companies in this domain, we insist on one key principle: there is no free lunch. If we provide a service for free, customers must give something in return. This can come in the form of a commitment to increased purchasing volumes, serving as a reference to another customer. In all cases, the company must strive to meet customer expectations of service quality exactly, not more, not less. If you can deliver a must-have service free of charge but at lower cost than competition, your company still can gain a competitive advantage over other vendors.

**Stop or Delegate Service Provision.** The second option is to simply stop a service, which thus far has been provided free of charge. This is particularly justified when a company realizes that customers really do not value the service in question. In such a situation, discontinuing a service will not lead to dissatisfied customers, nor will they switch to the competition.

Take the example of a manufacturer of industrial consumables we worked with. We probed into customers' value perceptions vis-à-vis a set of industrial services provided by the company. The supplier had a habit of providing customers with paper reports of monthly consumption analyses sent along with product shipments. When investigating customer value perceived in receiving this service free of charge, the finding was a surprising verdict: in one case out of two, customers discarded the report without even taking a single look at consumption statistics provided. Compiling monthly reports represented a costly task to the supplier. The vendor realized that stopping this free service would neither dissatisfy customers nor would such an action drive them into competitors' arms. Clearly, the service provided exceeded customer expectations. By simply discontinuing a service that was not needed, it could reduce costs without upsetting customers.

Beyond merely ceasing to provide a service, a supplier may also want to consider delegating a service to a distributor. Rather than not providing a too costly service anymore, the company finds a new way of serving the customer—at a lower cost. One manufacturer we worked with realized that a number of services in its overall portfolio could be performed in a much more cost-efficient manner by its channel partners. To provide a best-possible customer experience at a much better cost, the company deliberately shifted some of its services to its dealer network while keeping others to itself. Rethinking who does what and sharing activities in the overall services portfolio is particularly important when firms have to rethink their channel strategy in light of a new service-growth initiative and must develop a better value proposition not only for customers but also for their own distribution partners (see chapter 12).

**Transform a Service from Free to Fee.** The third option is to transform a free service to a paying service—that is, a free-to-fee transition. This is undoubtedly the most difficult challenge because customers have become accustomed to receiving a free service and hardly appreciate such a change without a compelling argument.

Companies often bend over backward to please customers and provide services such as prototyping, technical drawings, or training for free. Yet while the challenge of stopping to give free services away and starting to invoice customers for valuable services provided may appear daunting at first, we found a host of best practices and successful cases where companies turned around services from free to fee.

Consider the example of a manufacturer of industrial gases we worked with. Manufacturers in this industry ship millions of gas cylinders annually to hundreds of thousands of business customers, from small auto repair shops to university labs or factories. Cylinders represent a huge asset investment for gas suppliers and require vendors to carry a significant supply-chain cost. Considering that providing gas in small quantities represented a value-adding service, the company started to charge a small monthly rental fee for each gas cylinder delivered on-site. In parallel, through educational activities, it ensured that they understood the value of gas availability. The recurring billing for millions of gas cylinders not only resulted in substantial additional revenues and profits. It also sent a signal to customers that this was a valuable service. Introducing a price triggered new questions among customers: Do we really need that many cylinders on our premises? Can we get the job done with less? With heightened awareness created among customers, the supplier even started to offer a new inventory management service—for a fee. As it turned out, this was a win-win situation for both parties.

Customers could lower their inventory holding and management costs while maintaining the same volumes of gas consumption. The gas supplier could better allocate its assets to where they were actually needed. Finally, the supplier generated additional revenues through new services provided. However, this change was not made overnight and not in all countries simultaneously. Local market conditions, such as the supplier's relative market share or customers' willingness to pay for enhanced value-added features, facilitated or slowed down the introduction of this for-pay service. For example, the company launched the service first in markets where it commanded a very high market share. In addition, the supplier waited for introducing the fee in conjunction with an improved usage and enhanced safety feature added to its new cylinder regulator system.

Attention to detail when observing customers in their operations can go a long way in identifying opportunities to turn around free services into revenue and profit generators. Consider two examples. In the case of the above-mentioned gas supplier, the company noticed that customers frequently approached its delivery drivers for a helping hand to hook up gas cylinders with their equipment. While done with the good intention to help out, intervening in a customer's operations may also represent a potential risk. A wrongfully connected cylinder can potentially lead to considerable liability issues in case of an accident. Instead of banning drivers from giving a little helping hand, the supplier identified and packaged this activity as a new service it commercially introduced in the market.

The second example is no less instructive. For many years, a manufacturer of specialty chemicals (industrial pigments) had been accustomed to covering all delivery costs on behalf of its customers. Customers were not aware of the relative importance of shipping costs involved; especially in the case of pigments, delivery costs represented a minor percentage of overall amounts invoiced. However, while representing only small change to individual customers, supply-chain costs represented a significant portion of the vendor's supply-chain costs. Based on this observation, the president of one country organization of the supplier we worked with conducted an interesting experiment. In a sample of a hundred randomly selected clients, he unbundled delivery costs from the product sales price and then invoiced based on the commercial terms "ex works" instead of "free on destination." The overwhelming majority of customers did not realize the changes made since the impact on the final cost was minor. Only a dozen customers noticed the modification, and of these only a few demanded a return to prior conditions. For these customers, the supplier reinstated the initial shipment conditions. The vast majority of customers, though, did not request a change. By taking a new look at which services created value in the eyes of its customers and which didn't, it had successfully improved its margins.

These two examples illustrate situations in which firms managed to increase revenues or decrease costs; however, an immediate step from free to fee may at times appear to be too risky. Hence, companies may want to consider intermediary steps on the free-to-fee journey. Companies can first raise awareness that a service exists and establish the fact that it creates value for customers. They may then attach a price tag to the service without initially charging for it. For example, a steel producer we worked with created a loyalty program much like a frequent-flyer program in the airline industry. The manufacturer had actually defined a scale to assign points to customers based on the volume of steel ordered. Customers could then use these points to obtain free consulting services from the provider, such as assistance in improving their production processes. Clearly, the company communicated that consulting services had a dollar value. Once bonus points were consumed, customers had to pay for additional services or turn to third-party consultants.

In another case, a supplier provided a host of costly services free of charge. The company noticed that customers hardly used all services, but as long as they all were obtained for free, they would use selected services once in a while. To improve its overall costs, the supplier invited customers to select from a menu of services it currently provided; the company agreed to continue to provide half of the services pro bono in the future. For the other half, however, customers had to start paying for these services. This approach allowed the supplier to clarify the situation, save costs of services provided, and generate additional revenue from others.

Finally, a slightly different variation of such a free-to-fee transition consists of defining a free baseline service offering first and then add for-pay options on top of this generic free offer. For example, one manufacturer of steel products we worked with found itself tied up in a situation where it performed a host of complex calculations and technical simulations free of charge in return for the steel products customers bought. Despite a host of external engineering companies, which all charged for their consulting services, customers were understandably delighted to obtain as much technical support as possible free of charge. Against this backdrop, the company decided to clarify its offer; while basic calculations remained free, it introduced a fee for more complex calculation and simulation services involving a considerable amount of man hours needed.

All these cases above show that companies leave too much money on the table—too often. While there may be good reasons why firms decide to provide selected services free of charge, they are well advised to take a step back from time to time and ask, "Why do we provide this service for free? Does the customer give us something in return? Is the service really needed? Does it create value for customers? How much? What would happen if we stopped it tomorrow? Could we introduce a for-fee option? How?" There may be nothing wrong with free services, but if they are given away too often and systematically, then there may be a need to put the facts on the table and check your assumptions.

## How to Price Services

Once managers have addressed the challenge of free services, they can turn to the broader issue of how to price all services in their portfolios. Setting prices depends on the type of service offered. By now, you are familiar with our service typology discussed in chapters 2 and 5. Our typology is based on two dimensions: the distinction between two value propositions (the promise to perform a deed and the promise to achieve a result) and the distinction between a service targeted at the vendor's product and a service geared toward the customer's process. Figure 7:2 presents the underlying approaches to pricing in each of our four service categories.

Figure 7:2
Pricing Approaches for Different Service Types

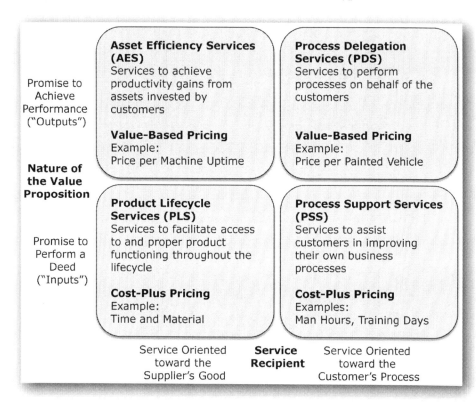

*Pricing Product Lifecycle Services.* In this first category, companies promise customers to allocate resources and perform an agreed-upon activity such as repairing a machine. As the starting points are inputs into the service delivery process rather than the value customers derive from the service, the prevailing pricing approach is cost-plus based. PLS are typically invoiced based on time and material used to perform a service. Which spare parts were needed? How many hours did a technician spend on-site? How much does it cost us to provide this service? What is our internally agreed-upon markup?

Oftentimes, customers are given the choice of paying a fixed price. Once a company knows its costs and required margins, there can be many benefits with fixed-price services. As a service manager of a pump manufacturer explained:

> *We're really trying to innovate with products that we can offer within a service environment. So we've got certain products, for instance fixed price servicing, which means that the customer in advance can know how much it's going to cost to repair that unit, and they can call us and tell us what pump they have and say they want a fixed price repair. That saves an awful lot of administrative work of making a quotation for that customer, and we can go straight in and dismantle the pump and see what's needed, order those spare parts, repair the pump, and get it back to the customer… We really try to always bring on new types of offerings that we can make it easier for our customers and easier for us. It's something that competition is catching on to, but we can have the edge for a certain time, and that gives us a competitive advantage.*

There is no doubt that revenues from spares and repairs can be extremely profitable in many industries. We have also come across many situations where profit margins on spare parts and technician hours were so incredibly high that one even can't decently report on examples here in this book. But this should not hide the fact that companies also often find it extremely hard to ask for a price for other PLS. Thus, profitable spare part and repair services must often compensate for mediocre prices and margins elsewhere. The underlying reason is that customers perceive many PLS as a must-have and display low willingness to pay for such services. Managers frequently find it difficult to differentiate many PLS from the competition and seek to standardize these basic services. Yet PLS can play a key role beyond merely enabling sales in that they are pivotal in establishing the supplier's reputation as a competent service provider. Firms can develop customer relationships and build trust through PLS as a prerequisite for expanding into adjacent, value-added service categories.

These characteristics have important implications for pricing PLS. Firms are often tempted to give away such services for free to secure equipment sales or simply invoice customers for time and material, according to a "break it, fix it" logic. To avoid tedious pricing negotiations, some firms even bundle PLS with goods sold into an "all-inclusive, take-it-or-leave-it" packing. With lack of better knowledge of how to price these services, managers thus resort to a heuristic of forcing PLS on the shoulders of customers—arguably not the best way of pricing PLS. To succeed in this category, managers must be mindful of the specific characteristics of these services and learn how to set prices in the most efficient and effective manner.

*Pricing Process Support Services.* While PLS are inherently product oriented, process support services are oriented toward the customers' processes. Like our first category, PSS are input-based. Vendors commit to making resources available, but they tend not to engage in signing contracts tied to results achieved. For example, a vendor may invoice an energy-efficiency audit based on the number of days needed for performing the service, not the amount of energy ultimately saved. Likewise, a supplier of executive education services may invoice a customer according to the number of days taught in a leadership and change management program instead of according to a transformation of teams ultimately achieved. Hence, the dominant pricing approach to PSS is equally based on a cost-plus approach.

*Pricing Asset Efficiency Services.* This category of services shifts the customer promise by committing to outcomes achieved. After all, customers don't want a forklift per se but the need to move pallets in a warehouse. Likewise, they don't necessarily want to buy ball bearings, but they need to keep a machine running and want to achieve more productivity from assets invested.

For Asset Efficiency Services (AES), the focus naturally shifts from a cost-plus to a value-based pricing logic. Instead of offering a fixed price for repairing an equipment every time it breaks, suppliers can create more value for customers by committing to availability of well-functioning equipment. Consequently, the pricing can now be linked to a performance indicator related to the vendor's product and agreed-upon between the buyer and the seller. For example, a forklift manufacturer may commit to 100 percent material-handling capacity available in a warehouse—all the time. The warehouse customer pays according to result achieved, and it's the supplier's task to ensure that there is always a well-functioning forklift in place. This might imply keeping one spare forklift on-site available 24-7.

Customers typically understand that AES go beyond enabling an equipment's basic functioning and must-have services. It is easier to sell AES separately from the supplier's core product offering. Shifting from cost-based to value-based pricing for these services often allows vendors to raise customers' willingness to pay for AES under the condition that the supplier can persuasively communicate the potential for value creation in form of productivity gains and/or cost savings.

To set prices appropriately for AES, companies need to secure unique resources and distinctive skills (see chapter 5). By investing in the products underlying AES, acquiring and safeguarding product usage and process data, and developing analytics skills, vendors can develop an ability to predict failure rates and take corrective actions better than the competition.

Building unique pricing skills for AES may require that a supplier accepts providing services at a loss for a certain amount of time for the sake of acquiring strategic data and experiencing its own learning curve. For example, an aircraft jet engine manufacturer we worked with was willing to take initially unprofitable maintenance contracts as a means to acquire unique usage data, learn over time how to redesign jet engines for better serviceability, and develop novel AES ahead of its competition.

Data and analytics represent a formidable driving force for future AES. But pricing of such services can remain tricky, especially when prices don't reflect risk taken by vendors. The barriers to entry are lower today, and the cost of communication, sensor hardware, and data processing has plummeted compared with twenty years ago, when manufacturers invested heavily in infrastructure. For example, jet engine manufacturer Rolls-Royce built an expensive satellite communication network to establish a digital link to its engines on aircrafts around the world. Today, this can be achieved much easier. Yet many companies still lack the data processing and risk assessment skills needed to correctly set prices for, and ensure profitability of, such services.

***Pricing Process Delegation Services.*** Many of the points developed for AES above also hold true for process delegation services (PDS). Suppliers can take their output-based value proposition one step further, committing not only to asset productivity achieved but also to take responsibility for outcomes of end-to-end customer processes.

We have seen in chapter 2 that one of the key motivations for customers to sign complex contract agreements for process-delegation services is the ability to delegate risk to suppliers and the assumption that a supplier has the expertise and skills to manage that risk better than the customer him- or herself. Without any form of risk delegation involved, there is no need for entering into a PDS agreement.

In line with the notion of risk transfer, PDS also often involve complex gain-sharing agreements. This requires that both parties jointly develop and agree upon changing existing performance metrics or develop new sets of performance indicators that serve as the basis for pricing PDS. For example, automotive coating supplier PPG and car manufacturer Fiat agree to switch from paying the supplier according to volumes of paint delivered to number of flawlessly painted cars. Likewise, commercial airlines started to pay jet-engine manufacturer Safran according to newly signed fly-by-the-hour agreements rather than based on engines maintained. Finally, a food-packaging company we worked with launched a new processing solution with a revenue stream linked to specific customer product targets. If the solution performed better, the supplier could get additional revenue, but if the performance was below the acceptable productivity range, the supplier would pay a penalty.

The example of the abovementioned food-packaging supplier illustrates that PDS bear the highest levels of risks of all four categories. When venturing into PDS, companies face the risk of committing to outcomes they cannot deliver or that can only be achieved by adding unforeseen resources. This risk is particularly acute when customers' actions, which the supplier cannot control, affect service performance—a classical moral hazard problem. Consider the following example:

*We provide construction firms with fleet management for their tools. Instead of buying equipment, customers pay a fixed monthly charge that covers all tool, service, and repair costs. That greatly simplifies their lives and cuts out lots of hidden costs. Yet, over time, we found that some construction workers changed their behavior once they knew that tools were now covered through a contract. They handled the tools less carefully, and we found ourselves with soaring costs for repair and shipments. We hadn't anticipated these costs, and it took us a while to learn how to keep these costs in check by introducing personalized tool labels and online tracking.*

This illustration shows that with the high levels of risk involved, the interests of both parties should be strongly aligned in process-delegation services. Setting prices for PDS in such an environment can easily turn into a nightmare for both the buyer and the seller. From a customer perspective, how does one trust a vendor that suggested prices reflect the value created in implementing a PDS contract? How to compare prices proposed by one PDS supplier to those of a next-best alternative? Similarly, from a vendor perspective, how does one set prices in such a way that the company can achieve its profit targets? What is the true value-creation potential? Which key performance indicators make most sense? Consider the following example of an outsourcing agreement negotiated between telecommunications company Hutchison Australia and network equipment and telecom service provider Ericsson as a case in point (see exhibit 6).

---

**Exhibit 6**
***Process Delegation Services:***
***The Case of Ericsson and Hutchison Australia***

With the introduction of third-generation (3G) telecommunications networks, first offered in the 2000s, technology providers such as Ericsson, the global market leader in telecom services, started to offer services to manage networks on behalf of its customers. The managed service contracts meant a breakthrough for the company's service business, growing from 16 percent of net sales in 2002 to 44 percent in 2015.

In 2001, Ericsson signed a contract for several hundred million dollars with telecom provider Hutchison Australia, a subsidiary of Hong Kong-based investment holding company Hutchison Whampoa Limited (HWL) for the delivery and rollout of a 3G mobile network. However, the contract faced technical problems and delays, and Hutchison was struggling to get the rollout cost under control. During a meeting between the two parties in 2002, the chief operating officer of HWL took the managing director of Ericsson aside and suggested, "Surely you could run this operation cheaper and better. Why don't you make a bid for running the whole network?" In a follow-up meeting with the board of HWL, Ericsson decided to present a bold value proposition: "We can run the network at a twenty to twenty-five percent cost saving to Hutchison." A small team of senior executives from both companies began to negotiate in order to land a deal within the next months. Despite initial suspicion—a Hutchison director recalls the CTO saying in a meeting, "As far as I'm concerned, this is like sitting down with your worst enemy, asking them to share a glass of wine and hoping they haven't poisoned it"—a strong emphasis was placed on collaboration, which turned out to be needed. For instance, Hutchison seemed not to have complete control of its own operations, and Ericsson had major concerns with the quality and reliability of the data that underpinned the performance targets.

The service-level agreements included penalties, but because of the fast negotiation process, the security surrounding it, and the lack of due diligence beforehand, it was not possible to verify the performance targets prior to signing the contract. During the transition stage, it turned out that there were major gaps between contract and reality and that many performance targets were unrealistic and impossible to achieve. The pricing of the contract was a key factor in resolving the problems; it was not a fixed price but a fixed margin contract. Furthermore, having an "open book" process enabled the parties to see the resources needed to meet the KPIs. By applying flexibility and openness, the KPIs were gradually renegotiated to align them with reality, and the contract survived.

*Sources:* Ericsson; Malmgren (2010)

The Ericsson example illustrates well the challenges of not only setting initial prices for PDS but also adjusting prices throughout the implementation process. These challenges cut across industries and markets.

Consider the example of fleet management on the case of tire manu-facturer Michelin. If customers' truck fleets comprise multiple types of vehicles used at different locations and in a broad variety of running sit-uations, the contractual agreement must cover not just one single price per mile but multiple prices to adjust for multiple combinations of vehi-cles and usage contexts. One can easily see how getting initial pricing right can become very challenging. At one point in time, the company must make a leap of faith, sign its first contract, learn the implementa-tion process, make adjustments fast, learn from its next contract, and so forth. From working with manufacturers on pricing issues, we learned that fast prototyping and engaging in your own learning curve represent effective ways for building unique PDS pricing skills.

## Aligning Prices with Your Core Value Proposition

We have seen that each of the four business service categories has its own pricing challenges, but there is still one more aspect we need to address that cuts across all four service types. Any of the above-mentioned ser-vice pricing initiatives are doomed to fail if they are not well aligned with the company's underlying value proposition to customers. Prices play a key role in positioning a service and communicating value to customers. Time and again, we have seen that when business customers misunder-stand prices, confusion is often rooted in a misalignment between the fundamental value proposition and chosen prices.

**Ingredients of Outstanding Value Propositions.** A good value prop-osition clearly identifies what customers gain from a business service and communicates effectively and efficiently how the service of one company stands out from those of others. Value propositions are built around the customer job to be done—that is, the fundamental prob-lem that customers seek to resolve in a given situation.[4] For example, a job to be done in business markets may be to reduce capital invested in assets. A customer-perceived benefit flowing from such a fundamen-tal customer goal may be, for example, to reduce unnecessary inven-tory levels. With a clear understanding of what customers ultimately seek to achieve, a service provider can then persuasively explain how its innovative inventory management service creates value for customers and price it accordingly.

Outstanding value propositions share five common characteristics. First, rather than enumerating a long list of (potential) customer benefits, they emphasize only those few value elements that truly resonate with a given customer or a group of customers. In short, they have a resonating focus.[5] Which are the one or two points of difference that will deliver the greatest value to a particular customer or customer segment? Second, great value propositions always include a competitive anchor. Customers can (almost) always choose between services of two or more suppliers. Or they may decide to perform a service themselves rather than asking for outside help. Hence, best-in-class value propositions identify next-best alternatives and communicate how a service provider can create more value than others. Third, effective value propositions don't just claim superiority; they quantify how a firm's business service affects those key performance metrics that truly matter to customers. Fourth, they document and back up their claim with a tangible proof. For example, by installing and monitoring its own electricity meters in customers' facilities, Schneider Electric can commit to well-defined energy savings in a retail customer's food mart. Outstanding value propositions back up their claims and provide a reason why benefits in form of productivity enhancements and/or cost savings can be achieved. Finally, good value propositions are sustainable; they are difficult to copy over time.

To convey their value proposition effectively and efficiently, best-in-class company Schneider Electric has developed tools that allow customers to understand and visualize value created and calculate their own ROI of service offerings proposed. To accelerate its service growth, technology provider SKF created Documented Solutions Program (DSP), a software capable of identifying and calculating the expected value of products, services, and combinations thereof (see also exhibit 2 in chapter 3). SKF has a competitive advantage in its ability to accurately predict customer value through DSP thanks to its large customer case database; up to 2015, the company has collected sixty-four thousand customer reference cases quantifying and documenting customer savings and productivity gains achieved.[6] SKF leverages the knowledge it gains from its DSP tool to craft competitive value propositions by bundling different value attributes to each customer segment and offer customized solutions and contractual innovations, including performance-based services.

In business markets, value propositions must be adapted to the needs and wants of individual decision makers inside the customer's organization. They need to have a resonating focus with each member of the buying center, as the example of construction tool manufacturer Hilti illustrates (see exhibit 7).

---

**Exhibit 7**
*Hilti Fleet Management:*
*Crafting a Distinct Value Proposition for Each Stakeholder*

Revenues and profits of construction firms are largely driven by their ability to perform construction projects according to specifications, on time, and within budget. If tools on-site are not available or if they do not work properly, workers cannot perform their duties, leading to delays and costs. Construction firms make money by using tools in the most effective and efficient manner; owning tools does not change anything in this case. Yet customers often realize the magnitude of hidden costs due to malfunctioning tools. Hilti realized it could help construction firms achieve significant productivity gains and cost savings by identifying and reducing those hidden costs. Consequently, the tool manufacturer changed its value proposition. Instead of selling tools, it began to offer its customers tool management solutions—the promise of having the right tool at the right time, always. Hilti now markets a contractual offering of tool fleet management, coupled with performance guarantees; however, this customer promise is not geared to all customers alike. Nor does it convey the same value proposition to all key stakeholders inside the company. A quick look at Hilti's brief video clips on YouTube reveals that the tool manufacturer has developed individual customer promises to the construction company's general manager, finance manager, or tool crib manager.[7]

---

How does price come into the equation when crafting a value proposition for service offerings? In business markets, value is generally defined as the worth in monetary terms of the technical, economic, service, and social benefits a customer receives in exchange for the price it pays for the offering[8]. As we saw earlier, a value proposition has to make the case about *net* value—that is, the extent to which a business service creates *more* value than the next-best competitive alternative. To have a strong value proposition in hand, one supplier's offering must be superior to that of the competition:

$$(Value_S - Price_S) > (Value_A - Price_A)$$

In this comparison, $Value_S$ and $Price_S$ represent the value and price of a service provider's focal offering, while $Value_A$ and $Price_A$ represent the value and price of the alternative offering as perceived by customers. Essentially, the difference between the two represents the incentive for a customer to favor the service of one supplier over the other. Note that in this equation, price is not part of value but a separate dimension. In other words, price can be considered as a "value capture" mechanism. Setting a price for a service offering serves as a distribution lever for sharing value between a buyer and a seller.

Combining the dimensions of value and price, a company can thus identify nine potential bases for developing a value proposition (see figure 7:3). Three of these value propositions, displayed in black (VP4, VP7, and VP8), are rather difficult to defend vis-à-vis customers. For example, offering less value at a higher price represents an avenue that is difficult to pursue over time. Next, one value proposition, displayed in dark gray (VP5), is undifferentiated and therefore weak. Finally, the framework displays five value propositions in light gray (VP1, VP2, VP3, VP6, and VP9), each with a strong potential of finding a resonating focus with customers.

With these fundamental platforms in mind, companies can clarify their offers, set them apart from others in the market, and even rethink their own portfolios. For example, Dow Corning, the leading global supplier of silicones we discuss in chapter 4, works with customers for innovation and performance improvements through a host of value-added services and solutions. This represents a perfect illustration of value proposition VP1: technical support, R&D services, and other activities all come at a higher price than volume-driven competitors. On the other

Figure 7:3
Nine Generic Value Propositions for Business Services

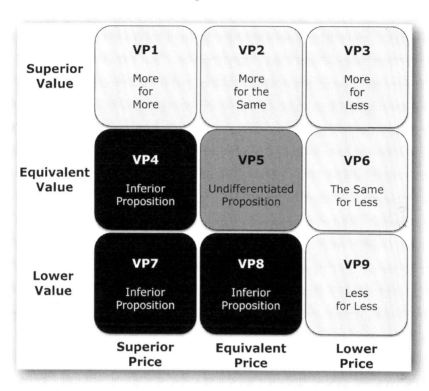

hand, the company also developed an entirely different value proposition in the same market but targeted at "no-frills" customers. Services are unbundled and cut down to a common core valued by cost-sensitive customers, all at a lower price. To effectively communicate this price-aggressive value proposition and to clarify differences between both simultaneously managed value propositions, Dow Corning created a separate brand, Xiameter. This is a perfect example of VP9 (see also chapter 4).

When it comes to competing though VP2, industrial gas supplier Air Liquide is a good example. At one point in time, both Air Liquide and its competitor, Air Products, offered basic inventory management services for gas cylinders at comparable prices. Yet when carefully assessing service elements provided, Air Liquide offered more for the same, such as automatic reordering of gas cylinders, when supplies reached a minimum-inventory level or operator-safety trainings, to name two examples. In other instances, Air Liquide provided a help desk available 24-7, while selected competitors certainly offered a hotline, too, but only during regular office hours.

VP3 is the most challenging value proposition: it promises superior value to customers at a lower price than competition. This value proposition is often used when companies want to set foot in a new market segment or grow their customer base to the detriment of the competition. It can be used effectively when suppliers know how to better affect customers' business outcomes. For example, with Empire Southwest, one of Caterpillar's main distributors in Northern America, a Southwestern mining company's tender, the company developed a customer solution that promised customers to extract more tons of copper annually (a higher performance) with less earth-moving machines than the competition. To get the job done, it had to leverage unique service skills.

Finally, many me-too suppliers and challengers use value proposition VP6 in business markets. This value proposition can be effective not only to undercut competition but also to grab market share. When companies know how to meet customers' expectations exactly, not more or less, by taking cost out of service provision, then they have a powerful value proposition in hand.

To conclude, the choice of value proposition depends on a firm's resources and skills, competition, and environment. It is common to see several value propositions coexist in the same market. The key imperative for firms is to deliberately choose one or more propositions and consistently implement its go-to-market approach.


## KEY QUESTIONS ABOUT CAPTURING MORE VALUE

In reviewing the implementation issues in this chapter, managers have to ask themselves ten fundamental questions:

1. Have we taken stock of the breadth and depth of services we already provide to customers today?

2.  Do we leave money on the table by providing too many services to customers free of charge or by not invoicing an adequate amount offered?

3.  Are we making the most of internal best-pricing practices across business units and/or geographic territories?

4.  Do we systematically seek opportunities for improving prices and margins in our service portfolio, for example, by discontinuing an unprofitable service, delegating service provision to a dealer, or raising a price?

5.  Have we successfully turned around services from free to fee?

6.  Do we predominantly practice cost-plus pricing in our company?

7.  Do we adapt our pricing approaches to the challenges and success factors in all four pricing categories?

8.  Do we have a fundamental understanding of our customers' job to- be-done? Do we understand the KPIs that ultimately matter to them?

9.  Are our value propositions generic statements, barely different from the competition's, with no tangible proof to back up our claims?

10. Do we use one or more of the five viable value proposition platforms and execute our go-to-market approach in line with value propositions chosen?

# CHAPTER 8

## SERVICE INNOVATION: HAVE YOU INSTITUTIONALIZED IT?

*Daring ideas are like chessmen moved forward; they*
*may be beaten, but they may start a winning game.*
—JOHANN WOLFGANG VON GOETHE

To be successful, a firm not only has to capitalize on its existing services; it must also innovate new services, matching the attention it brings to product-related R&D. This chapter should allow executives to examine how they can better institutionalize service innovation. Rapid technological advances and evolving customer expectations and needs require companies to develop their service portfolios continuously and systematically. Companies also need to break free from the common use of methods originating in product development, which are not always suitable for developing new service offerings. In this chapter, we provide a service framework that can be used to manage such innovation in a systematic manner.

The previous chapter allowed us to understand what to do to make better use of existing services, how to price these services, and how to find the adequate value proposition. With this now clearer in our minds, a new issue arises: how to identify new service opportunities. In chapter 5, we identify several possible growth trajectories. From process lifecycle services to process delegation services, the company can move gradually toward new services and hybrid offerings. It may offer support services to operations and ultimately services to meet more complex needs requiring supported processes and their redesign. But questions remain: How can new opportunities be identified? Which new service concept should be prioritized? When and where should resources be allocated to launch new services that will ensure future growth?

## Service Innovation Is Different

What is service innovation? Based on the definition of service that we present in chapter 2, we provide the following definition:

- *Service innovation* is the rebundling of diverse resources that creates novel value for the beneficiaries themselves or in their assets, activities, and processes in a given context.

This definition encompasses all types of services (including hybrid offerings) regardless of degree of innovativeness and what types of benefits they provide. It is also inherently customer-centric; it recognizes that value perception is customer unique and context specific, and it incorporates the customer as an active participant in the innovation process.

Investing resources in product development is obvious for any leading manufacturer. The very same companies typically invest only a negligible share of their development resources in new services, and even fewer pursue service research in a scientific sense. The old view of services as "innovation laggards"[1] prevails in many organizations, and service innovation often becomes a concern only once the new product is ready to launch. The following quotes from executives and managers responsible for service development illustrate some of the challenges:

- "Our product development process is not suited for services."
- "Service development takes place ad hoc."
- "Services can come from anywhere, often close to the business: customers and employees. It only needs an idea, but it takes a change management project to realize it."
- "Services cannot be evaluated in the same manner as products."
- "It comes to a stall when we want to launch and roll out the service."

The service innovation process is risky and may require significant investments in capital and human resources. At the same time, resources and experience are lacking in many companies. For example, a global manufacturer with 20 percent of revenues coming from services had thousands of engineers working with product development but only a small team working with service development at the headquarters. It is also increasingly difficult to erect entry barriers to prevent imitation by competitors, which exercises even more pressure on companies. They must not only make the right choices in terms of innovation but also try to shorten the time between the moment of defining a new service concept and its commercialization in the market.

In this chapter, we focus on a simple and structured approach to assist the company's innovation efforts. Innovation processes for new products or services pass through similar stages of development. These stages include idea generation to commercialization, through intermediate phases such as development and testing of concepts, analysis of customer desirability, technical feasibility, economic-viability study, and testing with pilot customers before market launch. A detailed description of all these steps is beyond the scope of this book; however, we wish to focus on the way to proceed to generate new service offerings. To do this, we will rely on straightforward tools, developed and tested with several industrial firms.

While product and service innovation have much in common, such as similar development stages, there are also important differences that managers must acknowledge. Service development requires the very same meticulous attention as product development. However, for any company pursuing both product- and service-led growth, it is necessary to understand the specificities of service innovation and manage it accordingly. As we discuss in chapter 3, one of the seven deadly sins of service-myopic firms is to think that services are just like products. Table 8:1 shows important differences between product development and service development processes.

Over the years, we have seen several companies develop compelling service concepts that failed because they were developed much like complex product development models. This view, which has traditionally dominated innovation practice, implies that models and theories

**Table 8:1**
**Product Innovation and Service Innovation: What's Different?**

| Dimension | Product Innovation | Service Innovation |
|---|---|---|
| Initiation | Centrally initiated, structured, technology driven: new technology or new use of existing technologies | Locally initiated, close to customers, ad hoc: New value creation potential identified |
| Strategic Perspective | Inside-out | Outside-in |
| Key Asset | Patents | Knowledge of customer latent needs |
| Development | Closed process, involving R&D and production | Open process, involving sales companies and service organizations |
| Tools and Methods | Stage-gate models | Service blueprinting, service engineering |
| Critical Resources | Production facilities, components, sub-systems, supply chains | Knowledge and skills, relationships and networks, including the resources of service partners |
| Stakeholders | R&D and other central units and functions | Local and central units, customers, partners/dealers |
| Marketing and Sales | Market to (push): management of customers and markets | Market with (pull): collaboration with customers and partners |
| Result | A tangible offering that is easy to understand | An intangible service that is difficult to visualize |

Source: Based on Kowalkowski (2016)

originally developed with manufacturing in mind are seen as equally applicable to a service context. Because such *assimilation perspective* suppresses differences between services and manufacturing, it undermines many unique characteristics of services. In contrast, a *demarcation perspective* on service innovation emphasizes the unique characteristics of services and, consequently, the need for different innovation models and processes.[2] Simply put, the service-specific hurdles we discuss in chapter 2—intangibility, active role of the customer, variability, perishability, nonownership, and shorter distribution channels—impose other requirements on development than products do.

While the development stages may be the same, the relative emphasis on each stage differs between product development and service development. In a workshop with service and business development managers from a variety of different industries, this difference was illustrated with the schematic representations in figure 8:1. The figure shows that product development is generally back heavy with many resources required for technology development and prototyping. Service development, on the other hand, is more front heavy with more time and resources needed for market introduction and pilot testing and to secure the sales and delivery infrastructures and capabilities.

**Figure 8:1**
**Differences in Resource Requirements between Development Stages**

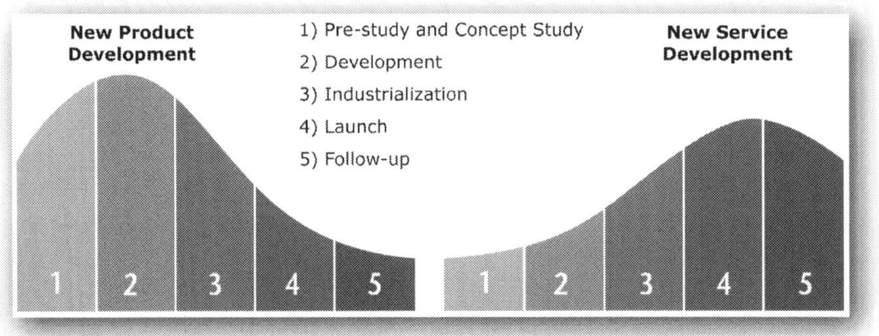

Source: Kowalkowski and Kindström (2012), p. 112

For a company that has successfully pursued product development for years or even decades, the mind-set change needed for service development can be tough. In addition, many firms lack both resources and support for service development and formal roles and experience within the organization. Typically, the responsibilities for service development may be assigned to a product manager on top of existing responsibilities. The successful service innovators that we have worked with have generally dedicated roles and units responsible for the development and marketing of new services. At the same time, however, companies must avoid too much silo thinking in order to foster design-to-service capabilities and hybrid offering development, which requires collaboration between product and service development teams. In exhibit 8 below, we explain why and how Volvo Group developed a service-specific innovation process.

## Exhibit 8
### *Volvo's Global Service-Development Process*

Volvo Group is an 110,000-employee-strong supplier of trucks, buses, and construction equipment, which includes the Mack and Renault truck brands. The company has actively pursued service-growth strategies for many years. As other multinational product firms, the company uses a global product development process (GDP), which is based on a traditional stage-gate model: prestudy, concept study, detailed development, final development, industrialization and commercialization, and follow-up. Since the development of software in many ways differs from the development of vehicles and engines, Volvo has a specific development process for such projects.

However, none of these processes was regarded as adequate for service innovation. The structures and processes of product development were too rigid; service innovation requires a more flexible and iterative process with more active customer involvement in the development and launch phases, increased collaboration between functions and central and local units, and securing resources and competences for sales and delivery. For example, the process has to consider that many innovative ideas emerge on a local level, in interaction with customers.

Consequently, the company set out to put together a global service development process (S-GDP). After a prestudy and several iterations, the first version was presented, and the process was tested in real life for the first time in pilot projects. Based on feedback from these projects, the process and documentation were revised and further refined. Since then, new versions have been launched, and Volvo employees can nowadays enroll for a course on the S-GDP. Anders Ekblad, the Volvo manager who initiated the project, explains, "Volvo identified a need for service development close to the customer and found a lack of a proper method. We have managed to take a major step in this direction by developing our own process, which also is integrated with the product-oriented development processes."

As figure 8:2 below illustrates, the process consists of five phases, each with several substeps: explore, conceptualize, build, pilot, and deploy. Emphasis is on the iterative characteristics of the process, which is visualized by the circular phases instead of traditional boxes and stage-gate processes. Interdisciplinary and holistic processes with means to systematically work with customer involvement and visualization are other cornerstones. In addition, three criteria need to be fulfilled for any service being developed: customer desirability, business viability, and technological and organizational feasibility. While some units systematically work with the entire process, others may pick parts of it depending on their purpose. For example, a sales company with ninety people may decide to use the S-GDP innovation toolkit when developing a new local service without having to go through all the phases of the development process.

**Figure 8:2**
**Volvo Group's Service Development Process**

*Source:* Volvo Group

## How to Identify Opportunities for New Services

How can companies identify novel ideas for service innovation? Unless the company is in the same seat as Apple—where Steve Jobs generally had an instinctive feel about customers' latent needs and desires—customers are a key resource for ideation. Furthermore, local units of the firm, such as sales companies and service organizations, and partners or dealers may provide invaluable inputs to the innovation process. Next, we will discuss some useful methods for customer involvement before showing how companies can go ahead to generate new services.

### Customer integration within service development

One of the key differences between product and service development concerns the degree of customer involvement. While customer involvement such as focus groups and pilot testing is part of many product development projects, it becomes even more vital for services. Involving users and other customer stakeholders means getting firsthand information about the firm's products and services in the use context. Depending on the stage of the innovation process, customers have different roles:[3]

- During the ideation and concept definition stage, customers are suppliers of ideas and makers of demands.
- During development, customers act as codevelopers and testers.
- Once the service is launched, customers become purchasers, coproducers, and feedback providers.

In many cases, service innovation appears as a direct response to new customer demands. It means that the company quickly has to decide how to seize emergent opportunities that are not planned for. The managing director of a leading forklift provider in the United Kingdom told us how his company managed an innovation opportunity that later became an integral part of their business:

> *The UK was the first country in material handling to demand rental for trucks [to a large extent]. And that was back in the mid-80s. What*

*happened in the UK was that a lot of our traditional customers were starting to demand their services entirely through their third-party distributors, and they were offering the distributors five-year agreements. So the third-party distributor immediately came back and said, "I want five years' use of machines. I don't want to buy them." So rental became the issue almost overnight, it seemed. So we had a requirement, we saw an opportunity, we produced the relevant cost-based plan, and we then promoted it. And that was the starting point. When this started to materialize, we also realized that service was a defining factor. You could use service as a reason to buy from us as opposed to from somebody else.*

In other cases, service innovation is the result of a deliberate and systematic process, whether it is developed at a local sales company or initiated by a central service development unit. In such innovation process, three different types of customer involvement methods can be used: improvement of existing services, incremental service innovations, and radical service innovations. Common methods related to each category are presented in table 8:2.

**Table 8:2**
**Categories of Methods for Service Innovation**

|  | Improvement of existing services | Incremental service innovation | Radical service innovation |
|---|---|---|---|
| Focus | Reactive | Reactive | Proactive |
| Methods | Usage data Critical incidents Complaint data | Surveys Focus groups Interviews | Lead user methods Customer test drive Ethnographical studies |
| Description | Methods based on existing information or information about common customer problems | Methods based on what customers have experienced in retrospect | Methods focusing on information about customers' use contexts and based on customer (real-time) behavior |

Source: Adapted from Kristensson et al. (2014), p. 75

Companies typically use data on product usage, critical incidents, and complaints to obtain customer information. While these methods are vital, they usually provide insights how to improve the existing offering rather than ideas for novel services. To gain further insights, many companies use traditional marketing methods such as customer surveys and focus groups. While these methods are rather straightforward and easy to conduct, they tend to only scratch the surface of customer experience and needs. To better understand the customers' businesses, in-depth interviews can be conducted. If you are close with your customers, they can tell you their jobs-to- be-done in an upright conversation, which you can then translate back to new services. However, it is important to ask the right questions. Consider the difference between the following two questions that will generate very different answers: "Do you want a microchip?" versus "Do you want better safety and control?" Most customers will answer based on how the market exists today, echoing what Henry Ford reputedly said: "If I had asked people what they wanted, they would have said faster horses."

In order to examine the underlying customer needs and identify their jobs to be done, companies should complement traditional marketing techniques with proactive, forward-oriented methods that focus on the use context. For example, lead-user methods zoom in on the processes, practices, demands, and ideas of leading customers. Several studies have found that lead users can provide more valuable ideas than internal employees. One such study was conducted within the 3M Company, which is known for its innovation capabilities. The experiment showed that lead users had more original ideas and that the probability of success, strategic importance, and estimated sales were higher compared with internal ideas (see table 8:3).

Another user-centered method is allowing customers to test drive the service by providing them with virtual or physical tools to test new concepts and capture new ideas in use situations. It can also include such things as customers keeping diaries about their service experience, be it machine operators or patients in hospitals.

Finally, ethnographic methods such as participant observation can be used to understand customer behavior and preferences in their

Table 8:3
**Lead-User versus Employee-Funded Ideas**

| Factor | Ideas from Lead Users | Ideas from Internal Employees |
|---|---|---|
| Novelty (scale 1–10) | 9.6 | 6.8 |
| Originality/Newness of Customer Needs Addressed (scale 1–10) | 8.3 | 5.3 |
| % Market Share in Year 5 | 68% | 33% |
| Estimated Sales in Year 5 | $146m | $18m |
| Strategic Importance (scale 1–10) | 9.6 | 7.3 |
| Probability of Success | 80% | 66% |

Source: Lilien et al. (2002)

natural environments within the context of a specific process, situation, product, or service. To get a 360-degree customer view, a wide range of organizations is using ethnography when innovating. Much like ethnographic studies in the consumer world, insights happen when you spend a day in the life of a business client. Spending a day in the production plant can be an eye-opener about internal supply-chain flows, and spending time with vehicle users can allow hands-on understanding of their daily service needs. To live in the shoes of the customer, companies like Volvo Trucks also carry out mystery shopper audits, which allow for improvement of existing services but can also enable new, innovative service concepts. Drivers employed as mystery customers enable the company to assess whether it is on the right track. As a service director puts it, "It is like an MRI scan of what we are doing in the workshop."[4]

### Understand the customers' customers

Customer integration can also provide valuable insights into the needs of customers' customers or end users. Such knowledge may be needed in order to craft a compelling value proposition that can increase the competitiveness of the customers. Consider a specialized, global steel producer operating on a market where the commodity magnet is inevitably pushing margins down. While continuous product innovation is pivotal, there is very limited room for increasing the product margins. Instead, the company is actively working with service innovation through research and development services, which focus on the needs of their customers and customers' customers. The company knows that many customers lack the resources and skills to pursue advanced R&D. When working with customers such as trailer manufacturers, the company can help their customers to develop lighter products with increased strength and longer life-span. In order to capitalize on its product expertise and develop such advanced services, the company needs to understand the needs of the end user and show how its research-and-development services can positively affect the bottom line of its own customers.

## Harness digital technology and big data analytics

Digitization is a key enabler for service innovation. Regardless of label—Industrial Internet, Industry 4.0, or Internet of Things, Services, and People—new technologies make competition based more on gathering and using informational content and less on product benefits. Intelligent machines, advanced analytics, and remote connectivity, in combination with low-cost sensors and data processing, are enabling a multitude of new services based on customer data. Any company pursuing service innovation needs to exploit the digital side in order to stay competitive. This includes working with intellectual property and patenting when it comes to such things as user interface, algorithms, and trademarks.

By utilizing integrated wireless sensors to make ball bearings the "brains of the rotating machinery," SKF can monitor the real-life performance of industrial machines. The company has seized the opportunities industrial Internet provides to move into digital services such as knowledge as a service, where the SKF cloud and its remote diagnostics center network is used to improve conditions-based maintenance of its partner customers. All companies should try to envision where the world of technology is headed in the years to come and what service opportunities it may bring. For example, Siemens use such retrospection ("Pictures of the Future" scenario[5]) to create road maps for how to realize the innovation potential.

As the disruptive effects of new technology are changing the competitive landscape, small and agile firms and ecosystems are increasingly competing with established industry incumbents. Companies like Rolls-Royce invested heavily in such expensive technologies as satellite communications over twenty years ago to create a digital link to the aircraft engines. Obtaining in-depth insights into the operation of its engines through numerous sensors enabled Rolls-Royce to develop its game-changing service model where customers are charged per hour for the use of its engines. All sensors are multipurpose, which means that they not only collect data on the different aspects of engine performance; they are also used to control the engine and provide information to the pilot. Today, however, not only can Rolls-Royce monitor its newest engines in the air and alert its airline customers if action is needed, but smaller players are also able to offer more and more advanced remote services. In addition, connected technology is also offered for products far less capital intensive than engines.

Despite all opportunities, companies must nonetheless resist the temptation of being purely technology driven. In this respect, technology is a double-edged sword; service innovation should depart in a profound understanding of customer value rather on what is technically possible to develop. Far too many service innovation projects depart in technical possibilities without knowing what specific customer job to be done the service should address or how it should be charged for. One firm we worked with walked into the technology trap when it developed its telematics services. Managers focused on imitating a main competitor's offering based on the very latest technology but without ensuring that the service resonated with actual customer needs. Customers were able to extract rich data about their fleet, but most of them had neither the time nor competence to properly analyze and interpret it. The company eventually had to revise the service package and more explicitly focus on operational efficiency and cost reductions in their value proposition.

## Generating ideas within the firm

Systematically identifying within the organization ideas that can materialize as commercially viable services is a profitable exercise, often rich in lessons, that allows the detection of innovative, potentially exploitable concepts. These sessions can include both internal and external stakeholders, and may range from a couple of hours to several days. In 2006, over seventy-two hours, IBM put together more than 150,000 people from 104 countries and sixty-seven companies in a virtual "innovation jam." Ten ideas were selected for further development and allocated a development budget of $100 million.[6] Since then, management consultant Capgemini and many other organizations have conducted similar jam sessions.

In most cases, however, idea generation takes place at shorter and more focused workshops. From working with companies in a diverse set of industries, we developed a straightforward method for generating and evaluating new service concepts. For example, in a workshop with an industrial equipment manufacturer, twelve marketing managers from various European subsidiaries identified no less than eighty ideas to boost business growth in services. After a day and a half of reflection, fourteen concepts were identified as priority candidates for the launch of pan-European service offerings across the subsidiaries. Thereafter, action plans were prepared to monitor the implementation of these projects and their performance in each country. Figure 8:3a shows a simple and effective template we have successfully used for group brainstorming sessions for service innovation.

Each participant completes the worksheet in figure 8:3a for three service concepts that he or she would like to see launched in the near future. To do so, the participant briefly describes the central idea of the new concept (step 1), specifies the two main reasons that justify this action (why the company should be interested to invest in this new concept, step 2), identifies two major obstacles to overcome on the path to commercialization of the new service (step 3), details the necessary support from management for successful development of the offering (step 4), and outlines the approach that should be taken to ensure a successful launch (step 5).

The process of providing answers to each of these steps then allows the participants to present their concepts and facilitates sharing and exchange of knowledge and experience within the group. This exercise is particularly fruitful if the workshop members do not immediately

### Figure 8:3
### Service Innovation Template

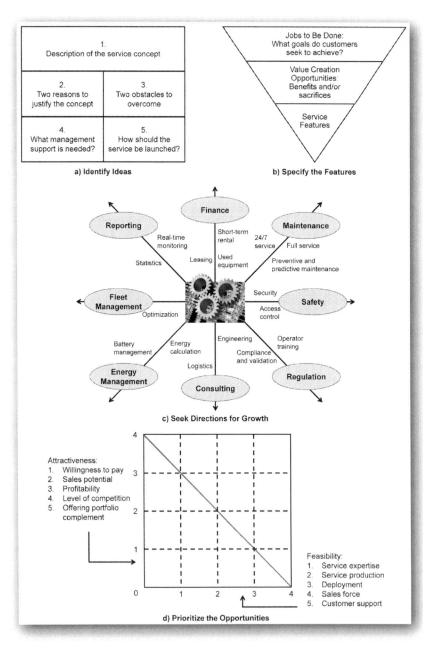

a) Identify Ideas

b) Specify the Features

c) Seek Directions for Growth

d) Prioritize the Opportunities

go to the characteristics of a particular service but instead focus on the customers' jobs-to-be-done and the problem that the concept can solve or the goal it can accomplish, such as reducing customer inventory. Participants can subsequently perform a more fine-grained analysis of areas of value creation in order to identify specific benefits that can relieve customers from pains, enable them to achieve more, or both. This leads to the formulation of essential features of the service that would match those value dimensions. The inverted pyramid in figure 8:3b refers to this approach.

We can illustrate our remarks with the example of a service provided by Fenwick, the biggest material-handling provider in France. In this industry, the company's customers have increasingly outsourced their noncore activities, and customers tend to make greater use of temporary forklift operators. However, the increase of temporary staff on an industrial site inevitably engenders increased risks in terms of safety, which requires better management of access to forklifts at the company premises. In order to solve this problem, Fenwick developed an access control system for driving authorization management. In this case, the customers could explain their problem but did not know how to solve it. Only by analyzing the situation and cocreating a testable concept was Fenwick able to launch and integrate a new solution for access control into its service portfolio.

In general, all companies should be interested in investing in profound understanding of their customers to be able to identify underlying needs and thereby anticipate the potential impact of new services on operations and processes. By consistently engaging in this exercise, the possibilities to reveal new business opportunities should increase. Figure 8:3c provides an example of a set of issues encountered by a customer who bought industrial equipment. Each of them can form the basis for service innovation.

For instance, bringing a product to compliance with national or international regulations is a low-hanging development opportunity for suppliers in many industries. Take the case of pharmaceutical, food, beverage, and cosmetics industries that use raw materials that may contain potentially allergenic substances or be contaminated by microbes. Accordingly, life science company EMD Millipore, part of the Merck

Group, offers its customers in each industry a portfolio of services such as certificates, monitoring production processes, assuring sterility, and detecting microbes and hazardous substances.

### Prioritize what to develop and launch

The systematic search of innovative ideas usually creates a long list of potential opportunities that will then need to be assessed and sorted according to the priorities that the company has made. The extent of work to do and the selection criteria to use ultimately depend on the specific context of each company; however, any company has to determine both the attractiveness and feasibility of the service concept. The combination of the two perspectives enables us to focus on the low-hanging fruits; it allows us to start prioritizing which service opportunities should be developed first, what may follow then, and what to discard already from the beginning. Figure 8:3d presents a simple approach of evaluating each new service idea in relation to these two critical questions:

- How attractive is the new service: should we develop and market it?
- Do we have the resources and capabilities to offer the service in the short, medium, and long terms?

Each of these basic questions induces a number of subquestions. To determine the attractiveness of a potential offering, managers have to answer several questions: What will be the adoption behavior of the customers, and what will they be willing to pay? What is our sales and profitability potential? What competition are we facing, and how will our competitors react? What impact will the new service have on the performance of existing product and service offerings?

The ability to implement the service brings us back to other questions: Do we have the expertise to define the service content and design the service process? What is our service production capacity? Do we have the service prerequisites—that is, resources—necessary to deploy the offering on the local market? Will our sales force be able to market and sell it? Can we monitor customer satisfaction and provide support? Will the quality meet customers' expectations?

Having innovative services and an attractive service portfolio is essential if the company is to successfully implement its service strategy. As we have discussed, companies should actively involve customers in their innovation processes in order to increase the success rate. However, equally important, they need to profitably deliver the new services. Therefore, the next chapter focuses on how to industrialize the service business. We will present service blueprinting—a customer-focused approach for service innovation and service improvement to drive and support service execution—and discuss how to boost productivity in service operations.

## KEY QUESTIONS ABOUT SERVICE INNOVATION

In order to implement and institutionalize service innovation within the firm, managers should ask themselves the following questions:

1. Do we use a specific service development process, or do we simply copy existing product development methods?
2. What obstacles do we face that hinder service development to get similar attention and support as product development?
3. Do our product development and service development teams adequately collaborate? What does it take to align the two development processes to support the development of new hybrid offerings?
4. What are the sources for new ideas for service innovation today? Are there other sources that we have not sufficiently explored?
5. To what extent can we identify and support local service initiatives, and do we know how to formalize and deploy them on other markets?
6. To what extent do we systematically involve customers in the different stages of the innovation process? Do we know who the lead users for service are?
7. Are we able to gain the insights we need into the needs of customers' customers or end users?

8. In what ways do we work with the digital side from a customer perspective?
9. How well can we assess the attractiveness and feasibility of our service concepts?
10. What can be improved in the process from idea to concept to launch?

# CHAPTER 9

## SERVICE PRODUCTIVITY: HAVE YOU BUILT YOUR SERVICE FACTORY?

> *Once service "in the field" receives the same attention*
> *as products "in the factory," a lot of new opportunities*
> *become possible. Companies must think of themselves*
> *as performing manufacturing functions when*
> *it comes to so-called "service" activities.*[1]
> —THEODORE LEVITT

In the previous chapter, we have seen that firms used to focus on products and physical assets, and infrastructures must dedicate specific resources for service innovation, overhaul R&D processes, and provide space for new service concepts to improve and grow their service portfolio overall.

Building a company's service innovation resources and capabilities usually results in another, not less important, dilemma: firms must strike the balance between the desire to constantly improve their portfolio of service offerings that resonate with customer expectations and the need to exploit these opportunities in a cost-efficient manner. As we have seen in chapter 4, our survey of 250 industrial firms underscores this omnipresent tension. Mastering profitable service growth depends largely on a firm's ability to not only generate revenues through new service offerings but also its knowledge and expertise of deploying such novel services in a cost-effective and efficient manner.

Hence, in this chapter, we discuss how companies can strike the balance between accelerating service innovation and cost-effective service industrialization. To this end, we will first discuss service blueprinting, a powerful technique for taking new service concepts from theory to practice or improving and differentiating existing offerings. Blueprinting can also contribute to achieving sweeping changes in service orientation throughout the organization.

With service blueprinting in mind, we will then explore how firms can improve efficiency and effectiveness in service deployment. We will discuss several approaches that firms must master for industrializing service operations. This will not only achieve top-line revenue growth but also secure bottom-line profitability in rolling out their service-growth strategy.

## Bringing Your Offer to Life: Service Blueprinting

There is widespread agreement today that understanding, cocreating, monitoring, and managing customer experiences rank among executives' top priorities. In a recent study of four hundred executives conducted by Accenture and Forrester Consulting, "improving the customer experience" topped the list of business priorities companies have for the next twelve months. This priority received the most number-one rankings (21 percent), followed by "growing revenues" (17 percent) and "improving differentiation" (16 percent).[2]

Across industries, in business and consumer markets alike, management teams have come to understand that differentiating through superior end-to-end customer experiences outweighs by far efforts to compete on product features or service attributes.

Customer experiences involve multiple aspects such as a brand or technology. They consist of individual contacts among a company, a customer, and other parties involved. Experiences are built up through a collection of such touch points in multiple phases of a customer's purchase of a product, a service, or an interaction in general.[3]

Against this backdrop, a company must understand how to cocreate such a customer experience for and with customers, what the above-mentioned phases and touch points are, and how to design and coordinate its own internal processes in order to meet customer expectations in a cost-efficient manner.

A major hurdle in designing and developing a service that resonates with the experience that customers really want is not only describing the overall concept but also the process by which the service is designed and deployed. Recall the challenges that manufacturers face when venturing into services. They are intangible and variable and often require flexibility and adaptation to changing customer contexts and needs. It may often become difficult to clearly define and communicate, both to customers and a company's own staff, the sequence of steps involved in a given service process. These difficulties can instigate frustrations and misunderstandings, both on the customer side and for a firm's own employees, which, in turn, can result in poor customer satisfaction, internal conflicts, and excessive service deployment costs.

To address the above-mentioned challenges, companies need to have a clear vision of the process flow and individual steps so that all stakeholders involved—management, employees, channel partners, and customers alike—can understand their respective roles in the coproduction process. Hence, in this chapter, we discuss service blueprinting, a robust, tried-and-tested approach for understanding and articulating those critical processes needed to bring a customer experience to life in the most effective and cost-efficient manner.

## Service Blueprinting: A Powerful Technique for Designing Services

A service blueprint is a picture or map that portrays the customer experience and the service system so that the different people involved in providing the service can understand it objectively, regardless of their roles or their individual points of view.[4]

The idea of a service blueprint emerged in the 1980s.[5] Blueprinting as a technique subsequently developed throughout the 1990s and 2000s. The seminal work by Mary Jo Bitner, Amy Ostrom, and Felicitas Morgan at Arizona State University's Center for Services Leadership (CSL) largely contributed to shaping and diffusing the technique over many years.[6] Today, many companies have adopted service blueprinting in service innovation and design workshops globally.

What is the origin of the blueprinting concept and the term itself? In the past, technical drawings of machine tools were reproduced on blue paper, called "blueprints." They specified the technical characteristics of the equipment and rendered all the instructions needed to correctly assemble it. Similarly, service blueprinting identifies all critical elements of a given service process and visualizes how the process must be designed and delivered. Thus, service blueprints can serve as a common language for management, frontline employees, back-office employees, and any other stakeholder involved.

The service blueprinting approach was originally developed as a technique to document the steps in the execution of a service process and to control the quality of operations to which it refers.[7] Over time, this versatile technique has been used to tackle many different services strategy and implementation challenges such as service innovation and testing of new concepts, positioning and differentiation, and cost reduction in service operations, to name a few. Today, blueprinting can be considered as part of the growing field of service-design thinking in which global consultants such as US design firm IDEO, leading service organizations, and academics continue to refine the technique and enrich understanding of service process-design and deployment through novel techniques such as customer journey mapping.

While no technique should be treated as a design silver bullet, service blueprinting has a number of outright advantages for practitioners:

- Blueprinting represents a hands-on technique for bringing customer-centricity to life. Many organizations want to become more customer focused, but executives often don't know where to begin and how to jumpstart a customer-centricity initiative. By its very nature, blueprinting is firmly grounded in the customer's perspective and induces everyone inside the organization to align around customers' needs and wants. Hence, blueprinting is a well-suited technique for building a more customer-centric organization.

- Blueprinting is a perfectly suited technique for bringing the voice of the customer inside the organization. It allows staff to explore and understand all stages of a service process from the customer's point of view. At the same time, blueprinting can reveal a lack of customer insights, blind spots, or internal beliefs about customer needs that don't reflect their real needs. Blueprinting contributes to deep insights about the job that customers want to get done.

- Blueprinting represents a powerful technique for service innovation. This approach allows staff to take new service ideas and to think through all the ramifications of bringing the concept to life.

- The technique is well suited for revisiting existing customer experiences in search of differentiation. For example, with growing commoditization in many markets, blueprinting can help a company to find new ways of differentiating a service from the competition's. How to stand out from me-too providers? What are the moments that matter to customers and how to set a service apart from competitors in these critical moments? These are typical questions that blueprinting can answer.

- Service blueprinting can become the starting point for cost-reduction programs. By visualizing all service processes end to end, a company can ask, "How can we provide the same for less?" Blueprinting contributes to a better understanding of how a company can provide customers with exactly what they need while taking cost out of the service-deployment process.

- Finally, in conducting service blueprinting workshops across different countries and industries, we have experienced multiple times that blueprinting can also serve as a highly valuable tool in human resources. Service blueprinting provides a common platform. It reunites everyone inside the company around the customer. The technique provides a common language; it enables everyone to see, touch, and understand how all pieces of the organizational puzzle must come together to bring a service to life. Blueprinting can be used as a means to motivate people inside the organization to work toward the common goal of creating not just good enough but outstanding customer experiences.

## How Service Blueprinting Works

A service blueprint visualizes how the key critical elements of a company's service system need to be integrated in a coherent process to create a desired customer experience. To better understand the foundations of this approach, let us make two important distinctions.

*Front-office versus back-office actions.* First, service experts often speak of front office and back office to describe the visible and invisible elements of service operations.[8] Like the image of the theater, we can apply the concepts of onstage and backstage. As in a play, the visible parts of a service process can be divided into two categories: those related to service staff (the actors) and those related to all tangible aspects surrounding the staff (the stage). Companies particularly pay attention to what happens "on the stage." They evaluate the quality of service by gauging employees with whom they interact; they make judgments based on the tangible elements they see or interact with during the course of the service delivery as well as the output of the delivery process.

*High-touch versus low-touch services.* The second distinction refers to the difference between high-touch services (interactive or provider-active services) and low-touch services such as self-service or machine-to-machine services. The nature of the service largely determines the degree of visibility of the operations. For example, high-touch services such as management consulting or industrial cleaning require customer interaction or a strong physical presence on the customer premises. In this case, the front-office service operations play a very important role. A relatively limited level of interaction with customer employees, in turn, characterizes low-touch services. Operations behind the scenes play a larger role. Examples of services classified as low-touch are remote monitoring of production processes or technical assistance provided by a call center.

The notions of front-end versus back-end activities and high-touch versus low-touch services are important in the design and deployment of a service. Let us now look at how the service blueprinting technique works.

## Service Blueprinting Components

Service blueprinting typically has five main components: the customer's actions when experiencing a service, the "onstage" visible actions performed by contact employees, the "backstage" invisible actions performed by contact employees, support processes involving other employees of the company, and the specific technologies and physical evidence related to the activities of the front stage. Figure 9:1 provides an overview of these five key elements of service blueprinting:[9]

**Figure 9:1**
**Principal Components of Service Blueprinting**

| | |
|---|---|
| Physical Evidence | |
| Customer Actions | |
| -User | |
| -Buyer | **Line of Interaction** |
| -Payer | |
| Onstage/Visible | |
| Contact Employee Actions | |
| -Supplier | |
| -Channel partners | **Line of Visibility** |
| Backstage/Invisible | |
| Contact Employee Actions | |
| | **Line of Internal Interaction** |
| Support Processes | |
| Other Employee Actions | |

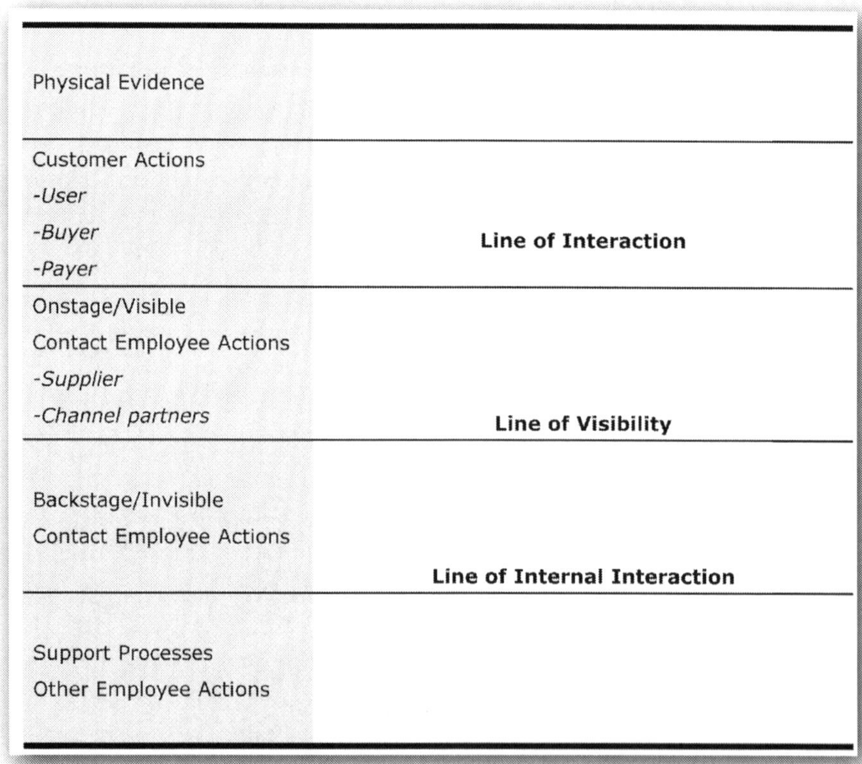

Source: Adapted from *Bitner, Ostrom, and Morgan* (2008)

*Customer Actions.* Customer actions refer to the sequence of steps that customers take before, during, or after purchasing and/or experiencing a service. As customers are the focal point of interest in such an exercise, service blueprinting naturally begins by exploring the breadth and depth of activities a customer performs in a service experience. For example, when observing a machine failure, a maintenance manager may first search for a manufacturer's customer service contact on a smartphone app. He or she may then call a helpdesk for scheduling an on-site visit by a field service technician. In short, the need for a repair service triggers a sequence of steps customers take for getting the job done. When conducting a blueprinting exercise in a business-to-business (B2B) context, identifying customer actions has an additional layer of complexity compared to exploring consumer actions. In B2B markets, customer organizations consist of multiple stakeholders that come together in a buying center. Hence, there is a need to distinguish between different roles—a user, a buyer, or a payer—when exploring customer actions in business markets.

*Onstage or visible contact-employee actions.* Once the main customer actions are identified, the visible onstage actions performed by contact employees should be delineated. The *line of interaction* separates the customer's actions from those performed by contact employees who are visible to customers. Each time the line is crossed, there is a moment of truth when the company can either positively influence the customer experience or run the risk of jeopardizing perceived service quality. For example, when performing on-site repair of industrial equipment, a frontline service technician may meet with a customer's maintenance manager and machine operator to discuss malfunctions noticed.

*Backstage or invisible contact-employee actions.* In a similar fashion, the *line of visibility* separates visible onstage actions and invisible backstage actions performed by contact employees. All actions above this line are visible to the customer; those that are below remain invisible. In the above-mentioned example of equipment repair, a service technician may pick up spare parts and tools needed for performing the on-site repair job.

*Support processes.* The fourth key component of service blueprinting consists of support processes. These processes are separated from the backstage contact-employee actions by the *internal line of interaction.* Support processes cover all activities performed by other employees within the company and include the technologies necessary for the proper production and deployment of a service. Examples of support processes are transmitting spare-part repair data to a handheld device for assisting a frontline service technician in performing an on-site repair job or preparation of background information by a staff member for a consultant's presentation to a client.

*Physical evidence.* Finally, for each customer action and for each critical interaction between them and the visible contact staff, the physical evidence that customers experience is added at the top of a service blueprint. These are all tangible items to which a customer is exposed during the service process. These elements largely affect customers' perception of service quality delivered. Examples of physical evidence are tools used by a frontline service technician during on-site equipment repair at a customer's factory or a smart phone app and/or website interface used for customer support.

## Steps in Creating a Service Blueprint

Managers can develop service blueprints for creating entirely new services, documenting, differentiating, or simply improving existing services, clarifying specific subprocesses within more complex service processes, or sharing with new employees how they provide a service in their company. From leading blueprinting workshops with companies in different industries, we have learned that a number of steps must be followed to bring such an exercise to fruition. Managers should follow the following steps when conducting a blueprinting workshop.

*Step 1—Define Your Scope.* The first step is to clearly define the scope of your service blueprinting exercise. For example, in one of our workshops, a manufacturer of industrial components wanted to redesign its postsales customer service process. In preparing for the blueprinting workshop, a number of preliminary questions needed to be answered. For example, for which individual customer or customer segment is the service blueprint developed? From the customer's point of view, when does the postsales service begin? When does this process stop? When does the service end? What role(s) does the customer have in the service process? Are third parties involved (such as distributors, installers, or system integrators)? Should they be part of the blueprinting assessment?

*Step 2—Assemble a Blueprinting Team.* The second step refers to building a team of those people inside the company who all contribute to providing a given service to customers. This team will obviously comprise all those who directly interact with customers in the process. But a blueprinting exercise also represents a great opportunity for including those who indirectly contribute to a successful process design and deployment. The technique providing a space for all employees involved to join forces around the same goals: exploring what truly matters to customers, understanding how each other's roles and responsibilities contribute to create the best-possible customer experience, and implementing the process in an effective and efficient manner.

*Step 3—Gain Deep Customer Insights.* Blueprinting exercises always start with identifying customer actions. Hence, there is a need to collect data and gain insights about what customers expect from the process to be assessed. Likewise, knowledge about how customers view their respective roles and involvement in the service experience is paramount. At first sight, this may appear as a truism. Yet from working with companies on service blueprinting over many years, we found that the number-one barrier to leading successful blueprinting assessments is the lack of deep customer insights shared by participants during workshops. When mapping customer actions on a blueprinting wall poster, we have found, time and again, that participants realized that they actually knew too little about the breadth and depth of customer actions. This step can reveal inconsistencies or differences in points of view not only between customers and the company but also among all those people inside the company who contribute directly or indirectly to the service provision. Bringing these differences to the surface and explaining the causes can be a very instructive exercise and can lead to revealing discussions within the company. For all these reasons, before heading into a blueprinting exercise, you need to take a step back and ask, "Do we have sufficient insights about our customers' journeys? To what extent do we know (or think we know) the sequence of steps and individual actions taken by our customers?" If you feel that there is too much speculation going on about what customers probably do or how they possibly experience the process, then you definitely need to collect more customer data and gain deeper insights before moving to the next step.

*Step 4—Blueprint the Service Process.* Once the team is in place with sufficient customer insights in hand, it can start visualizing customer actions. As a general rule, it is best to first focus on broad customer actions. This will allow the team to see the big picture first. There is always time to return to specific customer actions at a later stage and drill into specific activities. It is important that teams first agree upon the general sequence of customer actions. This represents the basis for all subsequent steps. Once the main steps of the customer journey are delineated, the team can then develop its blueprint further by exploring all other levels. Start with the onstage or visible contact-employee actions, and then move to the backstage or invisible contact-employee actions, and so forth. Teams should refrain from focusing too early, and in a too detailed fashion, on support process. Doing so might not only delay the overall blueprinting process but also risk blurring the picture and diverting the team's attention from those issues that truly matter.

In addition, some blueprints also include a *line of order penetration,* which is independent from a specific customer. For automated and semiautomated services in particular, customer independent and infrastructure support processes that involve IT systems often play a pivotal role. Finally, the identification of physical evidence elements usually represents the last step of the process. The blueprinting process often has to be refined through several iterations before a final, most comprehensive blueprint can be obtained.

*Step 5—Implement and Monitor Blueprinting Results.* As a result of the blueprinting exercise, teams typically identify a host of actions for improving existing service processes or launching entirely new services. Hence, detailed action plans can be developed for each department and individual people involved. In our experience, we found it extremely helpful to share the master blueprint with all parties involved and continue to work on its refinement in the weeks and months following the exercise. For example, benchmarking with competitors' processes can provide valuable additional information for differentiating and improving the company's own process. Detailed blueprints focusing on individual steps or subprocesses can complement the overall picture. Throughout the implementation process, it is essential, though, that all department-specific actions remain consistent with the master blueprint. Once actions have been implemented, there is a need for teams to reconvene periodically and monitor progress on an ongoing basis.

Figure 9:2 illustrates the blueprint of a remote-monitoring service we developed in a workshop with a supplier of high-voltage circuit breakers used in power plants. In this case, due to the nature of the service, we included a *technological interface* as an additional onstage level. The company explored a new concept of a service it had never offered before. Hence, the blueprint in figure 9:2 only depicts the main steps in the process; subprocess diagrams were developed at a later stage to document required internal support processes and support systems in greater detail. As with any other technique and tool, the chosen level of detail depends on a given project's purpose. In this particular case, emphasis was placed on visualizing actions of customers and frontline employees and their interactions throughout the entire process. Support processes for each step were also included as they affected both the customer's quality perceptions and anticipated service deployment costs. Finally, the team also explored key elements of physical evidence needed in the process.

To summarize, blueprinting represents a versatile tool in service design. It allows companies to take a new service concept from theory to practice. Blueprinting can further serve as a basis for positioning services relative to those of the competition. The technique is well suited for decommoditizing and actively differentiating existing service offers. The approach lends itself to developing key indicators for monitoring customers' service quality perceptions and for implementing corrective actions. It can also be used for assessing profitability of service processes and implementing cost-improvement programs. Further, blueprinting is an excellent tool for standardizing processes across business units of the same company and for aligning service processes among the firm, its distribution partners, or third parties in general. Finally, blueprinting represents an excellent catalyst for building a customer-centric organization and for aligning people around a common service culture.

**Figure 9:2**
**Blueprinting a Remote Monitoring Service**
**for High-Voltage Circuit Breakers**

| | | | | | | |
|---|---|---|---|---|---|---|
| **Physical Evidence** | Commercial Brochure; Supplier Website | Value Documentation Tool; Salesperson Demeanor | Service Contract Format and Content | Service Technician Uniform, Tools and Demeanor | Ergonomic Design Extranet Format and Content of Online Reports | Service Technician Uniform, Tools and Demeanor |
| **Customer Actions** | Decides to Explore the Use of Remote Monitoring System | Meets with a Technical Sales Person | Receives, Analyzes, Discusses and Signs Contract | Overviews Installation Process and Receives Training | Accesses and Reads Online Reports | Is Informed of Need to Provide Preemptive Maintenance → Supervises on-site Intervention of Field Technician |
| **Front Stage: Interface Technology** | | | | | Diffuse Data and Reports through Dedicated Extranet 24/7 | |
| **Front Stage: Visible Contact Employee Actions** | | Collects Background Data on Customer and Application | Presents Contract | Technician Installs Material and Software On-Site | | Technician Calls Customer and Schedules Maintenance Visit / Technician Maintains Circuit-Breaker On-Site |
| **Back Stage: Invisibles Contact Employee Actions** | | Prepares Contract | | Technician Sets Up Link with Supplier Database | | |
| **Support Processes** | Collect Technical Documentation; Design Brochure and Webpages | | Develop and Authorize Contract Details | Prepare Hardware and Configure Software | Remotely Collect and Analyze Data Produce Online Reports | Prepare Tools and Parts |

These benefits underline that blueprinting is highly useful not only for service design but also for industrializing services. Building upon this knowledge, we move on to the need to build the service factory by focusing on service productivity, which is the subject of the second section of this chapter.

## Industrializing Service Deployment

Once the company has developed its service portfolio, it should optimize all processes necessary to launch and implement these service activities. This is of particular importance as companies must not only seek new sources of services revenues but must also ensure that such new revenues result in healthy margins and contribute to overall profitability of the firm.

In the first section of this chapter, we see that blueprinting can be used for improving efficiency and effectiveness of service processes. Furthermore, in chapter 5, we also briefly touch upon unique capabilities companies need to secure in the area of service operations. We discuss that companies must emphasize repeatability and economies of scale in service deployment, ensure modularity of service elements, and learn to proactively manage service delivery costs for profitable service growth.

Because of the strategic importance of managing service costs for successfully mastering service-growth strategies, we return in this section to the imperative of industrializing service provision with a specific emphasis on service productivity. To secure profitability of service operations, firms must adopt a production-line approach to services. Four decades ago, famous Harvard professor Theodore Levitt already urged executives to transpose the principles of mass production into services.[10] These ideas, revolutionary at the time, were subsequently widely discussed and are mostly still relevant today. Esteemed at times, then vilified, these theories are now more nuanced, suitable for exchange and implementation. The industrialization of services followed a trend similar to that encountered in manufacturing of production principles; it increased gradually from mass production logic to a lean service production approach.[11] Even today, in terms of operations and productivity, service organizations in general are long behind manufacturing.

Nevertheless, despite the need to industrialize service operations, managers must be mindful of differences between goods and services. Productivity is typically defined as units of output divided by units of input. In service, however, there are often tradeoffs between productivity and service quality.[12] For example, a call center may raise productivity by hiring fewer employees. Yet longer waiting times will result in lower perceived service quality. Manufacturing-based productivity models are based on the *constant quality assumption*. Yet changes in manufacturing resources and systems affect service quality. These models ignore variations in quality due to the heterogeneity of services and the influence of customer participation in the production process. Therefore, using such productivity models in service is likely to give executives wrong directions for action.[13]

## Service Productivity

How, then, can the productivity challenges faced by companies in the service deployment phase be understood? While the discussion about lean principles in service is beyond the scope of this book, we want to highlight three interrelated dimensions of service operations that every company needs to manage: efficiency, effectiveness, and capacity utilization (see figure 9:3).

**Figure 9:3**
**The Service Productivity Triad**

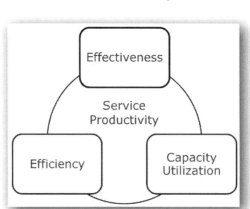

*Efficiency* focuses on the means necessary to achieve a certain output. These means are the inputs that the supplier—and its service partner—puts into the service process, such as human resources, technology, equipment, systems, information, and time. In service operations, companies frequently refer to predefined performance standards such as a specific number of sales calls per hour or the time it should take a technician to repair a broken tool. The more efficient the service organization uses its resources as inputs, the better the efficiency of the service. However, as services are generally cocreated in interaction with customers, customer inputs also need to be considered. For self-service processes where frontline employees only play a minor role, the most critical inputs can be those of the customer.

*Effectiveness* essentially concerns the ability of the firm to do the right things to achieve its objectives. In a service context, to be effective means before anything else to produce a level of quality expected by the customers. Outputs of any service process are twofold: *quantity* in terms of service volume and *quality* of the service process and outcome. Traditionally, productivity models have assumed constant quality and therefore focused on input efficiency and quantity of output. Because of the characteristics of service processes, however, the management of the perceived service quality has to be an integral part of the service operations. Conventional productivity measurements are valid only if the quality of the production output is constant, which could be the case for services such as automated online support.

*Capacity utilization* is also a fundamental element of service productivity. It deals with the questions of how the capacity of the service process is utilized and how demand is managed. As we see in chapter 7, it is an integral part of the profit equation of any service value proposition, and it is equally important from a productivity perspective. As we further see in chapter 2, in opposition to most manufacturers of physical products, service providers are seldom able to use inventories to cope with excess demand or excess capacity. A typical example is transportation services; there are a limited number of seats on each vehicle, and any unsold seat cannot be sold after departure. Overall, if demand matches supply, capacity utilization is optimal. If there is excess demand, the capacity is also utilized to full extent, but there may be a negative effect on the service quality such as long waiting time for a service technician. On the other hand, if demand is lower than what could be produced with available inputs, the capacity is underutilized and the utilization rate is lower than optimal.[14]

## Managing Productivity Dynamics and Tradeoffs

In services, measurement of productivity is often difficult as it is hard to determine the right performance indicators, taking into account the variability of service quality. Indeed, too often, traditional tracking of service operations is confined to the measurement of internal indicators of productivity or efficiency, neglecting possible indicators of effectiveness. What appears to be improved productivity in terms of better production efficiency may turn out to have a negative effect on customer-perceived quality, customer satisfaction and loyalty, and, ultimately, on the bottom line of the firm.

The service productivity triad in figure 9:3 shows that firms must strike the balance among all three interrelated elements. By focusing too much on efficiency, some companies may compromise customer satisfaction and jeopardize future sales.[15] Other companies may be tempted to customize their offerings to best meet the individual needs of each client. But while tailored offerings have many advantages from the customer's point of view, it is a potential pitfall for the service provider in that it is likely to jeopardize the overall profitability of the business. It is not possible to reinvent the wheel for each client without financial consequences. Similarly, excessive standardizing of service offerings and packages to maximize operational productivity run the risk of alienating some customers and losing market share.

How can this balance be achieved? First, it should conduct a series of marketing studies together with its customers. It must indeed gauge expectations with the desired quality and know the perceived value of the offering. The company can then make use of techniques such service blueprinting to optimize the design and operation of the process. It must invest in employee training and exploit digitization opportunities to cut costs and enhance performance. For example, a monitoring service can enable the company to anticipate potential failures and thus respond as soon as possible, avoiding the cost of mobilizing a technician.

Second, executives should consider the order in which the company launches its services. In a recent study, we included 513 German companies in mechanical engineering. Results show that the most profitable firms concentrated on industrializing their portfolio of services oriented toward their products first—that is, product lifecycle services and asset efficiency services. A broad portfolio of product-oriented services was found to help a company lay a foundation for more complex services such as process support services and process delegation. By systematically building the service portfolio and giving meticulous attention to the costs in service production and deployment, a company can reap the financial benefits of its service strategy.[16]

Finally, a supplier can influence customer behavior to optimize service operations. Many levers exist in this area. By having the opportunity to participate in preventive maintenance during off-peak periods, the supplier can provide better service while optimizing the use of its production capacity. Preventive maintenance plans enable Toyota Material Handling to schedule their service technicians well in advance, which enables a very high utilization rate and also consistent service quality. Some tasks such as troubleshooting may even be conducted by the client itself or by a specialized distributor who can assure the delivery in a more personalized way at a reduced cost.

The critical role of a loyal customer base for growing the firm's service business profitably was already highlighted in the large-scale study of German manufacturers.[17] Experts in services management rightfully underscore that managing service productivity should be seen as a mutual learning experience, where the provider and the customer are aligning their resources and production and consumption processes to each other.[18] Systematic and structured dialogue between the parties facilitates the learning process, which leads to better match between expectations and experiences—and has a positive long-term effect on service productivity. In fact, customer retention management is important from a productivity perspective; a high defection rate leads to lower productivity because the customer competence gap is constantly broad and because the cost to serve is lower compared to loyal customers with whom the company has more experience working.

## Unlock value and productivity through technology

With the information revolution and, more recently, the rise of industrial Internet, both high-touch services and high-tech service processes can benefit from technologies that can overcome the usual tradeoff between productivity and service quality if implemented correctly. A typical example is decision making enabled through data analytics, which catalyzes the shift from reactive to proactive and predictive service operations. In addition, backstage processes and support processes should be looked at as they are invisible to customers. Cost-cutting initiatives should target the nonvalue-added activities in those processes that can be automated or even eliminated.

When Toyota Material Handling initiated a mobile technology project to improve efficiency of field services business, it specifically targeted backstage activities. By implementing a system with handheld computers for each service technician, the company achieved a standardized service process for its European sales companies, which was both more efficient and more reliable. For example, the ratio between service technician and indirect employees increased from 3:1 to 5:1, and the company benefited from reduced cost for administration, increased cash flow, and improved quality and planning. Customers, in turn, benefited from faster response time and increased first-time fix, which led to improved customer satisfaction.[19]

Across industries, data and analytics have changed the way providers do business. For example, in the automotive industry, car-sharing companies car2go and Zipcar analyze usage patterns to ensure they have the right number of cars in the right neighborhood at any time. Opportunities for remote integration between devises and equipment also provide new service opportunities, more efficient service processes, and better utilization of capacity. Carmakers like Mercedes can provide customers with a unique ID and remotely track how the components in the car are wearing, which enables them to proactively prompt a service appointment. The customer ID can be further used to access various car and mobility-related services such as car2go, which it owns, through the "Mercedes Me" online portal.

However, as services are increasingly reliant on information about customer operations and product usage, customers have to trust the supplier and know that the data they share is in safe hands; alternatively, trust the supplier that they are not monitored in case they are unwilling to share certain data. Ford was forced into an embarrassing retraction at 2014 year's Consumer Electronics Show in Las Vegas after Jim Farley, then head of marketing, said, "We know everyone who breaks the law. We know exactly when you do it because we have a GPS sensor in your car. By the way, we don't supply that data to anyone." Although he later clarified that the company did not track anyone without his or her permission, the gaffe was already made.[20]

## KEY QUESTIONS ABOUT SERVICE PRODUCTIVITY

Before moving on to organizational issues, executives need to ask themselves whether they have secured the resources and competencies to strike the balance between service growth and efficient and effective service industrialization. To assess your strengths and weaknesses in this area, consider the following questions:

1. Do we rely on service blueprinting, customer journey mapping, or other voice-of-the-customer techniques as a starting point for developing new services?
2. When improving existing services, do we systematically start with collecting data about what customers need and want in terms of service experience?
3. Do we involve all internal departments and people who contribute to providing a service when exploring opportunities of service-quality improvements or cost reductions?
4. Do we use practical tools such as blueprinting for building a more customer-centric service culture in our organization?
5. In our company, do we take a production-line approach to services?

6. Do we succeed in balancing efficiency, effectiveness, and capacity utilization when deploying services in our company?

7. Can we work proactively and systematically to maximize the utilization of our service employees? Do we know how to cope with excess demand or excess capacity?

8. Do we systematically survey customers to identify opportunities for service-productivity improvements or service-delivery cost reductions?

9. Do we invest significant efforts in informing and educating customers about how they can contribute to service-productivity gains?

10. Do we leverage technology to make our services delivery processes more cost efficient while at the same time improving the service quality?

## CHAPTER 10

### TRANSFORMING SALES: IS YOUR SALES FORCE READY FOR SERVICES?

*Product salespeople are from Mars;*
*service salespeople are from Venus.*
—VICE PRESIDENT, SERVICE ORGANIZATION, CAPITAL-GOODS
MANUFACTURER

I n the previous chapter, we discussed how companies can both leverage opportunities for innovation and ensure service delivery in a cost-efficient manner. Striking this balance represents a critical milestone in any service-growth strategy. Yet knowing *what* to sell and controlling costs will not suffice for mastering the journey. The next critical stage for any company willing to grow through services is knowing *how* to sell its service offerings in the marketplace. Firms must decide how to organize and implement the right go-to-market strategy. In the final part of our book, we address how to align the company's sales organization (chapter 10) and partners (chapter 11) with its objectives and make the right organizational choices for implementing its service-growth strategy (chapter 12).

In business markets, companies often find that their existing industrial sales force represents a major hurdle in implementing ambitious service-growth strategy. Hence, in this chapter we provide guidelines for managers to assess whether their company's existing sales force is actually ready for achieving corporate service-growth goals and develop a road map for how they can successfully steer the transition from a product-centric to a service-savvy sales organization. This chapter draws on research we conducted among sales executives and salespersons in charge of growing service revenues beyond their firms' traditional goods-dominant sales.[1] We investigate the specificities of selling services versus selling goods, identify unique competencies and skills required for selling services, and discuss how these skills resonate with profiles of high-performing salespeople in the services arena. Finally, we lay out the steps that companies must take to transform their sales organizations.

## Companies Must Align Sales with Service-Growth Objectives

In working with companies around the globe on service-growth strategies, we found numerous examples of strong resistance to change from within the sales organization. Firms experienced high levels of churn among salespeople, even after extensive training. Managers found themselves with little choice but to fire and hire. Some even went as far as replacing 80 percent of their existing sales forces.[2] Others heavily invested in training and change management to accompany the transformation of their sales organization. As a general rule of thumb, companies we worked with found that only one-third of industrial salespeople easily transitioned from selling products to selling complex services and customer solutions. Another third of sales reps required substantial management support to master the process of selling value-added services on top of usual product sales. Finally, one-third of salespeople preferred to be reassigned to selling goods and continue to focus on what they did best.

These examples underscore the pivotal role of sales in the shift from a goods-centric to a service-centric business model. They also underline the need for management to take a step back, assess whether its sales organization is prepared for such a move, and, if needed, drive change throughout the entire sales organization. If "product salespeople are from Mars, while service salespeople are from Venus,"[3] as one of the managers we worked with explained, then companies need to take a step back and critically review whether their sales force is aligned with the corporate strategy of growing service revenues and profits in addition to goods-based sales.

## Magnitude of Change: How Important Is the Challenge of Transforming the Sales Organization?

We wanted to understand to what extent companies' sales organizations were prepared for implementing service-growth strategies. To this end, we interviewed sales executives and senior sales managers deeply involved in leading sales organizations in diverse industries and markets (see exhibit 9 for a brief description of our field study).

**Exhibit 9**
*Steering the Sales Force from Products to Services: Field-Research Findings*

This chapter draws on the finding of field research we conducted among sales executives and sales managers in B2B companies.[4] We first organized a workshop with eighteen senior sales managers and experts experienced in leading industrial services sales transformations. We (1) explored the strategic imperatives leading to change from product-centric to service-savvy sales organizations; (2) discussed barriers and enablers of the transformation process; and (3) shared best practices when steering the transition toward services and customer solutions in B2B manufacturing companies. After the workshop, summaries of findings were shared with all participants to ensure that analyses and interpretations were consistent with outcomes of workshop discussions. Based on initial insights gained, we developed a detailed interview guide for drilling deeper into the pressing issues faced by industrial salesforces. We then conducted in-depth interviews with twenty executives of seventeen firms, ranging in size from small and medium-sized companies to large, multinational firms. All participants were senior sales managers from manufacturing firms in diverse industries. We focused on interviewing senior (C-suite) level managers. In all firms, service-growth was considered a strategic priority. Aligning the sales force with corporate goals of services growth represented a major challenge in most organizations. Selection, compensation, retention, and training of services salespeople presented particularly pressing challenges to the firms in this study.

*Source:* Ulaga and Loveland (2014)

The companies in our field study reported that their sales organizations went through a substantial transformation process when moving from a goods-centric to a service-centric business model. All sales forces we studied were highly successful in product markets. Yet when allocating salespeople from product to services sales, firms consistently reported unexpectedly high variations of performance outcomes. Some firms reported differences in sales results of 300 percent or more between highest- and lowest-performing salespersons once salespeople were allocated from goods- to services sales. These results are striking, especially as salespeople had a well-established prior track record of high-performing product sales. Interestingly, a salesperson with stellar achievements in product sales is not necessarily a "star" salesperson in services sales. Consider the illustration from a capital equipment manufacturer in our field research:

> *Our service sales force sells a host of value-added services on our fleet of 170,000 machines installed and systematically place value-added services with these existing accounts. They also use a service to get a foot in the door with those customers that currently have a competitor's equipment. We expect of a service sales rep to generate €250,000 annually. Yet, the reality looks different. While our best service salespeople achieve €500,000 or more, some of our sales reps linger at €150,000 annually. That's definitely not enough to turn a profit. Our sales guys are all experienced in equipment sales, but they don't make the transition equally well to services.*

These performance differences inevitably lead to considerable churn among salespeople allocated to goods and services sales. Selling services required skills and abilities completely different from those required for selling goods, according to an executive from a major power utility: "We created a subsidiary to push our presence in energy efficiency services as a way to extract more value from selling electricity, a plain commodity. We offered our traditional sales reps to move to the subsidiary on a voluntary basis. After the first year, several salespeople asked to be reassigned to their former positions. Despite our training efforts, they just couldn't handle selling energy efficiency audits or performance-based contracts. They felt it was too much of a stretch…Those movements back and forth created all kind of hiccups, and today, we still haven't found the silver bullet."

The extent of these personnel problems appeared severe. Consider the following description by a senior sales manager:

> *We have a very successful international sales force in the telecom industry. Our salespeople are experienced in selling hardware and standard services. However, when we moved to selling complex solutions, we found that our sales organization was a major hurdle. I worked with a sales consulting firm to assess how well we were prepared. From our first audit, we learned that only sixteen out of 213 salespeople clearly had the skills to go after selling solutions. Clearly, the sales force appeared as a bottleneck if we were to make this transition a success. So we rolled out a major training program for our salespeople.*

Our field research thus clearly shows that changes in corporate strategy, such as a companywide push for service growth, inevitably affects the sales organization. The problem is not one of "good versus bad" salespeople but rather about the need to rethink how salespersons are selected, allocated to goods versus services sales, rewarded, and aligned with a firm's overall services strategy. One of the executives in our field study clearly summarized the pivotal role of the sales force in the service transition: "We believe that the people in these positions will be the limiting factor to getting ultimately to where we'd like to be with our services strategy."

## Are Service Sales Different?

More than thirty years ago, two researchers, Dubinsky and Rudelius,[5] asked a fundamental question: "Do you sell industrial services the same way as industrial products?" In surveying 154 sales reps, they found that salespeople indeed emphasized different selling techniques for industrial goods and services such that "because of the intangibility of service, the same selling techniques used to sell a product are not always applicable when used to sell a service." Today, the answer to their key question is still far from obvious. Sales experts have recommended various sales approaches and selling behaviors, such as adaptive selling, agility selling, consultative selling, customer-oriented selling, and relationship selling, or, more recently, challenger selling and value-based selling.[6] Yet there is also a consensus that current sales approaches and models insufficiently account for the growing sales complexity, especially in light of service transition strategies.[7] Clearly, in sales, we have "ignored one of the most important trends in contemporary business—the shift away from a traditional goods-based economy toward service-based offerings."[8]

In our study, we explored similarities and differences between selling goods and services. Managers explained that the traditional sales steps, from prospecting to closing and follow-up, applied to services sales, too, especially in the case of standardized product lifecycle services described in chapter 2 (e.g., extended warranty contract attached to an equipment sale). Selling service offerings in this category is comparable to a traditional goods sale that sales reps can easily handle. Consider the explanation of one of the sales managers we interviewed: "As long as we grew in services closely attached to our equipment sales, our sales force could easily handle these offerings. Selling a warranty extension or a financing offer is pretty straightforward. They are pretty standardized offers which any of our salespeople can sell. You need to listen to the customer, translate that into what we have and make the sale. To me, these services are off-the-shelf products. But when we went for those other offers, say a remote monitoring contract, well, all of a sudden, we ran into problems."

Selling services that fall in the remaining three of the four types of offering categories discussed in chapter 2 pose unique sales challenges. These categories are asset-efficiency services (such as a remote monitoring service attached to a medical scanner), process-support services (like an energy-efficiency audit), and process-delegation services (e.g., a performance-based construction tools fleet-management program).

Further probing the unique characteristics of services sales in these categories, we identified four critical areas in which services sales differ from goods sales (see table 10:1).

**Table 10:1**
**Comparison: Industrial Goods versus Services Sales**

| Key Aspect | Industrial Goods Sales | Industrial Services Sales | Key Capabilities for Selling Industrial Services |
|---|---|---|---|
| Underlying Tenet | Persuasion Model | Cocreation Model | Ability to gain deep understanding of customers' business model and key performance metric |
| Requirement Definition | Meet/exceed customer-initiated, goods-centric specifications | Discover/agree upon result-driven specifications | Ability to manage customer expectations: adroitly say "no" instead of getting to "yes" |
| Network Complexity | Limited number of stakeholders | Multiple stakeholders in customer and vendor organization | Ability to develop strong network ties in both customer and vendor organizations |
| Outcome Orientation | Focus on deal closing (hunter perspective) | Focus on share growth and contract renewal (farmer perspective) | Ability to tangibilize outcomes from the customer perspective |

Source: Ulaga and Loveland (2014)

***Underlying Tenet.*** A first difference refers to the underlying tenet for selling services in these categories. Selling the three categories of service offerings discussed in chapter 2 is grounded in a cocreation logic, unlike the traditional persuasion model grounded in goods-centric sales. They require a different mind-set for approaching customers. Consider the following example: "Selling a performance-based contract to a customer is an entirely different ball game than selling equipment…This is not about convincing the customer that our equipment is the best. It's about sitting down with the customer and designing the best-possible solution together. And if, in this process, we find that the customer needs fewer machines to get the job done than we initially thought, then just let the chips fall."

*Requirement Definition.* Second, in a goods-centric model, salespeople work to meet customer expectations based on customers' stated needs; thus, customers typically drive the process by issuing requests for quotes and initiating competitive bidding processes. Salespeoples' efforts are geared toward demonstrating the extent to which the vendor meets, and possibly exceeds, customer-initiated specifications better than the competition. For services sales in the three above-mentioned categories, though, sales reps face ill-defined customer specifications and must work with customers to clarify the "fuzzy front end" related to what they need. Both parties must explore, discuss, and agree upon specifications that will get the customer job done. In other words, they need to work together to define how goods and services can best be integrated for solving customers' problems.

*Network Complexity.* Third, in a goods-centric sales environment, salespersons interact with a more narrowly defined set of stakeholders in the customer organization (purchasing, maintenance, equipment operators). When selling services discussed in this chapter, sales reps must cast a wider net and interact with a broader network of stakeholders. Consider the following statement: "When we went after selling those complex cash management offerings to customers in retail banking, our sales reps were lost. All of a sudden, they had to talk not only to purchasing and IT but also to general management. They had to interact with the bank's marketing people and tell them how we could fit into their CRM strategy. Clearly, our salespeople were not used to talking to some of these folks."

Network complexity increases with respect to not just the customer organization but also the vendor's internal organization. As another sales executive explained, "When you sell an in-flight entertainment solution rather than just a system, the job becomes much more complex. You have to work with the customer, build that offer to suit a particular need. But you also need to reach out to your own people. How should the offer for this particular airline look like? Can we deliver on that promise? What about industrialization of that offer? You need to work with a lot of people to get that sale done."

*Outcome Orientation.* Fourth, expected sales outcomes greatly differ too. In a goods-centric sales context, the emphasis is on closing a deal, in line with transaction-oriented selling and the traditional "steps of selling."[9] By handling customer objections and overcoming resistance, goods-centric sales hunt down customers and convince them to buy. "Selling a product boosts your adrenaline levels. It's like a soccer game: you're in front of the goal, you have to score...In services, you need to spend time with the customer; you really need to understand his business. You need to care for his concerns."

In selling complex services, the outcome of the sales process shifts from deal closing to nurturing and growing a relationship over time. This opens up opportunities for adding more value in the relationship:

> *This is a different kind of sale. Instead of getting a foot in the door, selling services on top of our existing products requires identifying opportunities for doing more with customers. For example, we may have started out by selling heating equipment. That's a good start, but then we need to move up the ladder and grab more of a customer's business. Can we sell maintenance? Can we move to a performance-based contract? And what about taking over other jobs for that customer, such as cleaning or delivery of gases? This is easier said than done. Many of our sales reps prefer chasing down the next new account rather than sticking around and doing more with an existing customer.*

Clearly, highly value-added service sales reflect a farming perspective, geared toward ensuring continuity for the next contract and growing customer share, rather than a hunting logic. Collectively, the four characteristics discussed above clearly illustrate how the nature of selling complex industrial services differs from the traditional industrial goods sale.

## Which Sales Capabilities Do You Need to Secure?

Based on the differences in the nature of the sales process, managers in our field research also highlighted distinctive capabilities required for selling these demanding services (see table 10:2).

*Understanding Customers' Business Models.* First, selling complex industrial-service offerings requires a more fine-grained understanding of customers' business models and operations, as well as deeper

knowledge of how the vendor can contribute to reducing costs and/
or improving productivity on behalf of its customer. For example, one
executive mentioned that to sell a remote monitoring service aimed at
helping customers raise the productivity of high-voltage circuit breakers,
sales reps needed intimate knowledge of a customer's plant, work flow,
and key performance metrics:

> *To sell services and solutions, you need to have an intimate knowledge of
> the customer and the way he operates. In our company, we use a T-shaped
> model for describing the skills we want our salespeople to develop. On the
> one hand, there's the knowledge of the customer, his culture, his people,
> the way he operates. On the other hand, there's the knowledge of our orga-
> nization, our people, and our capabilities. And finally, there's a third
> part: how well do we know the customer's industry? Can we "surprise"
> the customer? Can we approach the customer and say, "Here's something
> you don't know that should be interesting for you"? It's all three things
> our salespeople need to know.*

***Managing Customer Expectations.*** Second, managers emphasized that service offerings required an ability to shape customer expectations in terms
of what can be achieved through a service offering. This also implies an
ability to clearly explain what a service won't be able to cover. In this selling context, salespeople thus play a pivotal role in crafting offerings and
designing contractual agreements. Contract negotiations largely make
or break profitability in subsequent service deployment. Managers in our
study highlighted an interesting aspect in this context: high-performing
services salespeople have an ability to adroitly say no (instead of the commonly described ability of getting to yes) to safeguard against service commitments that could jeopardize future profitability in contract execution:
"When selling services, you need to develop an ability to say no instead of
working toward getting the customer to say yes. Our product salespeople
have a tendency to throw in a warrant extension for free. Or they would
promise a training session free of charge just to get the customer to sign
the order. This is not how one should sell an industrial service."

***Developing Strong Network Ties.*** Third, sales managers in our field
research emphasized salespersons' ability to develop string network

ties in both the customer's and the vendor's organization. Managers explained that sales reps needed to demonstrate an ability to reach beyond their comfort zone and access key customer contacts they traditionally would not have targeted. Several participants explained that the more their firms moved toward selling value-added services, the higher salespeople had to reach in the customer's hierarchy. Managers also referred to capabilities deployed in favor of managing internal networks. As one manager explained, resource-intensive services require sales reps to compete for scarce resources inside the vendor organization: "The best of our service sales reps know whom to talk to in our organization. They know how to assemble the right team for delivering on what they promised. Our internal people face competing demands. They must decide whom they are going to work for. But whenever there's a bottleneck in terms of [human resources], these guys just have an ability to get the right people on board."

***Tangibilizing Customer Outcomes.*** Fourth, many advanced services imply some form of performance commitment (such as machine availability or pay-as-you-go agreement) rather than solely performing a task (like a break-fix agreement or repair of equipment within a preset timeframe). Hence, salespeople must develop an ability to persuasively sell outcomes instead of focusing on service attributes or functional benefits. As a manager explained:

> Some of our salespeople found it very hard to sell our fleet management to large trucking companies. Sell miles instead of tires. In every sales presentation, they kept falling back into showcasing the tire: "This is our tire; it's technologically superior. Our tire outperforms any competitor." But this is not what we wanted them to sell...At one point, I was so desperate that I fired off an e-mail to every salesperson in fleet management: "You are not allowed to show a tire on any slide in your sales presentations, full stop." The sales guys replied: "If I can't show the tire, what else shall we put in front of the customer?"

In summary, the complex services discussed in this chapter require a set of distinctive sales skills that flow from the very specific nature of the sales process. These characteristics also point at interesting personality traits of high-performing service salespersons—an aspect we address in the following section.

## Why Product Salespeople Are from Mars and Service Salespeople Are from Venus

In our research, we also explored to what extent high-performing service salespeople differ from other salespersons in terms of personality traits. Sales managers identified twelve personality traits, as well as general intelligence, a thirteenth critical factor, summarized in table 10:2. In this section, we focus on the eight most frequently mentioned personality dimensions and how they relate to services sales.

*Learning Orientation.* Salespeople with a strong *learning orientation* devote a significant amount of time to improving their sales skills. They view their sales capabilities as reflective of their own levels of effort.[10] In contrast, salespeople scoring high on *performance orientation* believe their skill sets are fixed. They focus on maximizing their performance at every task. Learning-oriented salespeople tend to perform better in services sales due to the nature of the sales process. Longer and more complex sales cycles require that salespersons spend more time with customers, meet with multiple stakeholders, collect data from a variety of sources, and explore how customer needs can be fulfilled through existing or new services.

In our study, firms struggling with achieving service sales goals were those in which performance-oriented salespeople dominated in sales forces. In a medical device company we studied, salespeople excelled in selling millions of dollars of medical diagnostics equipment. Yet sales of training modules to medical doctors remained well below expectations. Over the years, we found multiple cases where lack of learning orientation appeared as a major hurdle; as one manager stated, "You are going to have a problem with the guy who comes out of a training session and says, 'Yes, that's fine, but I knew all that already.' It's a rule, and I've seen it with more than forty (terminated) salespeople."

*Customer Service Orientation.* In markets where firms focus on "moving boxes," management often tends to view services as an afterthought, a necessary evil merely focused on enabling goods sales,

Table 10:2
Personality Traits of High-Performing B2B Service Salespeople

| Trait | Definition | Count* |
|---|---|---|
| Learning Orientation | Inclination to learn new materials and find answers to questions on one's own; working to continuously improve. Inclination to constantly improve one's task performance. Willingness to engage in self-directed learning. | 26 |
| Customer Service Orientation | Striving to provide responsive, personalized, quality service to customers. Putting the customer first. | 25 |
| Intrinsic Motivation | Intrinsic motivation implies enjoying a task for its own sake, rather than enjoying it because it is instrumental to some reward or gain. | 23 |
| General Intelligence | Ability to recognize patterns, analyze situations and ideas, and reason. | 19 |
| Emotional Stability | Overall level of adjustment and emotional resilience; ability to work well with job pressure and stress. | 16 |
| Teamwork Orientation | Propensity to work as part of a team; cooperative and participative in group projects. | 11 |
| Introversion | Tendency to be more reflective, introspective, and attentive to others. | 9 |
| Visionary Thinking | Inclined toward a global, intuitive, big-picture thinking style rather than a practical, detail-oriented style. | 8 |
| Nurturance | Inclination to use personal warmth to help others, a need to help others and attend to their needs. | 3 |
| Openness | Prone to seek out and engage in new ideas, procedures, techniques, and experiences, travel, cross-cultural activities. | 3 |
| Perfectionism/Rigidity | Having an orientation to detail, focusing on a task until it has been completed at every level. | 2 |

(*) N.B.: Number of times a personality trait was mentioned by managers
in our field research. Source: Ulaga and Loveland (2014)

handling customer complaints, and addressing service delivery hiccups. In contrast, customer service–oriented salespeople strive to provide responsive, personalized, quality service to customers. Managers in our research emphasized that customer-oriented salespeople not only put the customer interest first. They also manage to strike the balance between having both the customer's and the company's interests in mind. While providing customers exactly what they need, they also know how to approach customer relationships with an emphasis on making the most of the installed base of goods already sold. Customer service–oriented salespeople allocate more time to growing existing relationships, while less service-oriented salespeople tend to place more efforts on prospecting new customers. These findings resonate well with the distinction between hunters and farmers frequently observed in sales. While a high-performing goods salesperson typically hunts for the next transactional sale, the typical "farmer" relies on his or her strong customer orientation to grow service revenues in a relationship over time.

***Intrinsic Motivation.*** Intrinsically motivated salespeople enjoy the sales task for its own sake rather than because it is instrumental to sales compensation. Intrinsic motivation reveals why salespeople desire to learn more on the job and spend more time trying to improve their skill sets. Extrinsically motivated salespeople, in turn, focus more on the rewards and incentives associated with high performance. They also tend to enjoy competition more and seek to outperform their peers. As one of the managers we interviewed stated, "The day when the 'big sale' comes down, everyone is made aware of it. These are the extraordinary stories that circulate within the firm: the hero."

Such situations of hunting for the "next big whale" contrast with many services sales contexts. Indeed, selling multiple remote monitoring contracts for a few thousand dollars each annually may be less visible than one major sale. Yet, taken together, these contract sales may well exceed the profitability of one transactional sale over time.

Sales management must account for these differences. For example, outcome-based sales control systems resonate better with extrinsically oriented goods-centric salespeople, while behavioral-based sales control systems, on the other hand, are better suited for services salespeople. Such systems entail more monitoring and direction by supervisors and more subjective measures of performance. With behavioral control, the focus centers on inputs from salespeople, such as their work activities and sales strategies. This type of control engenders intrinsic motivation because a salesperson must focus attention and efforts on the sales process rather than its outcomes. As one executive explained, "Good service salespeople actually don't focus on, like, 'How much money am I actually going to be making?' Those guys are more comfortable selling services because they are less driven by the incentive plan."

*General Intelligence.* Managers in our research emphasized the importance of general intelligence[11] (or "g") because of the demanding nature of selling complex services. Personality traits such as learning orientation are important, but a desire to learn is not sufficient. The breadth and depth of knowledge required of the "T-shaped professional" means that effective salespeople must be able to incorporate and integrate large amounts of knowledge from many domains. Support for the importance of general intelligence thus emerged as a key trait, as the following quote about a firm's highly effective service sales force shows: "A lot of our people were quite technical and had kind of gone through project engineering and then into sales. The [successful] service person tends to be...quick to learn and look at nuances and differentiators of our product and service offerings. They see the bigger picture when it comes to understanding customer operations, and they are able to enlarge the scope of discussions. They are able to sell the entire project rather than focus the equipment at hand."

*Emotional Stability.* Two aspects of emotional stability emerged as important factors when selling complex services. First, emotional stability favors pursuing sales opportunities that are larger in size but that may also require a longer sales cycle and are riskier in terms of positive outcomes. Managers explained that high-performing goods-focused salespeople tend to feel less comfortable in such sales environments: "So the personal interest of a salesperson, it's necessarily to go for the value. It's much more complicated and has a greater chance of failing—you just don't know. A lot of salespeople actually tend to go for services when they can't do otherwise. If you give the salesperson the choice, 'Sell this widget starting at three million with the potential to bring in twenty-five million or sell another for ten to fourteen million, one-shot deal and never again,' don't fool yourself. He's the king. He'll always go for the lower sale."

Lower levels of emotional stability resulted in higher levels of resistance to change among salespersons. Managers in our study described their goods-centric sales force as "the most conservative group of employees inside the company."

A second aspect of emotional stability referred to interacting with customers. When selling complex services, salespeople typically face two important challenges. First, they frequently need to resist temptations of giving away services for free—a behavior often observed in goods sales to facilitate a sale. Second, they also need an ability to adroitly say no to customers during contract negotiations in order to maintain profitability during subsequent services deployment stages. The same holds for preventing service scope creep—that is, uncontrolled changes or growth of service quality within a service provided over time. In such situations, emotional stability helps a salesperson to step in and take corrective actions.

Another challenge for firms developing hybrid offerings has been getting both salespeople and buying firms to accept new ways of doing business and, as a corollary, disallowing salespeople from using the service elements of a hybrid offering as a freebie to ensure an at-risk sale. In moving to a service-centric business model, the firms had to learn how to manage the transition from free to fee, that is, to start invoicing customers for service elements that might have been offered for free. Managers explained that the salesperson was crucial in this transition, but many salespeople did not feel comfortable putting themselves on the line by attempting to make a simple relationship more complicated. The position of salespeople as organizational boundary spanners thus becomes riskier because, in changing their existing relationships, salespeople had to risk losing their customers by telling them things they might not want to hear: "This thing that I'm talking about and the transition we're going through, you could sit across the table from a customer and tell them that you think they're crazy. Customer calls at seven p.m. He only has the standard contract, but we will go because it is a really important customer. Now our job is to change that mentality inside [the organization]."

***Teamwork Orientation.*** Selling hybrid offerings requires teams to have more breadth. Thus, sales teams must include salespeople, sales managers, and even members from other functional units in the firm such as engineers and product planners. For such a team to function successfully, its members must prefer to work in a team setting and trust one another. For example, a sales manager for a firm selling industrial mining equipment noted a significant transition in how salespeople needed to allocate their time and to spend more time with other (non-sales) team members and members of the partner/buyer firm: "I want him [the service salesperson] to work with the other team members, and I want them all looking at the mine for solutions."

This behavior contrasts with the traditional lone wolf—that is, a salesperson preferring to work alone and inclined to hold low opinions of the competence of coworkers.[12] Instead, an emphasis on teamwork requires salespeople to give up independence and autonomy in exchange for being part of a collective group. No one salesperson can likely possess the requisite knowledge to perform an increasingly complex hybrid offering sale on his or her own. The sales team is not a hunting party but a diverse set of stakeholders and actors with different areas of expertise. Salespeople must give up their own sense of autonomy and expert status to work on teams with multiple experts to cocreate value with customers: "The service-savvy salesperson will bring in a subject matter expert, or even one of those transactional sales guys, and consult with them on capabilities, limitations, properties, etc. Do you see product sales guys doing that? No!"

***Introversion.*** Common wisdom has it that successful salespeople are extroverts—sociable, outgoing, and personally warm. They often must initiate contact with strangers and develop a broad array of relationships. Yet we found that introversion actually may be very beneficial for hybrid offering sales as the sales process requires a very methodical and detail-oriented approach. Extroverts tend to be easily distracted, less likely to pay attention to detail, and unable to persist in mundane tasks.[13] Hence, the sociable traits of extroverts may even be detrimental.

Research has shown that extroverts prefer extrinsic rewards, such as pay raises, benefits, and public acknowledgment of accomplishments, while introverts tend to be more sensitive to punishment. Some researchers even suggest that the core feature of extroversion is reward sensitivity rather than the inclination to be sociable.[14] Although introverts may not enjoy being the center of attention, they can work well with others on complicated tasks for which rewards are not explicit. The team-oriented, behaviorally controlled environment of hybrid offering sales does not provide immediate, distinctive, or frequent rewards, which may leave extroverts less satisfied and productive. Extroversion increases sales only if the rewards are explicit. For example, one salesperson who had just "landed a whale" described the feeling: "It's the adrenaline rush. 'I have the magic bullet, the ultimate weapon.' In services, that's less likely to happen. There's less of a strong moment."

*Visionary Thinking.* This trait relates to selling complex services in several ways. First, it allows salespeople to be more concerned with what is going to happen down the line instead of just a narrow focus on the next product sale. Second, visionary thinkers focus on bigger and broader opportunities. The trait facilitates sell more value-added services and complex solutions beyond traditional goods. Visionary thinkers envision and communicate the ability of teams to mobilize resources for attaining greater future success. Finally, because hybrid offering sales often require interaction with higher-level managers in customer firms, visionary thinking resonates with top management in customer organizations. Consider the following quote from a sales executive: "The higher you go in the management chain, the more 'strategic' people are. This is where they have the most vision on a problem."

*Other Personality Traits.* Several traits mentioned less frequently by participants still provide insights into sales of value-added services and customer solutions. For example, managers noted that salespeople needed to nurture the relationship throughout the sales process. *Nurturance* was especially important in situations where services needed to be customized and solutions required significant levels of cocreation. As one manager noted, services sales were more successful when salespersons were "very caring and nurturing."

Another trait discussed in our study referred to *openness*, which displayed similarities to learning orientation. Yet it also included a willingness to try new approaches or experience new cultures for their own sake.[15] Not only did services-sales forces need to learn how customers conducted their business, but they also had to be willing to try unorthodox methods or chase new ideas while keeping an open mind about what hybrid offerings they could cocreate. Consider this quote: "Some ideas…are filtered by the [product] salespeople, who tend to be conservative. They are probably a bit too conservative, and they will shoot down some ideas that might well be worth pursuing."

Managers further explained that salespeople needed *assertiveness* in a services sales context. Yet compared to a traditional product sale, the trait was beneficial in different ways. On the one hand, sales teams can become so interested in cocreating an offering that they may become overly focused on creating value for the customer, thus losing track of the vendor's own profitability. Thus, assertiveness contributes to ensuring that salespeople keep both parties' interests in mind. On the other hand, the transition away from a persuasion-based approach ("Always Be Closing") also suggests assertiveness can take on a different meaning in a services sales context. For example, one manager in the mining industry noted a new direction in hiring and training practices. Consider this observation: "We are moving away from the subject matter expert and making a hard sell or close but more toward information and building a relationship through our knowledge and our industry experience."

Finally, some managers suggested the traits of perfectionism and conscientiousness. Because of the complexity and long-term orientation of these offerings, a greater need to focus on details emerged, together with the deeper level understanding of the customer's business. To specify the results of this understanding, salespeople had to gain deep understanding of how both companies operate, which required a willingness to put forth substantive effort: "one must be absolutely flawless...To remain competitive in services, you need to commit to results."

In this chapter, we have seen that even firms with a dominant market position and a strong sales force often stumble when they venture into selling value-added services and customer solutions. Industrial services sales are not simply an extension of goods sales. Companies may be able to increase their sales of standard product lifecycle services, such as extended warranties attached to equipment, using their existing industrial sales force, but it would be inappropriate to expect competent, experienced, goods-centric salespeople to go about business as usual to sell complex combinations of goods and services in industrial markets. In particular, there often is a serious gap between the demands placed on existing industrial sales forces and their capability to sell complex services effectively, as evidenced by the high rates of turnover among (otherwise efficient and effective) sales reps.

In working with sales executives and studying salesperson behaviors, we identified distinctive characteristics of the services-sales process in contrast to a traditional goods-centric sale. These characteristics have important ramifications for the required sales capabilities and salesperson personality traits that are relevant to services sales. Some of the traits traditionally identified as relevant for high-performing salespeople in goods-dominant sales appear less important, irrelevant, or even detrimental in a services sales context. Likewise, selected traits that emerge as particularly beneficial for the sale of value-added services and customer solutions in business markets also appear insignificant or even problematic in a goods sales context. In summary, the profiles of a high-performing goods salesperson and a stellar performer in industrial services sales likely diverge on several key personality traits. Thus, our findings support the idea that while goods salespeople are from Mars, services and solutions salespeople appear to hail from Venus.[16]

Given the magnitude of change involved, we suggest that a firm's top management must get deeply involved in leading the transformation. A company's industrial sales force plays a pivotal role in ensuring a successful service-transition strategy. Steering the industrial sales organization from a goods- to a service-centric sales model requires full attention from C-level management. Such attention affects how salespersons are recruited, allocated, and trained; industrial firms also should take a fresh look at how they design their sales organization, develop coordination mechanisms for specialized sales forces, and redesign incentive structures to align the sales organizations with their overall corporate strategies.

Managers must find ways to further embed their sales forces in both their own firms and the customer organizations. With the stronger emphasis on teamwork and customer service, managers need to develop compensation schemes and performance appraisal systems that accurately reflect the process of creating and delivering hybrid offerings. Another managerial challenge refers to the need for more training and education of salespersons. Managers thus need a better picture of the specific competencies and skill sets of each member of the organization so that they can mobilize teams with the appropriate capabilities. Finally, with changes in compensation, training, allocation, and development of sales teams, managers must devote more effort to ensuring that services and solution sales are profitable for their firms. Investments in transforming the sales organization likely affect short-term profitability, a phenomenon we see in chapter 4. Service sales represent a double-edged sword: on the one hand, they are a strategic necessity with a strong opportunity for profits. On the other hand, there is a potential to mismanage or inadequately develop organizational capacities required of hybrid offerings. Moving forward, managers should take a serious look at how they implement these changes and gauge their progress.

## KEY QUESTIONS TO PREPARE YOUR SALES ORGANIZATION FOR SERVICE SALES GROWTH

In order to transform a sales organization from a product-centric to a service-savvy sales force, managers should address the following questions:

1. To what extent does the strategic shift toward a service-centric business model affect our company's existing sales organization?
2. Are there differences between selling goods and selling services in our market? Do these differences affect the nature of our selling process?
3. Which distinctive sales capabilities do we need for selling services?
4. What is the ideal profile of a service salesperson in our industry? Do we favor specific personality traits over others?
5. Do our salespeople possess the unique skills and personality traits needed for selling services?
6. Can we train our salespeople, or do we need to hire new ones?
7. What is the right mix of existing versus new service sales experts?
8. Do we need two parallel sales forces, one selling products and another focusing on service sales? If yes, how do we coordinate both sales forces?
9. Are our incentive systems aligned with our goals for service growth?
10. Do we provide adequate support (value-selling tools) to help our service sales organization reach its goals?

# CHAPTER 11

## ORGANIZING FOR SERVICES: ARE SERVICES INTEGRATED?

> *Companies claim to offer customer solutions, but most*
> *aren't set up to deliver them without specific changes in*
> *organizational structure, incentives, and relationships.*[1]
> —*RANJAY GULATI*

In order to reap the benefits of service, companies need to align the design of strategy and organizational structure. In order to succeed, they need to forge connections between internal boundaries and truly integrate services in the organization. This chapter deals with silo thinking and other organizational challenges that executives will face when moving into service. While there is no one-size-fits-all in terms of organizational design, there are fundamental guiding principles that can direct decision makers when dealing with organizational silos and determining to what extent the service business should be integrated into the organization.

To enable service-led growth, companies need the right organizational structure. The structure needs to support the systems and processes needed, and it should foster synergies and strategic linkages between the organization's businesses. Consequently, executives must understand the connections between the local and central service units and between the product and service organization. We first review how companies develop their service organizations when driving service growth. We then examine how to traverse organizational silos and deal with the organizational challenges arising from the need to combine product and service operations. Executives have to continuously consider balancing separation and integration, and centralization and local autonomy, establishing structures that support collaboration and systematic rules and procedures that allow decision making and information sharing to occur smoothly across organizational boundaries.

## Service Growth Requires New Organizational Structures

Why are organizational issues critical to manage in order to achieve success? Because service is an intruder, you can kill the entire service initiative if you do not give enough attention to organizational issues. An increased service orientation requires companies to get closer to their customers and understand what they truly value. The only way to do that is to change the organizational structure and relationships. For example, most of the firms we have worked with have created a separate service unit with profit and loss (P&L) responsibility to be able to focus wholeheartedly on the service business and show that it can make money. Studies show that the creation of a separate service unit has a positive effect on the services' financial performance.[2]

In order to enable its ambitious service-growth strategy—to more than triple service sales in ten years—aerospace giant Boeing launched a corporate reorganization in 2016 in which it elevated its service business. Boeing Global Services, which will be the company's third major business unit along with its commercial airplanes and defense, and space and security units, will be formed from the company's existing service units. The global services unit will bring together Boeing's core service capabilities to provide a broad portfolio of advanced services for its civil and defense customers.[3]

On the other hand, a separate service organization tends to strengthen the silo thinking that is apparent in many companies. Advanced services, and hybrid offerings in particular, require managers to harness resources across the internal boundaries of the firm, such as an integrated approach to product and service development, which we touch upon in chapter 8. In order to successfully organize for hybrid offerings, companies may have to create structures and processes that transcend—or even obliterate—its organizational silos. Depending on service strategy and service offerings, different organizational structures are appropriate. Next, we review how leading product companies have developed their service organizations when navigating the service transition.

## Organizational structures and change patterns differ

In order to distinguish different organizational structures, we can discern two distinct dimensions. The first dimension makes a distinction between product-focused and service-focused organizational structure. In a *product-focused* structure, strategic business units (SBUs) and other organizational entities are organized based on categories of products. For example, a paper and packaging product manufacturer can be organized along three product-focused SBUs: industrial packaging, paperboard, and printing papers. In such a case, the service business is subordinate to the product business in each SBU. In a *service-focused* structure, on the other hand, all functions related to service development, sales, and deployment are managed through one or more service-specific units. In practice, such companies have both specific product and service units.

The second dimension makes a distinction between geographically focused and customer-focused organizational structure. In a traditional *geographically focused* structure, the organization is designed along geographical positions. A typical example is multinationals organized in regions such as Americas, Asia Pacific, and EMEA (North and South America; Asia and Oceania; Europe, Middle East, and Africa) with each region being divided into local sales companies. Proximity to local customers, national regulations, cultural differences, and difficulties of managing a dispersed business are factors in favor of such a structure. In a *customer-focused* structure, the company complements its traditional design by organizing around specific customer-facing units. An example is the establishment of key account management (KAM) programs, which can be a powerful way to cut across silos in order to better serve the account.

Traditionally, many large companies have had a product-focused and geographically focused structure, such as central units based on product segments and national or regional sales companies. When moving into services, such structures tend to be inadequate. To reap the benefits of service, many companies therefore initiate profound structural change. For a product-centric firm with little experience of managing a service business, the first step for organic growth is typically to establish service units within the existing product-focused structure. In order to successfully grow the service, however, most companies need to establish separate service-focused business units. For companies aiming to grow through hybrid offerings and closer customer relationships, such a structure may nonetheless prove insufficient. Consequently, creating a customer-focused structure is a logical next step to take.

We will now review organizational change patterns along the two dimensions—product/service-focused and geographically/customer-focused structure—that companies pursue during their service journeys. The discussion is based on in-depth studies of thirty-two manufacturers in a broad range of industries such as electronic devices, equipment, machinery, and measuring instruments.[4] The organizational structures and changes are illustrated in figure 11:1. The numbers indicate how many firms of the total sample of thirty-two have restructured their organizations.

**Figure 11:1**
**Changes in Organizational Structure**

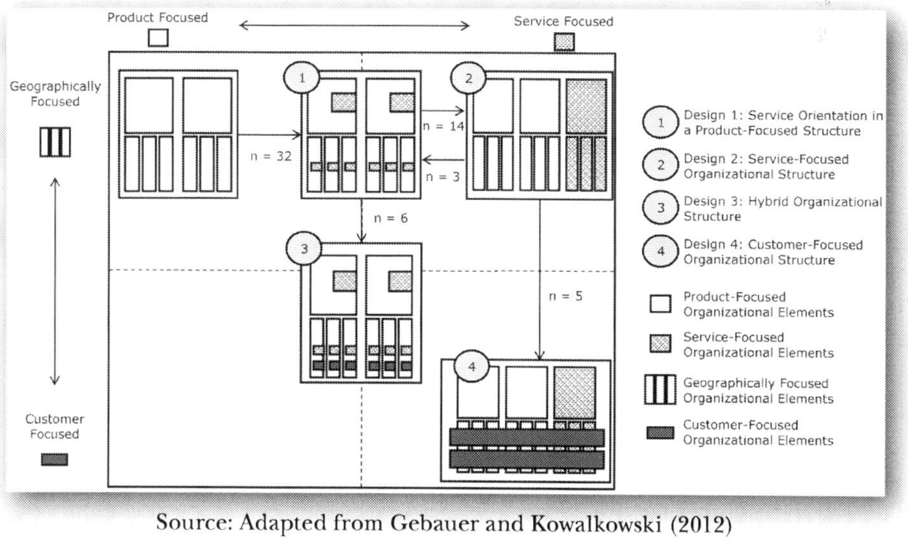

Source: Adapted from Gebauer and Kowalkowski (2012)

### Design 1: Service orientation in product-focused structure

For any company pursuing service-led growth, an internally oriented, product-focused structure is inadequate. A first step on the service journey is generally to establish separate service entities within the existing product units (design 1 in figure 11:1). Dedicated service managers have a responsibility to launch new services and, formally, have the same decision-making authority as product managers. Swiss company Bühler is a leading supplier of technologies and methods for processing grain into flour and feed for the production of pasta and chocolate, and in die casting, wet grinding, and surface coating. It is organized into five product-focused business areas within grains and food and three within advanced materials. The service business is linked to each product segment. In such a product-centric environment, however, it is generally difficult to get sufficient internal leverage and the resources and focus needed for grow. Consequently, many firms establish a separate service unit in order to grow their service business further (design 3). Alternatively, in order to become more customer-centric, companies that successfully implemented a service orientation in product-focused structure create some form of hybrid structure (design 2).

### Design 2: Hybrid structure

For companies wanting to become more customer-centric without too far-reaching an organizational change, a hybrid structure is a feasible option. Six of the thirty-two companies in the study arranged for a medium-level customer orientation by establishing dedicated front-office teams for key customers or specific customer segments. A typical example is Swiss-based Mikron Group, a manufacturer of productive systems solutions. The service organization is a separate back-office function that is integrated into its product-focused units, automation and machining. In order to place greater emphasis on customers, the automation unit reorganized itself according to a hybrid structure: it defined specific customer segments (automotive components, electrical/electronics, and medical/personal care). Rather than selling products to every customer on the local market, the salespeople became increasingly specialized in each segment.

Another arrangement that many firms in the study opted for was to focus on establishing a separate service organization rather than customer-specific units. Departing from design 1, fourteen of the thirty-two firms initiated such change, which we discuss next.

### Design 3: Service-focused structure

Moving to a service-focused structure implies creating one or more dedicated service business units. The service-focused SBU has full responsibility for service operations and strategic service business development, which means that the unit can focus exclusively on service-led growth. Many firms with a dedicated back-office service unit in the central organization also have separate service organizations with specific service sales teams on a local level, although the service focus can differ greatly between regions and local markets. For instance, a company can have local service organizations that sell, deliver, and actively develop new services on mature markets with large installed bases, whereas the structures remain product focused on emerging markets with many greenfield projects.

Wärtsilä of Finland—a global leader in lifecycle power solutions for the marine and energy markets—is an example of a company that has adopted a service-focused organizational design. In order to sustain its competitive advantage and become more service-centric, the company created a separate service division with global reach. Today, the services division is larger than its traditional, sector-specific power plants and ship power divisions. In other cases, companies have a separate service division while at the same time providing services also through the product-focused units. A case in point is the German engineering company Voith. When the company established its industrial services division, its management was able to commit itself fully to service-led growth. By means of acquisitions, it further strengthened its service business. In parallel, however, the firm has sold service companies that no longer fit the service division's industry-focused concept, and it also provides services to other segments through its three product units.

While a service-focused structure enables many firms to capitalize on its service business, there are also cases where firms decide to reintegrate their service business into its product units. Saurer was a Swiss manufacturer of textile machines and one of the three firms in our study that reestablished a product-focused structure. Due to its growing reliance on China and other Asian markets where domestic competitors had significantly lower prices, the company was increasingly facing customers who demanded services that were free or integrated into the premium price of their machines. As a result of these customer expectations, the company reintegrated services into the product units (design 1). Dürr, a painting and assembling system manufacturer, even had to sell its service business because of a lack of synergy between the product and service businesses. After the sale, the remaining services related to the painting assembling systems were reintegrated into the product-focused units. The majority of firms, however, either kept a service-focused structure or moved further to a customer-focused structure.

### Design 4: Customer-focused structure

While a service-focused structure (design 3) has many benefits, it may also have downsides for companies seeking to grow through service. An evident risk is that the knowledge and expertise is housed within organizational silos. Companies will then have trouble harnessing their competences across the internal boundaries and realizing synergies between the product and service businesses. In terms of customer relationship management, another common problem is the lack of coordination between the product and service units serving the same customer. Such behavior may cause confusion among customers and create uncertainty and tensions internally. In addition, a newly formed, independent service unit runs the risk of having limited authority and influence on the other parts of the organization. In order to become more service-centric and work closer with customers, many firms therefore create a customer-focused structure. Companies setting up this structure must be able to track the profitability of its product and services as well as service-centric performance metrics such as profitability and share of customers' wallets.

The matrix organization of a German supplier of processing and packaging technology is a case in point. On one hand, it is organized into three business units responsible for machines, systems, and services. On the other hand, it is structured into two customer segment-specific units: chocolate and confectionary, and pharmaceutical. The two segments differ significantly in terms of customer needs and require very different sales competencies. In the chocolate industry, the packaging process changes frequently because of the high number of new confectionary products being introduced. The packaging process for pharmaceuticals is more stable because of long product lifecycles. The company's customer-facing units share product and service functions, including pricing, marketing, R&D, human resources, and controlling. However, they have authority over what product-service combinations to offer and flexibility in the appropriate price for their customers within the price range recommendations stipulated by the product and service units.

A common practice of customer-focused firms is the management of KAM programs. The striving to holistically serve a large and global customer base and to create and capture more value from the relationships is manifested in the fact that global KAM is becoming the norm in many industries. It has also served well as a response to centralized procurement and other changes in customer practices.

A KAM organization within a customer-focused structure can also be the means to take the edge off situations with uncoordinated service prices. Due to customers' tendency to achieve synergies across borders in their procurement operations, it is risky to have geographically uncoordinated prices. For instance, an equipment manufacturer we worked with was facing a situation where many multinational customers placed order requests to multiple sales companies. These units then sent uncoordinated proposals back to the customers, which led to competition between sales companies and—inevitably—to price reductions. Such challenges have traditionally been a concern for mainly the product business. However, the growing demand for value-add activities such as remote services and global specialist services, which are less local than traditional field service used to be, means that such practices may also cause a threat to service-led growth.

In some companies, KAM has been practiced for many years, whereas the ideas in other cases are newer. For instance, in the process of better serving its global customers in the oil and gas business, French company

Vallourec, the global leader in premium tubular solutions, launched its KAM program in 2013. Toyota Material Handling Group, the world's leading supplier of counterbalanced trucks and warehouse trucks, is a successful example of a company that has had a KAM organization in a customer-focused structure for a long time. Over the past fifteen years, the number of KAM units has increased both nationally and regionally as well as globally. In order to become a preferred supplier, it has become essential to have a broad spectrum of services and financing alternatives available and to have similar service levels and terms and conditions regardless of local market. This is particularly important when doing business with international customers such as IKEA, the world's largest furniture retailer.

## From framework to implementation

The four organizational designs and change patterns offer guidance for executives seeking to restructure their companies toward customer and service focus. It is relatively easy to develop an action list with which to implement one of the four designs. The sequence of change suggests that companies should start to increase their service orientation within existing product-focused structure. In general, large differences in local market characteristics can favor a geographically focused structure, whereas a customer-focused structure is advantageous when (1) customer segments rather than types of products should form the basis for how to organize, (2) similar service levels and terms and conditions apply regardless of local market, and (3) customers increasingly sign international service agreements and pursue centralized procurement.

As the company extends its service business, the organization needs to facilitate the change (designs 1 and 3). More extensive service agreements and hybrid offerings require even closer customer collaboration and possibly integration, which requires a more customer-focused structure (designs 2 and 4). If the company adopts a customer-focused structure, however, it needs to be able to track service-centric and customer-specific performance metrics. Executives contemplating a change in the organizational design should therefore focus on finding alignments between the two dimensions in figure 11:1. In exhibit 10, we illustrate how Ericsson, one of the companies in our study, has restructured.

## Exhibit 10
### *Ericsson's Path to Customer Solutions*

Since the mid-1990s, telecoms equipment maker Ericsson has successfully developed a broad range of service capabilities and new organizational structures to facilitate its strategic transformation from hardware manufacturing to systems integration and service operations. Today, Telecom Services is one of the company's two core businesses, with the ambition to "simplify the management of every element in the operator network."

In order to integrate the different product units' disparate service business, the stand-alone division Ericsson Services was established in 1999 (design 3: service-focused structure). The following year, all service businesses were further consolidated into Global Services, which became one of Ericsson's five business units. As a back-office unit, it was responsible for the development of a global service portfolio and the supply of staff and resources to help the front-office units to develop and sell customer solutions. In 2002, the company merged its two product units to create the Systems business unit, a back-office unit responsible for the development of standardized product platforms for different generations and standards. Just as the Global Services unit did, the Systems unit worked with the front-office units to customize products tailored for Ericsson's key customers (design 4: customer-focused structure).

Since the early 2000s, Ericsson has had a clear goal to provide its customers complete telecom solutions and has dramatically increased its sales of services and solutions. It has also outsourced much of its manufacturing to contract manufacturers. As part of its service-led transformation, in 2003, Ericsson folded its 120 local companies in 140 countries into twenty-eight market units. The change continued in 2010, when it went from its twenty-eight market units to ten regions. It also created a global network of customer-facing units (CFUs), with a single channel to each customer, such as Deutsche Telekom, Telefónica, and Vodafone. In this structure, the back-office products and services are provided by the CFUs, and a central-level strategic center is responsible for coordination between the units. Throughout the transformation, Ericsson has also made strategic acquisitions to develop its service leadership. For instance, in 2012, it bought Telcordia, the US software and services company, for $1.2 billion, which Hans Vestberg, then Ericsson's CEO, described as a "perfect fit."

To accelerate its transformation and meet changing customer requirements in an increasingly competitive market, Ericsson implemented a new structure in 2016 with 5G, Internet of Things, and cloud in focus. The new customer-focused structure has five business units aligned around type of customers and type of business: network products and network services with a focus on incremental improvements and IT and cloud products, IT and cloud services, and media as targeted growth areas. According to Vestberg, the structure should better leverage the combined strengths in products and services, support end-to-end accountability, and align financial reporting with strategy execution in a simpler and more transparent way. Today, the services business, with sixty-six thousand employees, manages one billion subscribers and accounts for 44 percent of annual net sales of SEK 247 billion. Together, the services and software businesses account for almost 70 percent of sales.

*Sources:* Bessant and Davies (2007); Ericsson; *Financial Times;* personal communication

While it is rather straightforward to change formal structures, such as creating new units or merging existing ones, the modifications in corporate culture and human resources are longer-term tasks. For instance, all four patterns discussed change the authority and responsibilities of existing organizations. Consequently, the organizational changes should go hand in hand with other corresponding changes in the company's business model, including changes in incentive systems and financial metrics. As we have previously discussed, such wide-scale changes generally cause internal resistance and require strong leadership skills and the involvement of all units concerned to increase the acceptance in organization. The process should be systematic and transparent, incorporating frequent feedback loops between the phases of formulation and implementation of changes in the organizational design.

## Striking a Balance between Organizational Designs

As we have discussed, depending on organizational design, the degree of separation between service and product units differ. While the creation of a separate service unit with P&L responsibility has a positive effect on the performance of the service business, there is a risk of driving separation too far, thereby adding to a silo mentality. Similarly, the establishment of customer-facing units such as key account units and pilot organizations for vanguard service projects can be a prerequisite for customized service solutions. However, too much autonomy and flexibility can lead to a proliferation of inefficiencies and less homogeneous service operations. Any firm pursuing service-led growth has to break down the silo thinking while striking a balance between these two tensions.

## Break Down the Silo Mentality

Any leader wanting to integrate services in the organization will have to confront resistance and cope with interdepartmental turf wars resulting from silo thinking. Silo thinking is a mind-set when certain departments are reluctant to share information and resources with others in the same organization. This type of mentality becomes particularly problematic when companies want to inculcate a customer-centric service culture in the firm. Instead of focusing on collaborating to solve the customer's jobs to be done, each (product and service) unit jealously protects its own interests and power.

In order to break down obsolete silos and align the organization with the overall service strategy, the leadership has to identify the root cause of these issues and how to navigate the internal political landscape. In some cases, new structures that obliterate existing silos have to be created, but in other ones it can be enough to restructure without discarding the silos. Regardless of the magnitude of the reorganization needed, however, management has to see the big picture; it needs to understand the connections between the different parts of the organization, the motivators and incentives upon which people act, and what changes are needed to achieve service growth.

Many of the challenges boil down to leadership conflicts and weaknesses, such as those discussed in chapter 6. No real sense of urgency, a weak guiding coalition that lacks legitimacy in units affected by the change, and lack of commitment to the vision service strategy and necessary measures to be taken are all factors that stand in the way. To break down the silo mentality, leaders must gain support in the management teams affected, who in turn have to incentivize their staff. They need to convincingly show how the new organization will benefit the company and secure commitment and accountability among the key decision makers. This includes working in parallel with hard measures—incentives, metrics, and allocation of power—and softer cooperation-promoting ones such as to foster a culture of service-centric cooperation.[5]

One of the companies we worked with serves as a cautionary tale of how silo thinking can destroy a big strategic initiative of the CEO. The company was a fully integrated organization—from sourcing materials, refining, inbound logistics, component manufacturing, systems integration, operations, and dismantling. On paper, it made perfect sense to create a holistic solutions business—a one-stop shop for customers. The solutions initiative was a way to bring people together, and the company assigned a vice president of the solutions business who had to draw on the SBUs. However, he very soon came up against the brick wall of silo thinking. Conceptually, every SBU understood the concept and how to collaborate. However, once profit sharing was brought to the table, it came to an end; the directors could not agree upon shared objectives and how to split profits, change power structures, and revise incentives. In short, silo thinking destroyed the solutions initiative.

## Separation or Integration?

In terms of balancing separation and integration, the organization needs a structure that facilitates flows of knowledge and experience between back and front offices and between product and service units. While formally separating the service businesses, there is a need to establish structures that accommodate this form of organizational learning. Especially when becoming more customer-centric (designs 3 and 4), it becomes vital to establish a central organization responsible for coordination between units, balancing back-office push for standardization and front-office pull of customization. For instance, to come closer to its customers, Cisco established a central marketing organization residing between the back and front offices (similar to Ericsson's strategic center in exhibit 10). The marketing organization took responsibility for coordinating the integration of offerings and technologies and also established a cross-silo solutions engineering team to facilitate the development of hybrid offerings.[6]

When setting up a central-level strategic center that transcends existing boundaries, the company needs employees who possess two specific generalist skills. First, these employees need multidomain skills, which is experience about more than one type of service (or product) as well as in-depth knowledge of customer needs. Second, they need to possess boundary-spanning skills, which means being able to overcome existing silos within the firm.[7]

## Central or Local Decision Making?

How do successful companies manage to take stock and overcome silo thinking? We have seen that organizations that achieve both local responsiveness and global efficiency typically have a high degree of mutual interdependence between the back and front offices.[8] In many cases, a strategic service unit with global decision-making authority to burst through silos when needed plays an important role in this process. As a senior vice president in charge of a wide-scale digital service transformation at an SBU pointed out, the global service director's mandate to hire and fire globally was pivotal for its success. Central structures are also needed to support business development, such as global IT systems and platforms and risk evaluation tools, to encourage and assist local service champions and to help local units with competence and skills, such as profitability assessments of local service contracts.

When Toyota Material Handling Group implemented its mobile business system for its service technicians, organizational interdependence was a key factor for the success. The local sales companies lacked the capabilities and resources needed for in-house funding, implementation, and maintenance of such a system. By managing the project at business unit level (in Europe), Toyota was able to allocate the internal resources needed and initiate collaboration with leading software and hardware providers. In order to create local acceptance and thus secure commitment for implementation, a number of voluntary sales companies were actively involved in the development process, providing feedback and dedicating time and resources. The project became a major success, with cost savings and quality improvements above expectations. Since the rollout, new sales companies have voluntarily implemented the system and new, enhanced versions are being launched on a regular basis.

What is then the right balance between centralization and local autonomy? In essence, companies need to match their capabilities with the strategic requirements put on the service business. If the primary aim is to leverage global skills and scale to increase efficiencies (such as developing and refining standardized service processes, modules, and portfolios and software applications that are linked to the company's technical and product platforms), more centralized strategic and operational decision making is required. On the other hand, if there is large variety between markets, a strong local presence and sensitivity for local and customer-specific differences become more important. The latter is particularly important for service-led growth; too much centralized decision making will make the company less agile and therefore less capable of seizing emergent service opportunities.

When we looked at organizational issues in one of our large-scale survey studies, we found that in order for companies to thrive as they move from product-oriented to customer process-oriented services, they should decentralize the decision-making authority to lower levels in the hierarchy.[9] When providing such complex offerings in particular, people who are closest to customers should have the mandate to act on their behalf.

When discussing how to best organize for service, the managing director of a sales company told us about a vanguard app-based service he initiated, revealing the cumbersome processes he would have to go through in order to get approval from the corporate IT division. Because of all the bureaucracy, he was told by his superior in the central organization to proceed by flying below the radar in order not to lose the first-mover advantage. Evidently, the rigid centralized processes did not accommodate for rapid, technology-driven service innovation in the local organization.

What if the central organization is still stuck in the service desert? In such a case, it becomes even more important not to curb local autonomy as leading local units, rather than the central organization, are the ones that will have to drive the company's service-growth initiatives. As we have seen in some of our cases, leading local units can become service champions, promoting best practices and acting as catalysts for increased service orientation at other subsidiaries as well as at headquarters.

## Fostering collaboration between central and local units

To strengthen the integration between local management and central decision makers and foster a culture of cooperation, some of the firms we have worked with encourage their managers to change position— from central to local service organizations and vice versa—for a period of time. For instance, to better link local management to central decision making, managers from the central organization can work for local ones. An example is the active recruitment of notable local managers and specialists to new roles in centrally initiated projects and also longer-lasting positions in the central service organization. Such initiatives can cultivate the central-local bonds between the units without being perceived as coercive and can help build service capabilities across the organization.

Even when the integration between central and local units and back and front offices is well functioning, the transfer of knowledge and services across independent sales companies is often challenging. In order to absorb and compile knowledge from local markets and make it accessible for other local service organizations, globally linked processes are needed. As we discuss in chapter 8 on service innovation, many new service concepts are developed rather unplanned as a response to local, customer-specific needs. If successful, these customized services are later standardized and formalized and offered to a larger customer base. In order to allow the experience and knowledge gleaned from vanguard service projects to readily be applied at other markets, however, globally linked processes managed by a central organization are typically required. The central unit takes the role of a knowledge broker, facilitating knowledge and information exchange and providing formal and informal linkages between the local service units. For example, the regional organization may form and fund a service market forum, where representatives from the local service organizations meet on a regular basis.

In one case, the regional service organization of a European truck manufacturer appointed a local service director, with a good name and over thirty years' experience in the business, as a mentor for newer, less advanced sales companies. In this way, local units received much-needed support, and the overall awareness about the local organizations and market conditions increased. In another case, the service director at a central business development unit of a US pump manufacturer identified a successful process service in Australia. Spurred by the success, he saw the potential to support the company's service-growth initiative in Europe by launching the concept and thereby strengthening the overall service portfolio. By allocating central resources and securing commitment from leading sales companies, the service could be formalized, adopted to local market conditions, and launched.

## KEY QUESTIONS ABOUT ORGANIZATIONAL STRUCTURE

In order to truly integrate services in the organization, managers should ask themselves the following questions about organizational structure:

1. Is our organization aligned with our service strategy?
2. What are the biggest structural roadblocks that impede service growth—on a central and local level—and how do we overcome them?
3. Do we have what it takes to discard the root causes of silo thinking that obstruct service growth?
4. How well do we harness our global service expertise?
5. Have we decentralized the decision-making authority to lower levels in the hierarchy so that the people who are closest to customers have the mandate to act on their behalf?
6. Are we able to balance back-office push for standardization and front-office pull of customization?

7. Do we attract and provide attractive career paths for customer-focused employees with the abilities to overcome existing silos within the firm?

8. To what extent are we enabling local units to act as service champions, and to what extent does the central decision making block local service initiatives?

9. How well do we foster cooperation and coordination between central and local service units?

10. How well do we foster cooperation and coordination between product and service units?

Apart from integrating services in the organization, the company may provide services through a network of external service providers. The reasons for such design can range from a deliberate strategic choice to use partners to fill gaps in capabilities to a competitive service market where powerful system integrators act as middlemen between the company and its product users and jealously protect any attempt to break into their service domains. How to best manage the service channel will be scrutinized in the final chapter.

# CHAPTER 12

## CHANNEL-PARTNER MANAGEMENT: ARE YOU ALIGNED?

*Establish channels for different target markets and
aim for efficiency, control, and adaptability.[1]*
—PHILIP KOTLER

In order to build a structure for service-led growth, a company must integrate services into its organization. However, equally importantly, it also needs to achieve alignment with its channel partners. The final chapter of this book should therefore enable executives to better define a suitable dealer strategy. Many executives neglect how deep the service-strategy decisions go in terms of redefining the dealer relationships; the more advanced the service, the more a company has to touch upon these issues. In addition, if a company makes the wrong decisions, the things we discuss in the earlier chapters will hit a wall. In this chapter, we will first evaluate factors that determine whether service activities should be done by the firm or delegated to partners. Several market-specific, company-specific, and offering-specific factors influence this decision. Finally, we will broaden the perspective from market channels to value constellations in networks.

### Defining a Dealer Strategy

Traditionally, many companies deeply rely on their channel partners to ensure a well-structured flow of products optimized from the production site to the end customer. To really take on the service job, an extensive network of dealers is needed to cover the territory and ensure customer access to service. However, if the external partner is not aligned, the company can destroy its entire service strategy. Many of the service ideas we have discussed require local presence. Therefore, the way a company organizes this presence becomes critical. Typically, this has been done though channel partners, especially in traditional product firms. When a company relies on its channel partners for service growth, executives must ask if their company is aligned.

Distributors are often powerful intermediaries, and while they in some cases may actively oppose any service-growth initiative, they can in other cases be the ones driving such initiatives. For example, Empire Southwest is among the three largest dealers of Illinois-based company Caterpillar, a global leader in earth-moving products. Empire Southwest has annual sales of approximately $900 million per year and has more than sixteen hundred employees throughout Arizona, southeastern California, and northern Mexico. Not only does Empire Southwest sell Caterpillar's equipment, but it also has its own service organization offering maintenance, repair, and rebuilding services, including extensive service agreements.[2] It is an example of how a dealer became a proactive channel partner and a best-practice example at the forefront of selling performance-based solutions.

To realize its value proposition, Caterpillar needs to foster ties with users of its equipment and also forge partnerships with Empire Southwest and other dealers who sell and service that equipment. Many dealers enjoy notable face time with their customers and are heavily involved in their decision-making processes. The manufacturer operates through a global network of independent dealers in over 180 countries and refers to those dealers as "a critical competitive differentiator" and "the foundation" of its worldwide success.[3] Compared to companies such as John Deere, which has over two thousand dealers in the United States alone, Caterpillar operates through few—approximately fifty—but powerful dealers.

Another example is New York-based lift truck supplier Raymond, which provides material-handling services and logistics solutions through the members of its Raymond Sales and Service Center network, such as Abel Womack in the northeastern United States and Andersen in Michigan, Ohio, and Florida. However, Toyota Material Handling Group—the owner of Raymond Corporation—pursues a very different strategy in Europe, with tight control through ownership. In most European markets, services are provided through an extensive in-house service network. While independent dealers can supplement these networks, such as in more remote areas, service executives regard the internal arrangement as a major competitive advantage when competing with rivals who rely solely on independent service partners for building both customers relationships and the internal service factory. Similarly, Linde Material Handling, which we discuss in chapter 2, has pursued very different strategic channel choices in different markets.[4]

Given that even the same company may have radically different channel-partner arrangements depending on strategy leads us to the following questions: What determines which channel strategy to take and when to rely on dealers or other channel partners for service provision? Under what circumstances should companies rely on these external parties?

## Should You Do It Yourself or Delegate?

Several different factors influence the type of channel arrangement companies opt for. The most fundamental question is whether the company should perform front-office service activities through the internal organization, such as local sales and service companies, or rely on its local channel partners. The strategic decision about which type of dealer strategy to have has implications for issues such as how to control the service channel, manage the service portfolio, and interact with customers and already built customer equity. Many things boil down to the issue of which roles and positions existing channel partners currently have.

The ideal network (from the supplier's point of view) is typically not identical to that in real life, which is the result of the company's legacy and previous strategic decisions as well as actions of other network members. In other cases, legislation sets the boundaries for what may be possible, such as stipulating that manufacturers cannot own their dealers. Therefore, service directors (and even the company as such) may have limited possibilities to influence the existing channel model in the short term. In the longer term, however, or when launching new service initiatives, managers should have a clear view of how to align with the company's partners.

To manage individual dealers and service partners as well as the overall value network along the company's service transformation, managers should review the current situation and reflect on how well it serves its objectives: What would the ideal service-channel model look like if we could design it from scratch? How does it differ from our existing service network? Given our existing service network and our ideal one, what would the most desirable yet attainable arrangement look like? What strategies and actions need to be taken to achieve this channel arrangement?

Established companies often have an extensive partner network in place that, if properly harnessed, can be used to propel service-led growth. As in the case of Caterpillar, the collaboration with dealers may go back in time several decades and be more or less institutionalized, with cultural fit laying the groundwork for cooperation. While such structure can be a key source of competitive advantage, it can be the direct opposite if the cooperation is not working well. For instance, a dealer may act in an opportunistic and disloyal manner and be unwilling to embrace the service transformation initiated by the supplier. A typical example is dealers using counterfeit parts to cut cost and boost the own profitability at the expense of the manufacturer, an action that may affect both the manufacturer's parts sales and brand equity negatively. This is most common if the dealers sells multiple brands and has limited loyalty to the supplier.

While "incumbent inertia"[5] is a challenge for any established company needing to instill change, it can be even greater when the reluctance—or even hostility—to change is widespread among channel partners. Any attempt to bypass dealers ("cutting out the middlemen") or make other moves that may be regarded as entering the dealer domain can lead to channel conflicts too risky to take. Instead, suppliers have to overcome resistance by convincingly showing product-centric dealers how service-led growth can make them too more competitive and profitable. This includes aligning rewards and incentives, ensuring efficient information exchange, and actively investing in service sales support and other service capability-building activities. Before we further discuss the management of a dealer-partner network, we will review cases where companies have the option to decide whether to do services in-house or delegate them.

For many companies, the network and collaboration are less established and functional than in the case of Caterpillar. Many companies operate through a combination of in-house service organizations, like company-owned dealers, and independent distributors and dealers. Furthermore, companies can have the option to acquire independent dealers in order to come closer to customers. This leaves executives with the choice of determining if an in-house or external option is most favorable. In table 12:1, we list challenges that companies have to manage when deciding upon its service-channel structure. By understanding the challenges, executives can better evaluate the options at hand. The inability to overcome some of the challenges may also explain why some companies, despite not having an "optimal" configuration of internal and external arrangements, do not change.

**Table 12:1**
**Challenges with Internal and External Service Delivery**

| Internal Channel | External Channel |
| --- | --- |
| Large fixed costs. | Many dealers are product centric. |
| Establishing an internal organization requires resources and support; organic growth takes time, and growth through acquisition requires integration. | Manufacturer and dealer have different incentives for and interests in the service business: assessment of competences and commitment needed for service initiative is required. |
| Reduced flexibility. | Ensure loyalty to brand when selling spare and wear parts. |
| A wide range of (changing) competences is needed. | Both manufacturer and dealer seek to build relations with the customers. Dealers have the day-to-day relationship. |
| Potentially fewer resources for the product business. | Offering standardized, international or multi-state service agreements if dealers are local. |
| Internal coordination between units and markets. | External coordination with multiple parties. |
| Risk for channel conflict with (previous or existing) partners. | Assessment of competences and commitment needed for service initiative. |

In practice, many companies get set for a hybrid-channel model combining internal and external delivery, thereby reaping the benefits of both. While some services may be beneficial to conduct in-house, others are more suitable to rely on channel partners for. For example, a company can rely on dealers for the sales and delivery of traditional, product-oriented services like maintenance and repair but use its own application specialists and engineers to provide more advanced services like testing, optimization, and customized design.

## Factors Influencing the Service-Channel Strategy

Based on our discussions with service executives, we have distilled key factors influencing the service-channel choices. Essentially, we can divide these factors into three distinct categories: offering specific, firm specific, and market specific (see figure 12:1). While there is no silver bullet, decision makers can attack the issue of channel choice from these three angles. While certain factors are in favor of an internal option and others of an external one, a hybrid-channel model is a third option that many firms such as Toyota Material Handling pursue.

**Offering-specific factors.** When designing the service channel and crafting channel-partner strategies, a key question is to what extent services are part of the company's core business and core offering. A study of 477 publicly traded US manufacturers found positive effects on firm value when the service business was closely related to the product business of a company.[6] From a shareholder perspective, mainly channel partners should therefore perform service operations if the degree of service relatedness is low. On the other hand, if a service business is highly profitable and difficult to imitate, service volumes are high (and highly predictable), and product lifecycles long, a direct customer approach is favorable. Similarly, an internal channel model is supported by services critical for building and maintaining customer relationships and key to ensure customer performance. For a complete opposite situation, obviously, service partners can instead take a larger role.

The dependence on service partners may also differ depending on service. In chapter 10, we discuss the concepts of front-end versus back-end and high-touch versus low-touch services. A traditional, reactive repair service is a locally conducted front-end, high-touch service.

**Figure 12:1**
**What Factors Influence the Service-Channel Strategy?**

| | Internal Channel | External Channel | Hybrid Model |
|---|---|---|---|
| **Offering-Specific Factors** | • Service is part of the core offering<br>• Large, predictable service volumes<br>• Service is a lucrative business<br>• Services are difficult to imitate<br>• Amalgamating the product and service business provides synergies<br>• Products are expensive and have long lifecycles<br>• Services are essential for understanding customer needs and building customer equity and relationships<br>• Services are critical for ensuring correct product operations | • The core business equates the product business<br>• Low or unpredictable service volumes<br>• Service business not more profitable than products<br>• Services are easy to imitate<br>• Low degree of product-service relatedness: the two businesses serve distinct customer needs<br>• Products are relatively cheap and have short service life<br>• Customers expect extensive service also on competitor brands | • The extent to which a service links to the core product business varies greatly across the portfolio<br>• Fluctuating service volume: channel partners can assist during peak seasons<br>• Some services are more profitable than other<br>• Products are complex and require an extensive set of services and skills |
| **Firm-Specific Factors** | • Service centricity and customer orientation<br>• In-depth knowledge of the role of the products in the customer's process<br>• Interdependence between internal units<br>• Possession of valuable and scarce resources for service<br>• Global efficiency, standardized processes, and uniform systems on local level<br>• Resource slack in internal service organization | • Product centricity<br>• No strategic intent to increase service orientation<br>• Competences to build partnerships with, and exert control over, service channel partners<br>• Limited financial and human resources<br>• High overhead costs and internal inefficiencies vis-à-vis service providers<br>• Weak market presence, limited geographical distribution | • Different knowledge and skills depending on service or market<br>• Potential for higher-value offerings by combining service skills with those of complementary partners<br>• Different presence on different markets and territories |
| **Market-Specific Factors** | • Low product industry growth, large service market and installed base<br>• The service market is counter cyclical<br>• Customers seek to buy value (performance, uptime, etc.), not products<br>• Customer demand for international service agreements<br>• Dealers and other partner firms lack interest in service business<br>• Customers seek closer ties with strategic suppliers | • High product industry growth, limited service market, small installed base<br>• Competitive service market<br>• Customers are product-centric and reluctant to pay extra for value-added service<br>• Partners possess key resources and market positions<br>• Cultural fit between company and partners: partners have a strong service mindset, are loyal, and more hungry for new business<br>• Expensive or complicated to acquire channel partners | • Heterogeneous markets<br>• Successful pooling of internal and external service capabilities<br>• Large variety between segments/industries<br>• Customers are geographically dispersed: partners can complement internal service operations<br>• Partners have different competences on different markets<br>• Partners have different positions depending on market |

When moving to proactive service such as preventive maintenance, back-office activities like analytics and planning come to play a more important role. Similarly, new digitization-enabled services, such as John Deere's Operations Center website for farmers, allow more back-end and low-touch service processes, which potentially reduce the reliance of dealers. In the case of equipment theft-protection services, rather than the dealer, the most important service partner would be the local security firm with whom the supplier collaborates.

Furthermore, manufacturers generally struggle to perform service on competitor brands as efficiently as on its own products (in analogy with the design-for-service capability we discuss in chapter 5), which leads many companies to rely on service partners in cases where customers expect service on products manufactured by multiple companies. Konecranes of Finland, a market leader in industrial cranes and crane service with six hundred sales and service locations worldwide, is, however, an exception. Among the over 450,000 units covered by its service agreements, the majority comes from other manufacturers. Its ability to provide expert maintenance for any brand of equipment is the company's key to success. In 2015, operating margin for its equipment business was 1.5 percent, while the service business was 10 percent.[7]

**Firm-specific factors.** Overall, service-centricity is a key factor in favor of internal service provision. Product-centric firms invest few, if any, resources in the service business and therefore typically rely on channel partners for service. Many firms find an internal channel model advantageous when seeking to build closer bonds with customers and better understand the customer's operations and business needs. It also facilitates a hybrid offering strategy because, as an executive put it, "you control the integration of product and service components." Since customer relationships are valuable assets, there is a risk in any type of external collaboration that the parties disagree upon the "ownership" of each customer interface, including the management of customer and service data. Interdependence (as discussed in the previous chapter), transparency, and efficient information exchange between units also benefit the in-house option.

On the other hand, if in-house service processes are inefficient and overhead costs high or service quality below par, collaboration with channel partners is a better option. Limited financial and human resources and the desire to be flexible also favor external arrangements. In particular, collaboration with channel partners in geographical territories with scant customer base enables a better reach while avoiding large investments and fixed costs. In addition, the agility and entrepreneurial spirit of many local dealers is difficult for an incumbent firm to emulate. However, unless supported and trained by the supplier, channel partners may lack the cutting-edge skills needed for more advanced services. In order to offer such services, the company can either establish collaboration with specialist firms or develop the skills in-house.

**Market-specific factors.** The fundamental conditions for services tend to differ greatly between different markets and regions of the world, like mature and emerging markets. Overall, services become more important when product growth is sluggish and volatile. In order to cater the persistent growth in the service business and drive shareholder value, an internal channel model may become more important in slow-growth industries. On the other hand, in high-growth product industries, companies may even destroy firm value if they invest heavily in services.[8] Under such condition, channel partners would naturally play a larger role in companies' service initiatives. If the service market is limited and the installed base small, an external design is also more favorable. However, a small service market may be the result not only of inherent market characteristics but also of too loose control and partner firms lacking competence and interest in developing their service businesses.

Two factors in favor of an in-house option is growing customer demand for hybrid offerings and consolidation of their supplier bases, which implies larger purchases from fewer suppliers. As we briefly discuss in the previous chapter, international service agreements may stimulate uniform services across local markets, something that local service players are unlikely to be able to offer. Product-service integration may also be more efficient if the number of external partners is kept at a minimum. In addition, on turbulent markets in particular, it is important to be close to customers in order to adapt to ever-changing conditions. On the other hand, extensive hybrid offerings are likely to also require competences the supplier does not have internally. Working with external parties typically enables greater flexibility and agility. For example, regional partners may know culture, regulations, suppliers, and labor in their markets. They may also take on financial risk, while the supplier provides product and service platforms, sales and service support, and training activities. In cases such as Caterpillar, cultural fit helps the company actively working to leverage the capabilities of its dealers.

The most important factors are perhaps those related to the service partners themselves: Do our partners have the mind-set it takes and commitment we need? Is there a cultural fit between our partners and us? Do they possess the resources needed? For example, Amazon discovered the potential disadvantage of relying on external delivery networks over the 2013 Christmas season in North America. The network of UPS, the United States' biggest express parcel service, became seriously congested for the holiday shopping season, which meant that many customers did not receive their Christmas deliveries in time for December 25. In a bold step to increase control of its logistics operations, Amazon signed a leasing agreement with Ohio-based Air Transportation Services Group for twenty cargo jets in 2016.[9]

To summarize, the dynamics of the three types of channel choices in figure 12:1 means that, all other things equal, an internal option would be favorable given service-centricity. However, due to market characteristics and highly skilled partners, increased reliance on dealers may become more viable. Overall, while many factors we have discussed may favor an internal channel model, such as a lucrative service market and intent to work closer with customers, one or a few factors, such as service-minded, agile partners with strong market positions, may offset these benefits for the advantage of a hybrid or external arrangement (or vice versa). Consequently, managers need to understand the potential influence of each key factor in combination.

## Integrating and Orchestrating the Channel

Once you have a channel-partner strategy in place, how do you then work with your partners to implement the strategy and achieve an integrated experience across channels? Companies like Swiss-based agribusiness Syngenta go after assisting farmers through value-added services and solutions to achieve better performance outcomes from farming. In a world where seed is commodity, differentiation opportunities lie in the application of processes. Typical offers that flow from this are its GroMore rice crop–protection protocol and Hyvido barley cashback-yield guarantee. While the strategic initiatives are easy to follow, this opens up questions of how to commercialize these types of hybrid offerings, also in terms of working with channel partners. If you, like Syngenta, work with a distribution network, do you have the right partners?

### Service partner portfolio building

Managers should evaluate their channel partners and define what kind of profiles the company actually needs. If there is a mismatch between current partners and needed profiles, the company must determine how to best proceed—strengthening existing relations or investing in new ones. In order to succeed, managers should consider the following five steps:

1. *Define the partner profiles.* What kind of partners do we actually need for our services and markets? How deeply do we need to work with our partners: do we need to exercise tight control, or is loose control sufficient? How do the new (service) requirements differ from our current demands and expectations?
2. *Screen and select profiles.* Can our existing partners fulfill the requirements (and if so, what does it take), or do we need to seek new partnerships?
3. *Build the portfolio.* How do we establish a consistent customer experience across our different channels? How do we strengthen existing relations, dissolve those that impede us, and establish new ones?
4. *Work with partners.* How do we ensure collaboration, coordination, and competence development? Do we have the knowledge, skills, processes, and structures in place to support and work more actively with our channel partners?
5. *Orchestrate the channels.* How do we exercise the control needed, including incentive alignment, definition of responsibilities, distribution of risk, and conflict resolution?

Depending on market conditions and service strategy, different companies take different approaches to managing their dealer relationships and value networks. For example, water technology company Xylem is working with service-led growth through initiatives such as its TotalCare service portfolio to ensure performance of water and wastewater equipment.[10] While working through distributors in the United States, it implemented a "three-way multichannel" strategy for its Swedish service business, which means that they have (1) an in-house field service organization, (2) authorized partners with exclusive territories, and (3) independent service partners. In towns and territories with one or few customers only, it would be chronically unprofitable to work with an in-house design. Furthermore, workshops are personnel intensive, but a service technician only generates revenue approximately one tenth of a salesman's, and additional costs include service vans, equipment, and environmental permits. Xylem Sweden has classified its authorized and independent service partners in different categories, each with different demand and levels of support. The premium category means that the authorized partner is a "genuine" representative of the company with a top-quality workshop. Consequently, it enjoys the highest discounts on parts and most support.[11]

The concepts of coordination and collaboration, which we discussed from an internal perspective in the last chapter, can be applied also to the management of channel-partner relationships.[12] While managing a partner network is not the same as managing across internal silos, the need to align incentives, define responsibilities, distribute risk, and find efficient ways of exchanging information are the same. In many cases, companies need to actively support their partners with activities like service planning, analytics, certifications, and other forms of training to make their operations more professional. Coming back to the case of Caterpillar, despite its market success, the company believes its dealers may be missing out on $9 to $18 billion annually in easy-to-capture revenue, such that they need to enhance their service operations to boost their share of the global service market. Despite the integration of diagnostic technologies into Caterpillar machines, dealers have not capitalized on these assets sufficiently to grow their service business. As the group president in charge of dealer relations acknowledged, neither has the company sufficiently "directed them to do it or helped them to do it."[13] Another case in point is Michelin, one of the three major industry players in the world. Its initial move into the solutions business failed partly because of its inability to align its channel partners (see exhibit 11).

**Exhibit 11**
*Michelin's Fleet-Management Solution and the Role of Dealers*

Michelin is a worldwide leader in the tire industry with a 2014 market share of 13.7 percent. In 2000, it launched Michelin Fleet Solutions (MFS), a comprehensive tire-management solution for the European transportation market, with payments directly linked to the number of kilometers driven per vehicle. The model enabled customers to convert their tire-related costs to a variable cost tied to the vehicle use. Michelin's profitability, in turn, would depend on its ability to ensure operational excellence and follow service quality standards. The strategic initiative proved to be a major challenge for the strongly product-centric firm, being a premium manufacturer and provider of tires.

To expand its service-business model throughout Europe, Michelin decided to capitalize on its network of third-party distributors that would turn into close-service providers (figure 12:2 illustrates the interdependence between the parties). While Michelin would step in for selling and negotiating the contracts, their dealers would be responsible for execution. Michelin, however, substantially underestimated the challenges with this channel arrangement both in terms of time and money required.

First, dealers were dissatisfied to see the company enter the service domain, fearing that they would lose local sales and independence. Rather than invoicing their customers, they were now invoicing Michelin for their services, which was a major shift. Second, while Michelin thought that most of the job was done once a contract was signed, it was the other way around. Some dealers were cutting corners, and the company was unable to fully guarantee consistency of the service to its customers, especially those with international operations. Implementation was particularly difficult as the clients' trucks moved throughout Europe, making coordination of maintenance much more challenging. After three years, due to poor execution and operations, profitability was dreadful and expansion far below expectations.

Key lessons:

- A company working with external service providers must think proactively from the initiation; otherwise, there will be plenty of hiccups and firefighting. Dealers must not feel they are being downgraded and that the company is competing with them.

- Dealers will take a larger overall responsibility, but if they do not deliver, it will backfire on the manufacturer. Major investments in quality control, auditing, and training of employees may be needed to ensure a consistent service quality, a truly optimized tire management, and that the dealers will not deteriorate the company's brand and image.
- If properly executed, however, partnering relationships with strategic advantages can be built. The manufacturer's bargaining power will increase if it starts bringing business to its dealers, making them see the value of working closely aligned with the company.

**Figure 12:2**
**Michelin's European Rollout**

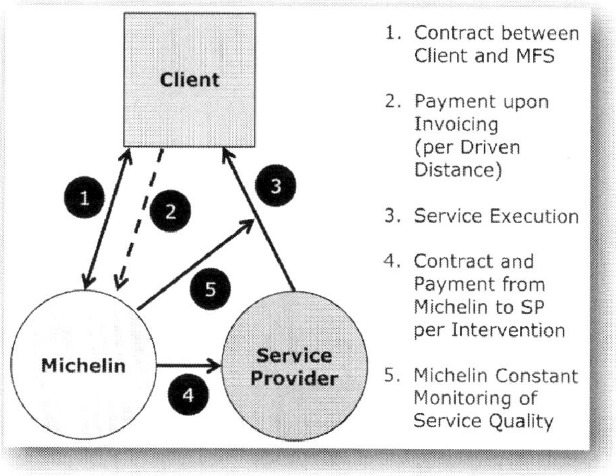
Client
Michelin
Service Provider
1
2
3
4
5
1. Contract between Client and MFS
2. Payment upon Invoicing (per Driven Distance)
3. Service Execution
4. Contract and Payment from Michelin to SP per Intervention
5. Michelin Constant Monitoring of Service Quality

*Source:* Michelin; Renault et al. (2010)

Another example comes from Husqvarna, a leading turf equipment manufacturer and competitor of Toro, which recently launched its first fleet-service package to enable safer and more productive landscaping operations. Being a new-to-the-industry service innovation—remote services was new ground to the company and its dealers and customers—the company gave meticulous attention to really understanding the needs of not only their customers but also their independent, multibrand dealers when developing the concept. Furthermore, training and quality assurance were made of the dealers being selected, and the sales companies carried an active role during the first years to ensure that customer value was achieved. While this particular service is still in its infancy, a well-established case is that of Cisco's channel-management practices, which is presented in exhibit 12.

## Exhibit 12
### Cisco's Shift from Selling Volume to Selling Value

As the first major company in the IT industry, Cisco switched from a volume-based to a value-based channel-management model in March 2001. Channel partners typically lead the design and installation of its networking solutions, integrating hardware, software, and third-party products. These partners, referred to as VARs (value-added resellers), also provide presales and postsales services to support the customized solutions.

In the 1990s, Cisco complemented its direct sales and delivery model for key account customers with VARs to expand its reach. These partners received a volume-based discount from list price on every Cisco offering sold, which added to the pressure on their margins. Even more problematic, it allowed large-volume players to drive out smaller dealers who did not enjoy volume discounts but added significant customer value through their expertise. Another major problem was the insufficient expertise of many partners due to a lack of structure for formal partner training and certification. Furthermore, partners lacked exclusive territory; there could be multiple VARs in one area competing for the same customer.

To enable the shift, Cisco developed a structured program for change. A key component was partner training and certification: the company focused on efficient training—technical knowledge, product positioning, and lifecycle services—and rigorous certification of individuals that is annually renewed. Eight years later, more than eighty thousand individuals at partner firms were Cisco Certified. Partners can benefit from both depth and breadth of certifications, and hundreds of courses are available for free online. It also enabled cobranding based on the training achieved, which significantly boosts partner credibility. Furthermore, Cisco encouraged partners to develop their own services and applications and provides rewards for such solutions. In fact, partners are able to reveal demand opportunities that are not visible to the company.

In the value-based model, equal rewards go to partners with similar capabilities regardless of how much Cisco products and services they sell. In addition to the baseline discount that is available to all partners, in order to tie incentives to value-added outcomes, Cisco provides additional transaction-specific rewards based on opportunity identification, sales of newer technologies and services (and achieving customer satisfaction targets), sales of partner-led solutions, and upgrading the installed base of Cisco products. To ensure that rewards are retained as margin by the partners rather than turning into customer discounts and affecting the retail price, Cisco waits with some of these payments until several months after the transaction. In addition, the company measures the impact of its programs on partner profitability.

Key lessons:

- The value-based model provides a workable approach when channel partners have to make up-front investments but do not have exclusive territories in which to regain them.
- Volume-based compensation does not align well with a value-based model.
- Channel arrangements and reward systems should be flexible enough to accommodate changing market conditions and technological change.

Eight years after the shift, 280,000 individuals in fifty-five thousand independent VARs, system integrators, service providers, and network consultants drove over $30 billion worth of sales, which corresponded to over 80 percent of Cisco's revenue. Channel managers do not believe that the two systems can peacefully coexist; while volume can follow the value-add focus of a value-based model, volume-based behavior tends to lower the actual retail price and destroy the opportunity for partners-led innovation.

*Source:* Kalyanam and Brar (2009)

## Broadening the Perspective: From Channel to Value Network

The idea that value is being created in a linear value chain is still widespread among managers. Because such view of business as value stacking stands in the way of service growth, in chapter 3, we even refer to it as one of the seven deadly sins of service-myopic firms. Managers have to think beyond such sequential, goods-centric mental models and instead espouse the principle that value is increasingly cocreated in networks with customers and partners that work together to mobilize value creation. Successful network orchestration enables new ways of gaining customer insights and service-innovation ideas from outside the boundaries of the own organization.

The value network does not have to become very complex for suppliers to find themselves walking a tightrope between the interests of different parties. In the case of Xylem, the company has deep systems knowledge and expertise in water and wastewater applications, being able to offer specialist-engineering services, such as loss calculations and pipework configuration modeling, that very few other firms can compete with. Xylem provides the training, system, and technical support for services such as remote service to the authorized dealers who sell and deliver them. It is also keen to help consultants with their expertise (energy efficiency), as customers often hire those firms to specify the requirements for new constructions and other major purchases. However, independent contractors and consultants also influence what the company can offer. Too extensive offerings like subsystems may cause channel conflict with major contractors and knowledge-intensive services with engineering consultancy firms. To be successful, Xylem needs well-established relationships with these key parties in order to develop mutually beneficial value propositions.

By joining forces with external partners, a company can harness the collective competences of this extended resource base and build clout to facilitate competitive, network-based value propositions and powerful ecosystems. Consider the case of a leading North European machine-to-machine (M2M) service provider who we worked with. It generally operates through independent dealers who supply the services and interact with customers. However, in order to succeed and keep pace with the rapid technical development (such as securing over-the-air operator management of M2M services), it needs to collaborate with network partners covering everything from IT consultancy to software development and security. With eight different types of partners, the network rapidly becomes complex. The number of possible network ties between companies points at some of the challenges of translating technology and skills into advanced services. Rather than technology itself, what sets the limits for many service concepts is a lack of network orchestration— that is, the ability to influence and develop the network through collaboration, coordination, and alignment across firm boundaries.

By taking a network perspective on service growth, managers can better identify opportunities and threats of the new competitive landscape. It can mean that companies that seem poles apart and operate in different industries may indeed become competitors. For instance, by providing fleet vehicle tracking services, ExxonMobil's has become a competitor to Google in telematics. Autonomous driving is rapidly becoming a disruptive force in the auto industry. Vehicles are becoming increasingly sensor-packed, and moves such as the $300 million industrial partnership between Uber and Volvo Cars to develop a self-driving car[14] and General Motors' $1 billion purchase of driverless car start-up Cruise in 2016[15] show that companies increasingly see themselves in the business of providing "mobility" (that is, a service) rather than only making cars. In the case of commercial vehicles, manufacturers like Daimler and Volvo, who have their own proprietary telematics systems, are facing competition from specialized IT firms that strive to integrate multibrand fleet data into their systems. These examples show that traditionally well-defined boundaries in rather stable industries may swiftly change or become obsolete. Therefore, firms need to continuously scan the environment for new service opportunities to reconfigure and thereby strengthen their value network in tandem with alignment with existing channel partners.

## KEY QUESTIONS ABOUT CHANNEL-PARTNER ALIGNMENT

In order to align with dealers and other network partners, managers should ask themselves the following questions:

1. Are we looking to secure more service margins for us? If so, what are the channel implications?
2. Would selling more advanced services and hybrid offerings require more control than we currently have? If so, how do we achieve that control?
3. What are the key factors—internal and external—that influence our channel design?
4. What is the right mix of internal and external channel design?
5. Are our channel arrangements and reward systems aligned with our service strategy? What are the biggest roadblocks?
6. Do our service-channel partners have what it takes to support our service strategy?
7. Do we know how to share risks and responsibilities with our channel partners?
8. Do we provide sufficient support and capability development to help our dealers grow the service business?
9. Do we systematically evaluate our channel partners?
10. To what extents do other network players influence our service operations?

# CONCLUSION

In these turbulent times, adopting a truly service-centric mind-set has become paramount for sustaining competitive advantage. In many industries, service growth has simply become a matter of survival. Yet, drumming up a few new service ideas and crafting commercial brochures won't do the trick! Instead, companies must begin to strategically compete through service. As we have seen, beyond a minimum threshold, venturing into the service space will inevitably affect the very foundations of your company's strategy and will often require taking a fresh perspective on existing and new service business models.

Our book *Service Strategy in Action (S2iA)* offers practical guidelines for designing and implementing your service-growth strategy. While the path might be fraught with challenges and roadblocks, our twelve-step road map provides clear directions for how your company can profit from services in business markets. In each chapter, we introduce hands-on frameworks and tools that you can apply to your firm. End-of-chapter questions allow you to assess your strengths and weaknesses at each stage of this journey. Working through each of our twelve chapters will help you craft and implement your own service-growth strategy.

Beyond a thorough understanding of *what* needs to be done, one of the unique aspects of our book is that we also provide guidance on *how* to lead others. Like with any major strategic initiative, leadership and change management skills lie at the heart of a successful service-growth strategy.

We always value your input and are delighted to provide a platform for sharing ideas and thoughts on service growth. Please join us at www. ServiceStrategyInAction.com to continue this discussion.

—Christian Kowalkowski and Wolfgang Ulaga

# ABOUT THE AUTHORS

Christian Kowalkowski is Associate Professor of Industrial Marketing affiliated with the Institute of Technology at Linköping University in Sweden and Hanken School of Economics in Finland. He has developed Sweden's first university course on industrial service development and has rapidly established himself as a leading authority in the field of B2B service strategy research. For over a decade, through research, consulting, and educational activities about service strategy and implementation, he has worked with market-leading multinationals in various product industries.

Wolfgang Ulaga is the AT&T Professor of Services Leadership and Co-Executive Director at the Center for Services Leadership, W. P. Carey School of Business, Arizona State University, USA. Over the past twenty years, he has worked with B2B firms in diverse industries around the globe on designing and implementing service-growth strategies. Dr. Ulaga is a frequent keynote speaker in Europe, Asia, and North America. He regularly leads executive education programs and workshops on new service-business models, service innovation, service portfolio design, service pricing, and transforming industrial sales forces from product-centric to service- and solution-savvy sales organizations. Dr. Ulaga is a globally recognized thought leader of B2B service strategy. His work has been published in the most prestigious global journals, including *Harvard Business Review* and the *Journal of Marketing*. He has received numerous awards and recognitions for excellence in teaching and research, including an honorary doctorate from Turku School of Economics in Finland for his "pioneering, high-quality research on customer value and servitization strategies in the field of business-to-business marketing as well as his exceptional ability to combine the requirements of science to practical relevance both in academic research, executive education and teaching of marketing."

# NOTES

## Chapter 1: The Service Imperative

1.  2014 World Bank figures, accessed September 20, 2016, http://data. worldbank.org/indicator/NV.SRV.TETC.ZS/countries?page=6.

2.  Jeremy Clegg and Hinrich Voss, *Chinese Overseas Direct Investment in the European Union* (London: ECRAN (Europe China Research and Advice Network), 2012).

3.  Reuters, "China's HNA Group to Buy Ingram Micro for $6 Billion," February 18, 2016, accessed September 22, 2016, www.reuters.com/ article/us-ingram-micro-m-a-tianjin-tianhai-idUSKCN0VQ2U0.

4.  See the website of the franchise www.tidedrycleaners.com.

5.  Figures retrieved from www.petsmart.com, accessed April 15, 2016.

6.  Antoine Gara, "PetSmart's $8.7 Billion LBO Is Already Paying Off for Consortium Led by BC Partners," *Forbes*, February 18, 2016, accessed September 22, 2016, www.forbes.com/sites/antoineg-ara/2016/02/18/petsmarts-8-7-billion-lbo-already-is-paying-off-for-consortium-led-by-bc-partners/.

7.  PetSmart 2010 and 2013 Annual Reports and Business Wire press release: "PetSmart Announces Fourth Quarter and Fiscal Year 2014 Results," accessed September 22, 2016, www.businesswire.com/news/home/20150304005081/en/ PetSmart-Announces-Fourth-Quarter-Fiscal-Year-2014.

8.  Theodore Levitt, "Production-line Approach to Service," *Harvard Business Review* 50, no. 5 (1972): 41–52.

9.  Jon Ostrower, "Boeing Reorganizes into Three Parts: Airliners, Fighters and Spare Parts," *CNN Money*, November 21, 2016, accessed

December 9, 2016, money.cnn.com/2016/11/21/news/companies/boeing-reorganization/.

10. Metso 2012 Annual Report. As of 2014, Metso Group demerged its pulp and paper business to a new, independently listed company, Valmet Corporation (www.valmet.com).

11. United Technologies 2014 Annual Report and Otis company website (www.otis.com).

12. 2014 World Bank figures, accessed May 18, 2016, http://data.world-bank.org/indicator/FB.ATM.TOTL.P5.

13. Carsten B. Henkel, Oliver B. Bendig, Tobias Caspari, and Nihad Hasagic, *Industrial Services Strategies: The Quest for Faster Growth and Higher Margins* (New York: Monitor Group, 2004), 15. See also see the study completed in 1998 by VDMA, the German Association of Mechanical Construction, published under the title *Dienen und Verdienen* (Frankfurt/Main, Germany: VDMA Verlag).

14. *The Economist*, "Top Floor, Please," March 16, 2013 issue, p. 67, accessed September 23, 2016, http://www.economist.com/news/business/21573568-things-are-looking-up-liftmakers-top-floor-please.

15. Daniel Thomas, "Huawei Sets out Third Stage of European Strategy," *Financial Times*, February 22, 2016, accessed September 22, 2016, www.ft.com/intl/cms/s/0/2b580046-d637-11e5-8887-98e7feb46f27.html.

16. Christian Grönroos, *Service Management and Marketing: Managing the Service Profit Logic*, 4th ed. (Chichester: John Wiley & Sons, 2015).

17. Ivanka Visnjic Kastalli and Bart Van Looy, "Servitization: Disentangling the Impact of Service Business Model Innovation on Manufacturing Firm Performance," *Journal of Operations Management* 31, no. 4 (2013): 169–80.

18. Robert C. Blattberg and John Deighton, "Manage Marketing by the Customer Equity Test," *Harvard Business Review* 74, no. 4 (1996): 136–44.

19. Roland T. Rust, Katherin N. Lemon, and Valarie A. Zeithaml, "Return on Marketing: Using Customer Equity to Focus Marketing Strategy," *Journal of Marketing* 68 (January, 2004): 109–27.

20. Rolls-Royce company website, accessed June 10, 2016, http://www. rolls-royce.com and Emma K. Macdonald, Michael Kleinaltenkamp, and Hugh N. Wilson, "How Business Customers Judge Solutions: Solution Quality and Value in Use," *Journal of Marketing* 80, no. 3 (2016): 96–120.

21. Information is based on Philips's press release: "Philips Provides Light As a Service to Schiphol Airport," April 16, 2015, accessed September 22, 2016, www.philips.com/a-w/about/news/archive/ standard/news/press/2015/20150416-Philips-provides-Light-as-a-Service-to-Schiphol-Airport.html.

**Exhibit 1**

Adam Bryant, "Xerox's New Chief Tries to Redefine Its Culture," *New York Times*, February 20, 2010, page BU1 of the New York edition, accessed September 23, 2016, www.nytimes.com/2010/02/21/ business/21xerox.html.

Henry Chesbrough, *Open Services Innovation: Rethinking Your Business to Grow and Compete in a New Era* (Chichester: John Wiley & Sons, 2010).

Eric (Er) Fang, Robert W. Palmatier, and Jan-Benedict E. M. Steenkamp, "Effect of Service Transition Strategies on Firm Value," *Journal of Marketing* 72 (September, 2008): 1–14.

Andrew Hill, "The Right Fit for Doing a Deal," *Financial Times*, December 7, 2011, accessed September 23, 2016, www.ft.com/cms/s/0/ a4c428f6-1ffc-11e1-8462-00144feabdc0.html.

Dana Mattolini, "Xerox Chief Looks Beyond Photocopiers Toward Services," *Wall Street Journal*, June 13, 2011.

Anjli Raval, "Xerox Says Shift to Services Is Paying Off," *Financial Times*, January 24, 2014, accessed September 23, 2016, www.ft.com/cms/s/0/bac264c8-662e-11e2-bb67-00144feab49a.html.

James Shotter, "UK Groups Lag Behind in Adding Services," *Financial Times*, May 29, 2012, accessed September 23, 2016, www.ft.com/cms/s/0/890ae896-a1bd-11e1-ae4c-00144feabdc0.html.

Xerox 2012, 2013, 2014, and 2015 Annual Reports.

Xerox Press Release, "Xerox to Separate into Two Market-Leading Public Companies Following Completion of Comprehensive Structural Review," January 29, 2016, accessed September 23, 2016, www.news.xerox.com/news/Xerox-to-separate-into-two-market-leading-public-companies.

Amy Yee, "Xerox takes road towards reinvention," *Financial Times*, November 4, 2004, accessed September 23, 2016, www.ft.com/cms/s/0/d5de5270-2e07-11d9-a86b-00000e2511c8.html.

## Chapter 2: B2B Services

1. Service management professor Evert Gummesson citing an unknown source: Evert Gummesson, "Lip Service: A Neglected Area in Services Marketing," *Journal of Consumer Services*, 1 (Summer, 1987): 19–22.

2. Adopted from definitions by Grönroos (2007), Lovelock and Wirtz (2007), and Vargo and Lusch (2004): Christian Grönroos, *Service Management and Marketing: Customer Management in Service Competition*, 3rd ed. (Chichester: John Wiley & Sons, 2007); Christopher Lovelock and Jochen Wirtz, *Services Marketing: People, Technology, Strategy*, 6th ed. (Upper Saddle River, NJ: Pearson Education, 2007); Stephen L. Vargo and Robert F. Lusch,

"Evolving to a New Dominant for Marketing," *Journal of Marketing* 68 (January, 2004): 1–17.

3.  Christopher Lovelock and Jochen Wirtz, *Services Marketing: People, Technology, Strategy*, 6th ed. (Upper Saddle River, NJ: Pearson Education, 2007).

4.  Cathrine M. Dalton, "A Passion for Pets: An Interview with Philip L. Francis, Chairperson and CEO of PETsMART, Inc.," *Business Horizons* 48 (2005): 473.

5.  See note 3 above.

6.  Lovelock and Gummesson (2004) claim that marketing transactions that do not involve a transfer of ownership—rent, hire, and lease— are distinctively different from those that do. Christopher Lovelock and Evert Gummesson,"Whither Services Marketing? In Search of a New Paradigm and Fresh Perspectives," *Journal of Service Research* 7, no. 1 (2004): 20–41.

7.  For information about Empire Southwest, see the "About Us" page on the company website: www.empire-cat.com.

8.  For information about AVNET, see the company website: www.avnet.com.

9.  Christian Grönroos provides thoughtful insights into this subject in his 2007 book, *Service Management and Marketing: Customer Management in Service Competition*, 3rd ed. (Chichester: John Wiley & Sons). He argues that the main dividing line is not between possible distinctions between products and services. That is, the type of resources needed (products, service activities, and information) in facilitating and supporting customers' assets, activities, and processes is not important; it is the business logic and culture that matter. Consequently, any firm can be a service-centric business because it is ultimately a strategic choice (similarly, a service

provider could have a product-centric culture and business logic). However, product firms are likely to struggle more with such a transformation due to the strong product centricity prevailing in most of these organizations.

10. Goutam Challagalla, R. Venkatesh, and Ajay K. Kohli, "Proactive Postsales Service: When and Why Does it Pay Off?" *Journal of Marketing* 73, no. 2 (2009): 74, 76.

## Chapter 3: Building a True Service Culture

1. Winter Nie, Wolfgang Ulaga, and Athanasios Kondis, *ABB TURBOCHARGING (A): Leading Change in Certain Times.* IMD Case Study No. IMD-3-2430, available at The Case Center, UK, web accessed www.thecasecentre.org.

2. Valarie A. Zeithaml, Mary Jo Bitner, and Dwayne D. Gremler, *Services Marketing*, 6th ed. (New York: McGraw Hill-Irwin, 2013). For other definitions of organizational culture, see, for example, S. M. Davis, *Managing Corporate Culture* (Cambridge, MA: Ballinger, 1985); H. S. Becker, "Culture: A Sociological View," *Yale Review* (Summer 1982): 513–27; Edgar H. Schein, *Organizational Culture and Leadership* (San Francisco, CA: Jossey-Bass, 1985), 168; and Rohit Deshpandé and Frederick E. Webster, Jr., "Organizational Culture and Marketing: Defining the Research Agenda," *Journal of Marketing* 53, no. 1 (1989): 3–15.

3. Christian Grönroos, *Service Management and Marketing: Customer Management in Service Competition*, 3rd ed. (Chichester: John Wiley & Sons, 2007), 418.

    For a definition of a service-oriented culture in manufacturing companies, see Heiko Gebauer, Bo Edvardsson, and Margareta Bjurko, "The Impact of Service Orientation in Corporate Culture on Business Performance in Manufacturing Companies," *Journal of Service Management* 21, no. 2 (2010): 237–59. Other references related to service culture and service orientation are David E. Bowen, Carn Siehl, and Benjamin Schneider, "A Framework for

Analyzing Customer Service Orientations in Manufacturing," *Academy of Management Review* 14, no. 1 (1989): 75–95; Christian Homburg, M. Fassnacht, and C. Günther, "The Role of Soft Factors in Implementing a Service-Oriented Strategy in Industrial Marketing Companies," *Journal of Business-to-Business Marketing* 10, no. 2 (2003): 23–51; Paul Matthyssens and Koen Vandenbempt, "Creating Competition Advantage in Industrial Services," *Journal of Business & Industrial Marketing* 13, no. 4–5 (1998): 339–55.

4.  Terrence E. Deal and Allan A. Kennedy, *Corporate Cultures: The Rites and Rituals of Organizational Life* (Reading, MA: Addison-Wesley, 1982).

5.  Christian Grönroos, *Service Management and Marketing: Customer Management in Service Competition*, 3rd ed. (Chichester: John Wiley & Sons, 2007).

6.  Lance A. Bettencourt, Robert F. Lusch, and Stephen L. Vargo, "A Service Lens on Value Creation: Marketing's Role in Achieving Strategic Advantage," *California Management Review* 57, no. 1 (2014): 44.

7.  Ibid., 44–66.

8.  Wolfgang Ulaga and Werner Reinartz, "Hybrid Offerings: How Manufacturing Firms Combine Goods and Services Successfully," *Journal of Marketing* 75 (November, 2011): 12.

9.  For more information on ASML, see the company website: www. asml.com.

10. Gebauer et al. (2005) first coined the term "service paradox" to describe such situations. The U-shaped relationship between shareholder value and relative size of the service business has been first documented by Fang et al. (2008) and confirmed by Eggert et al. (2014). The service paradox is further discussed in the next chapter.

Complete references:

Andreas Eggert, Jens Hogreve, Wolfgang Ulaga, and Eva Münkhoff, "Revenue and Profit Implications of Industrial Service Strategies," *Journal of Service Research* 17, no. 1 (2014): 23–39.

Eric (Er) Fang, Robert W. Palmatier, and Jan-Benedict E. M. Steenkamp, "Effect of Service Transition Strategies on Firm Value," *Journal of Marketing* 72 (September, 2008): 1–14.

Heiko Gebauer, Elgar Fleisch, and Thomas Friedli, "Overcoming the Service Paradox in Manufacturing Companies," *European Management Journal* 23, no. 1 (2005): 14–26.

11. See Kowalkowski et al. (2015) for further discussion about service growth trajectories and hybrid offerings:

Christian Kowalkowski, Charlotta Windahl, Daniel Kindström, and Heiko Gebauer, "What Service Transition? Rethinking Established Assumptions about Manufacturers' Service-led Growth Strategies," *Industrial Marketing Management* 45, no. 2 (2015): 59–69.

**Table 3:1**

David E. Bowen, Carn Siehl, and Benjamin Schneider, "A Framework for Analyzing Customer Service Orientations in Manufacturing," *Academy of Management Review* 14, no. 1 (1989): 75–95; Jay R. Galbraith, "Organizing to Deliver Solutions," *Organizational Dynamics* 31, no. 2 (2002): 194–207; and Denish Shah, Roland T. Rust, A. Parasuraman, Richard Staelin, and George S. Day, "The Path to Customer Centricity," *Journal of Service Research* 9, no. 2 (2006): 113–24.

**Exhibit 2**

Fredrik Nordin, Danilo Brozovic, Christian Kowalkowski, and Mats Vilgon, "CASE: Managing Customer Relationship Gaps at SKF," *Journal of Business Market Management* 8, no. 2 (2015): 455–63.

Joe Sinfield, Ned Calder, and Ben Geheb, "How Industrial Systems Are Turning into Digital Services," *Harvard Business Review*, June

23, 2015, accessed September 23, 2016, https://hbr.org/2015/06/how-industrial-systems-are-turning-into-digital-services.
SKF 2010–2015 Annual Reports.


## Chapter 4: Service Strategy

1. This strategic issue is raised by Jay R. Galbraith, "Organizing to Deliver Solutions," *Organizational Dynamics* 31, no. 2 (2002): 194–207.

2. 2015 figures, retrieved from Schneider Electric 2015 Annual Report.

3. BASF Corporate Report 2003.

4. BASF Vision, Values, Principles, accessed July 5, 2016, www2.basf.us/careers/pdfs/Vision_Values_Principles_e.pdf.

5. V. Kasturi Rangan and George T. Bowman, "Beating the Commodity Magnet," *Industrial Marketing Management* 21, no. 3 (1992): 215–24.

6. Scott D. Anthony and Joseph V. Sinfield, "When the Going Gets Tough, the Tough Get Innovating," *IndustryWeek*, October 8, 2008, accessed September 22, 2016, www.industryweek.com/companies-amp-executives/when-going-gets-tough-tough-get-innovating.

7. Andreas Eggert, Jens Hogreve, Wolfgang Ulaga, and Eva Münkhoff, "Revenue and Profit Implications of Industrial Service Strategies," *Journal of Service Research* 17, no. 1 (2014): 23–39.

8. Eric (Er) Fang, Robert W. Palmatier, and Jan-Benedict E. M. Steenkamp, "Effect of Service Transition Strategies on Firm Value," *Journal of Marketing* 72 (September, 2008): 1–14.

**Figure 4:1**
Rogelio Oliva and Robert Kallenberg, "Managing the Transition from Products to Services," *International Journal of Service Industry Management* 14, no. 2 (2003): 162.

**Figure 4:2**
V. Kasturi Rangan and George T. Bowman, "Beating the Commodity Magnet," *Industrial Marketing Management* 21, no. 3 (1992): 219.

**Exhibit 3**
Thomas Fischer, Heiko Gebauer, and Elgar Fleisch, *Service Business Development: Strategies for Value Creation in Manufacturing Firms* (Cambridge: Cambridge University Press, 2012).
IBM 2015 Annual Report.

Jeff Sommer, "Apple Won't Always Rule. Just Look at IBM," *New York Times*, April 25, 2015, page BU4 of the New York edition, accessed September 23, 2016, www.nytimes.com/2015/04/26/your-money/now-its-apples-world-once-it-was-ibms.html.

Jim Spohrer, "IBM's Service Journey: A Summary Sketch," *Industrial Marketing Management*, 60 (2017), 167–172.

Richard Waters, "Semiconductor Sale a Vital Part of IBM's Strategic Realignment," *Financial Times*, February 7, 2014, accessed September 23, 2016, www.ft.com/cms/s/0/f563bea0-8fa5-11e3-9cb0-00144feab7de.html.

**Exhibit 4**
Christian Kowalkowski, Daniel Kindström, Thomas Brashear Alejandro, Staffan Brege, and Sergio Biggemann, "Service Infusion as Agile Incrementalism in Action," *Journal of Business Research* 65, no. 6 (2012): 765–72.

## Chapter 5: Resources and Capabilities

1. Luis V. Gerstner, Chapter 14, "Services—the Key to Integration," in *Who Says Elephants Can't Dance?* (New York: HarperCollins Publishers), 133.

2. Morris A. Cohen, Narendra Agrawal, and Vipul Agrawal, "Winning in the Aftermarket," *Harvard Business Review* 84, no. 5 (2006): 129–38.

3. Winter Nie, Wolfgang Ulaga, and Athanasios Kondis, *ABB TURBOCHARGING (A): Leading Change in Certain Times*. IMD Case Study No. IMD-3-2430, available at The Case Center, UK, web accessed www.thecasecentre.org.

4. Treacy and Wiersema (1993) and Olson, Slater, and Hult (2005) respectively: Michael Treacy and Fred Wiersema, "Customer Intimacy and Other Value Disciplines," *Harvard Business Review* (January–February, 1993): 84–93; Eric M. Olson, Stanley F. Slater, and Tomas M. Hult, "The Performance Implications of Fit among Business Strategy, Marketing Organization Structure, and Strategic Behavior," *Journal of Marketing* 69, no. 3 (2005): 49–65. See also the discussion on service culture in chapter 3.

5. T. K. Das and Bing-Sheng Teng, "The Risk-based View of Trust: A Conceptual Framework," *Journal of Business and Psychology* 19, no. 1 (2004): 87.

6. Gary D. Eppen, "Effects of Centralization of Expected Costs in a Multi-Location Newsboy Problem," *Management Science* 25, no. 5 (1979): 498–501, and Harry Markowitz, *Mean-Variance Analysis in Portfolio Choice and Capital Markets* (New York: Blackwell, 1987).

7. Theodore Levitt, "Production-line Approach to Service," *Harvard Business Review* 50, no. 5 (1972): 41–52.

8. Roland T. Rust and Ming-Hui Huang, "Optimizing Service Productivity," *Journal of Marketing* 76, no. 2 (2012): 47–66.

## Chapter 6: Vision and Leadership

1. Chloé Renault, Frédéric Dalsace, and Wolfgang Ulaga, *Michelin Fleet Solutions: From Selling Tires to Selling Kilometers.* ECCH Case Study. Web Accessed: www.thecasecentre.org.

2. John P. Kotter, "Leading Change: Why Transforming Efforts Fail," *Harvard Business Review* (March–April, 1995): 59–67.

3. Eric (Er) Fang, Robert W. Palmatier, and Jan-Benedict E. M. Steenkamp, "Effect of Service Transition Strategies on Firm Value," *Journal of Marketing* 72 (September, 2008): 1–14.

4. Nokia was the world's biggest handset maker from 1995 to 2011.

5. *Financial Times*, "Stephen Elop's Memo in Full," February 9, 2011, accessed September 22, 2016, http://www.ft.com/intl/cms/s/0/37ecf3fe-3432-11e0-993f-00144feabdc0.html#axzz3RteSbbdv.

6. Stephen Elop's e-mail to employees, 2014, accessed April 3, 2016, https://news.microsoft.com/2014/07/17/stephen-elops-email-to-employees/.

7. Lucy Kellaway, "'Hello There': Eight Lessons from Microsoft's Awful Job Loss Memo," *Financial Times*, July 27, 2014, accessed September 22, 2016, www.ft.com/intl/cms/s/0/013511fa-13dd-11e4-8485-00144feabdc0.html?siteedition=intl#axzz3RteSbbdv.

8. John P. Kotter, "Accelerate: How the Most Innovative Companies Capitalize on Today's Rapid-Fire Strategic Challenges—And Still Make Their Numbers," *Harvard Business Review* 90, no. 11 (2012): 43–58.

9. E. Cornet, R. Katz, R. Molloy, J. Schädler, D. Sharma, and A. Tipping, *Customer Solutions: From Pilots to Profits* (New York: Booz Allen & Hamilton, 2000).

10. Adam Bryant, "Xerox's New Chief Tries to Redefine Its Culture," *New York Times*, February 21, 2010, page BU1 of the New York edition,

accessed September 23, 2016, www.nytimes.com/2010/02/21/business/21xerox.html.

## Chapter 7: Capturing More Value

1. For additional insights, see Werner Reinartz and Wolfgang Ulaga, "How to Sell Services More Profitably," *Harvard Business Review* 86, no. 5 (2008): 90–96.

2. Michael Steiner, Andreas Eggert, Wolfgang Ulaga, and Klaus Backhaus, "Do Customized Service Packages Impede Value Capture in Industrial Markets?," *Journal of the Academy of Marketing Science* 44 (2016): 151–65.

3. Find more information about Air Liquide's total gas and chemical management at www.cn.airliquide.com/en/electronic-semiconductors-tft-lcd-3/services-2/total-gas-and-chemical-management.html, accessed September 23, 2016.

4. Clayton M. Christensen, Scott D. Anthony, Gerald Berstell, and Denise Nitterhouse, "Finding the Right Job for Your Product," *MIT Sloan Management Review* 48, no. 3 (2007): 38–47.

5. James C. Anderson, James A. Narus, and Wouter van Rossum, "Customer Value Propositions in Business Markets," *Harvard Business Review* (March, 2006): 91–99.

6. SKF 2015 Annual Report, www.skf.com.

7. Hilti's Tool Fleet Management conveys a distinct value proposition to each decision maker inside a customer's organization. See, for example, the promise made to a tool crib manager: https://www.youtube.com/watch?v=7PfBhAt1ylY, accessed September 23, 2016.

8. James C. Anderson, Nirmalya Kumar, and James A. Narus, *Value Merchants: Demonstrating and Documenting Superior Value in Business Markets* (Boston, MA: Harvard Business School Press, 2007).

**Exhibit 6**
Ericsson 2003 and 2015 Annual Reports.

Mike Malmgren, "Managing Risks in Business Critical Outsourcing: A Perspective from the Outsourcer and the Supplier" (Published PhD diss., Linköping University, Linköping, Sweden, 2010).

## Chapter 8: Service Innovation

1. See Pavitt (1984) and Barras (1986): Keith Pavitt, "Sectoral Patterns of Technical Change: Towards a Taxonomy and a Theory," *Research Policy* 13, no. 6 (1984): 343–73; Richard Barras, "Towards a Theory of Innovation in Services," *Research Policy* 15, no. 4 (1986): 161–73.

2. Rob Coombs and Ian Miles, "Innovation, Measurement and Services: The New Problematique," Innovation Systems, in *The Service Economy: Measurement and Case Study Analysis*, ed. J. S. Metcalfe and Ian Miles (Boston, MA: Kluwer Academic), 85–103.

3. Nadine Dörner, Oliver Gassmann, and Heiko Gebauer, "Service Innovation: Why Is It So Difficult to Accomplish?," *Journal of Business Strategy* 32, no. 3 (2011): 37–46.

4. Catherine Bernard and Alastair Macduff, "The Dealerships' Mystery Customers," *Volvo Group Magazine* (February, 2015): 31.

5. Siemens, "Pictures of the Future," *The Magazine for Research and Innovation*, Fall 2001.

6. Osvald M. Bjelland and Robert Chapman Wood, "An Inside View of IBM's 'Innovation Jam,'" *MIT Sloan Management Review* 50, no. 1 (2008): 31–40.

**Figure 8:1**
Christian Kowalkowski and Daniel Kindström, *Tjänster och helhetslösningar: nya affärsmodeller för konkurrenskraft* (Malmö, Sweden: Liber, 2012), 112.

**Table 8:1**
The table is based on table 11.1 in Christian Kowalkowski, "Service Innovation in Industrial Contexts," in *Service Innovation: Novel Ways of Creating Value in Actor Systems*, ed. Marja Toivonen (New York: Springer (Translational Systems Sciences, vol. 6), 2016), 238.

**Table 8:2**
Per Kristensson, Anders Gustafsson, and Lars Witell, *Tjänsteinnovation* (Lund, Sweden: Studentlitteratur, 2014), 75.

**Table 8:3**
Gary L. Lilien, Pamela D. Morrison, Kathleen Searls, Mary Sonnack, and Eric von Hippel, "Performance Assessment of the Lead User Idea-Generation Process for New Product Development," *Management Science* 48, no. 8 (2002): 1042–59.

## Chapter 9: Service Productivity

1. Theodore Levitt, "Production-Line Approach to Service," *Harvard Business Review* 50, no. 5 (1972): 41–42.

2. Accenture, "Improving Customer Experience Is Top Business Priority for Companies Pursuing Digital Transformation," News release, October 27, 2015, accessed November 21, 2016, https://newsroom.accenture.com/news/improving-customer-experience-is-top-business-priority-for-companies-pursuing-digital-transformation-according-to-accenture-study.htm.

3.  For a definition of a customer experience, see Lemon and Verhoef (2016, p. 71). They define a customer experience as "a multidimensional construct focusing on a customer's cognitive, emotional, behavioral, sensorial, and social responses to a firm's offerings during the customer's entire purchase journey." Katherine N. Lemon and Peter C. Verhoef, "Understanding Customer Experience Throughout the Customer Journey," *Journal of Marketing* 80 (November, 2016): 69–96.

4.  Valarie A. Zeithaml, Mary Jo Bitner, and Dwayne D. Gremler, *Services Marketing: Integrating Customer Focus Across the Firm*, 6th ed. (New York: McGraw-Hill Irwin, 2013), 235.

5.  G. Lynn Shostack, "Designing Services That Deliver," *Harvard Business Review* 62 (January–February, 1984): 133–39; G. Lynn Shostack, "Service Positioning through Structural Change," *Journal of Marketing* 51 (January, 1987): 34–43.

6.  Mary Jo Bitner, Amy L. Ostrom, and F. N. Morgan, "Service Blueprinting: A Practical Technique for Service Innovation," *California Management Review* 50 (Spring 2008): 66–94.

7.  G. Lynn Shostack, "Designing Services That Deliver," *Harvard Business Review* 62 (January–February, 1984): 133–139.

8.  Christopher Lovelock and Jochen Wirtz, *Services Marketing: People, Technology, Strategy*, 6th ed. (Upper Saddle River, NJ: Pearson Education, 2007).

9.  Based on Mary Jo Bitner, Amy L. Ostrom, and F. N. Morgan, "Service Blueprinting: A Practical Technique for Service Innovation," *California Management Review* 50 (Spring 2008): 66–94.

10. Theodore Levitt, "Production-Line Approach to Service," *Harvard Business Review* 50, no. 5 (1972): 41–52; Theodore Levitt, "The Industrialization of Service," *Harvard Business Review* 50, no. 5 (1976): 63–74.

11. David E. Bowen and William E. Youngdahl, "'Lean' Service: In Defense of a Production-Line Approach," *International Journal of Service Industry Management* 9, no. 3 (1998): 207–25.

12. Roland T. Rust and Ming-Hui Huang, "Optimizing Service Productivity," *Journal of Marketing* 76, no. 2 (2012): 47–66.

13. As pointed out by Christian Grönroos and Katri Ojasalo, "Service Productivity: Towards a Conceptualization of the Transformation of Inputs into Economic Results in Services," *Journal of Business Research* 57 (2004): 414–23.

14. Ibid.

15. Roland T. Rust and Ming-Hui Huang, "Optimizing Service Productivity," *Journal of Marketing* 76, no. 2 (2012): 47–66.

16. Andreas Eggert, Jens Hogreve, Wolfgang Ulaga, and Eva Münkhoff, "Revenue and Profit Implications of Industrial Service Strategies," *Journal of Service Research* 17, no. 1 (2014): 23–39.

17. Ibid.

18. See note 13 above.

19. Christian Kowalkowski, "Managing the Industrial Service Function" (Published PhD diss., Linköping University, Linköping, Sweden, 2008).

20. Andy Sharman, "BMW Sounds Alarm Over Tech Companies Seeking Connected Car Data," *Financial Times*, January 15, 2015, accessed November 21, 2016, www.ft.com/intl/cms/s/0/685fe610-9ba6-11e4-950f-00144feabdc0.html#axzz3RcmWMfOG.

## Chapter 10: Transforming Sales

1. Wolfgang Ulaga and James Loveland, "Transitioning from Product to Service-led Growth in Manufacturing Firms: Emergent Challenges in Selecting and Managing the Industrial Sales Force," *Industrial Marketing Management* 43 (January, 2014): 113–25.

2. Werner Reinartz and Wolfgang Ulaga, "How to Sell Services More Profitably," *Harvard Business Review* (May, 2008): 90–96.

3. Wolfgang Ulaga and Werner Reinartz, "Hybrid Offerings: How Manufacturing Firms Combine Goods and Services Successfully," *Journal of Marketing* 75, no. 6 (2011): 5–23.

4. See note 1 above.

5. Alan J. Dubinsky and William Rudelius, "Selling Techniques for Industrial Products and Services: Are They Different?," *Journal of Personal Selling and Sales Management* 1 (Fall/Winter 1980–81): 65–75.

6. For a review of traditional sales approaches and behaviors, see, for example, Barton Weitz, H. Sujan, and M. Sujan, "Knowledge, Motivation, and Adaptive Behavior: A Framework for Improving Selling Effectiveness," *Journal of Marketing* 50, no. 4 (1986): 174–91; R. L. Spiro and Barton A. Weitz, "Adaptive Selling: Conceptualization, Measurement, and Nomological Validity," *Journal of Marketing Research* 27, no. 1 (1990): 61–69.

7. Christopher R. Plouffe, Brian C. Williams, and Trent Wachner, "Navigating Difficult Waters: Publishing Trends and Scholarship in Sales Research," *Journal of Personal Selling and Sales Management* 28, no. 1 (2008): 79–92; Brian C. Williams and Christopher R. Plouffe, "Assessing the Evolution of Sales Knowledge: A 20-Content Analysis," *Industrial Marketing Management* 36, no. 4 (2007): 319–408.

Harri Terho, Andreas Eggert, Alexander Haas, and Wolfgang Ulaga, "Implementing Sales Strategy in Business Markets: The Role of Salesperson Customer Orientation and Value-Based Selling," *Industrial Marketing Management* 45 (2015): 12–21.

8. Christopher R. Plouffe, Brian C. Williams, and Trent Wachner, "Navigating Difficult Waters: Publishing Trends and Scholarship in Sales Research," *Journal of Personal Selling and Sales Management* 28, no. 1 (2008): 87.

9. William C. Moncrief and Greg W. Marshall, "The Evolution of the Seven Steps of Selling," *Industrial Marketing Management* 34, no. 1 (2005): 13–22.

10. Michael Ahearne, Son K. Lam, John E. Mahieu, and Willy Bolander, "Why Are Some Salespeople Better at Adapting to Organizational Change?" *Journal of Marketing* 74 (May, 2010): 65–79.

11. Andrew J. Vinchur, Jeffrey S. Schippmann, Fred S. Switzer, and Philip L. Roth, "A Meta-Analytic Review of Job Performance for Salespeople," *Journal of Applied Psychology* 83, no. 4 (1998): 586–97; John E. Hunter and Ronda F. Hunter, "Validity and Utility of Alternative Predictors of Job Performance," *Psychological Bulletin* 96, no. 1 (1984): 72–98.

12. Terri Feldman Barr, Andrea L. Dixon, and Jule B. Gassenheimer, "Exploring the 'Lone Wolf' Phenomenon in Student Teams," *Journal of Marketing Education* 27 (April, 2005): 81–90.

13. Terry D. Blumenthal, "Extraversion, Attention, and Startle Response Reactivity," *Personality and Individual Differences* 31, no. 4 (2001): 495–503.

14. Richard E. Lucas, Ed Diener, Alexander Grob, Eunkook M. Suh, and Liang Shao, "Cross-Cultural Evidence for the Fundamental Features of Extraversion," *Journal of Personality and Social Psychology* 79 (September, 2000): 452–68.

15. John M. Digman, "Five Robust Trait Dimensions: Development, Stability, and Utility," *Journal of Personality* 57, no. 2 (1989): 195–214.

16. See note 3 above.

**Exhibit 9**

Wolfgang Ulaga and James M. Loveland, "Transitioning from Product to Service-led Growth in Manufacturing Firms: Emergent Challenges in Selecting and Managing the Industrial Sales Force," *Industrial Marketing Management* 43, no. 1 (2014): 113–25.

## Chapter 11: Organizing for Services

1. Ranjay Gulati, "Silo Busting: How to Execute on the Promise of Customer Focus," *Harvard Business Review* 85, no. 5 (2007): 98.

2. For example, Oliva, Gebauer, and Brann (2012) found a positive effect in their analysis of 216 manufacturers in the high-value durable equipment industry moving into the service business. Rogelio Oliva, Heiko Gebauer, and J. M. Brann, "Separate or Integrate? Assessing the Impact of Separation between Product and Service Business on Service Performance in Product Manufacturing Firms," *Journal of Business-to-Business Marketing* 19, no. 4 (2012): 309–34.

3. Jon Ostrower, "Boeing Reorganizes into Three Parts: Airliners, Fighters and Spare Parts," *CNN Money*, November 21, 2016, accessed December 9, 2016, money.cnn.com/2016/11/21/news/companies/boeing-reorganization/. Boeing News Releases/Statements, "Boeing Names New Senior Leaders, Launches Integrated Services Business," November 21, 2016, accessed December 9, 2016, boeing.mediaroom.com/2016-11-21-Boeing-Names-New-Senior-Leaders-Launches-Integrated-Services-Business.

4. The study is published in Heiko Gebauer and Christian Kowalkowski, "Customer-Focused and Service-Focused Orientation

in Organizational Structures," *Journal of Business and Industrial Marketing* 27, no. 7 (2012): 527–37.

5. In addition to such hard and soft measures to promote cooperation, Gulati (2007) also highlights the importance of customer-focused companies to focus on activities to support coordination and capability building.

6. Gulati, "Silo Busting," 98–108.

7. Ibid.

8. Bartlett, Ghoshal, and Beamish (2008) refer to such structure as transnational organization: Christopher A. Bartlett, Sumantra Ghoshal, and Paul Beamish, *Transnational Management: Text, Cases and Readings in Cross Border Management*, 5th ed. (Burr Ridge, IL: McGraw-Hill/Irwin, 2008).

9. Andreas Eggert, Jens Hogreve, Wolfgang Ulaga, and Eva Münkhoff, "Revenue and Profit Implications of Industrial Service Strategies," *Journal of Service Research* 17, no. 1 (2014): 23–39. We also refer to this study in chapters 4 and 10.

**Figure 11:1**
Based on figures 1 and 2 in Heiko Gebauer and Christian Kowalkowski, "Customer-Focused and Service-Focused Orientation in Organizational Structures," *Journal of Business and Industrial Marketing* 27, no. 7 (2012): 527–37.

**Exhibit 10**
John Bessant and Andrew Davies, "Managing Service Innovation," in *Innovation in Services* (DTI Occasional Paper no. 9, June 2007): Department of Trade and Industry, UK, 61–96, accessed September 23, 2016, www.servicemanagement.cz/soubory/innovation%20in% 20services.pdf.

Direct communication with management.

Ericsson 2015 Annual Report.

Ericsson Press Release, "Ericsson Accelerates Transformation to Drive Growth and Profitability," April 21, 2016, accessed September 23, 2016, www.ericsson.com/news/2005398.

Ericsson White Paper, "Managed Services' Impact on the Telecom Industry," March 2007, accessed February 3, 2010, www.ericsson.com/technology/whitepapers/3115_Managed_services_A.pdf.

Andrew Parker, "Ericsson to by Telcordia for $1.2bn," *Financial Times*, June 14, 2011, accessed September 23, 2016, www.ft.com/cms/s/0/1aafdc46-967c-11e0-afc5-00144feab49a.html.

## Chapter 12: Channel Partner Management

1. Philip Kotler and Peggy H. Cunningham, Chapter 17: "Designing and Managing Value Networks and Marketing Channels," in *Marketing Management* (Canadian Eleventh Edition) (Harlow: Pearson Education Canada).

2. See the website of the franchise: http://www.empire-cat.com.

3. James B. Kelleher, "From Dumb Iron to Big Data: Caterpillar's Dealer Sales Push," *Reuters Business News*, March 20, 2014, accessed September 23, 2016, www.reuters.com/article/us-caterpillar-dealers-insight-idUSBREA2J0Q320140320.

4. Linde Material Handling had a successful in-house distribution network in France with tight control and a buy-back channel. In Germany, on the other hand, management made a different decision, and the company concentrated itself on the design, production, and sale of its products, leaving distributors to sell the best portion of services. Despite selling the same equipment and serving

the same customer segments, the French model has proven much more successful for service growth.

5. Lieberman and Montgomery (1998) consider the root causes of such unwillingness or inability to change to be i) lock-in to a specific set of fixed assets, ii) reluctance to cannibalize existing offerings, and iii) organizational inflexibility: Marvin B. Lieberman and David B. Montgomery, "First-Mover Advantages," *Strategic Management Journal* 9 (Summer 1998): 41–58.

6. Eric (Er) Fang, Robert W. Palmatier, and Jan-Benedict E. M. Steenkamp, "Effect of Service Transition Strategies on Firm Value," *Journal of Marketing* 72 (September, 2008): 1–14.

7. Konecranes 2015 Annual Report.

8. See note 6 above.

9. Leslie Hook and Robert Wright, "Amazon leases 20 Boeing 767 Freight Jets for Air Cargo Programme," *Financial Times*, March 9, 2016, accessed September 23, 2016, www.ft.com/intl/cms/s/0/6f3867e8-e617-11e5-a09b-1f8b0d268c39.html.

10. See the website of the company's service offering: www.xylemtotalcare.com.

11. Christian Kowalkowski, "Managing the Industrial Service Function" (Published PhD diss., Linköping University, Linköping, Sweden, 2008).

12. This is further discussed by Ranjay Gulati, "Silo Busting: How to Execute on the Promise of Customer Focus," *Harvard Business Review* 85, no. 5 (2007): 98–108.

13. See note 3 above.

14. Volvo Cars press release, "Volvo Cars and Uber Join Forces to Develop Autonomous Driving Cars," August 18, 2016, accessed September 23, 2016, www.media.volvocars.com/us/en-us/media/pressreleases/194795/volvo-cars-and-uber-join-forces-to-develop-autonomous-driving-cars ().

15. Christian Shepherd, "Volvo Seeks Edge on Driverless Car Technology," *Financial Times*, April 7, 2016, accessed September 23, 2016, www.ft.com/intl/cms/s/0/96f256c8-fc6e-11e5-b5f5-070dca6d0a0d.html.

**Exhibit 11**
Michelin Group Fact Sheet 2015, "Michelin, A Better Way Forward."

Chloé Renault, Frédéric Dalsace, and Wolfgang Ulaga, *Michelin Fleet Solutions: From Selling Tires to Selling Kilometers*. ECCH Case Study. Web Accessed: www.thecasecentre.org.

**Exhibit 12**
Kirthi Kalyanam and Surinder Brar, "From Volume to Value: Managing the Value-add Reseller Channel at Cisco Systems," *California Management Review* 52, no. 1 (2009): 94–119.

# BIBLIOGRAPHY

*Accenture,* "Improving Customer Experience Is Top Business Priority for Companies Pursuing Digital Transformation," 2015, News release (October 27). Accessed November 21, 2016. https://newsroom. accenture.com/news/improving-customer-experience-is-top-business-priority-for-companies-pursuing-digital-transformation-according-to-accenture-study.htm. ().

Ahearne, Michael, Son K. Lam, John E. Mahieu, and Willy Bolander. "Why Are Some Salespeople Better at Adapting to Organizational Change?" *Journal of Marketing* 74 (May 2010): 65–79.

Anderson, James C., Nirmalya Kumar, and James A. Narus. *Value Merchants: Demonstrating and Documenting Superior Value in Business Markets.* Boston, MA: Harvard Business School Press, 2007.

Anderson, James C., James A. Narus, and Wouter van Rossum. "Customer Value Propositions in Business Markets." *Harvard Business Review,* March 2006, 91–99.

Anthony, Scott D., and Joseph V. Sinfield. "When the Going Gets Tough, the Tough Get Innovating." *IndustryWeek,* October 8, 2008. Accessed September 22, 2016. www.industryweek.com/companies-amp-executives/when-going-gets-tough-tough-get-innovating.

Barras, Richard. "Towards a Theory of Innovation in Services." *Research Policy* 15, no.4 (1986): 161–73.

Bartlett, Christopher A., Sumantra Ghoshal, and Paul Beamish. *Transnational Management: Text, Cases and Readings in Cross Border Management.* 5th ed. Burr Ridge, IL: McGraw-Hill/Irwin, 2008.

*BASF.* Corporate Report, 2003.

*BASF* (unknown) Vision, Values, Principles. Accessed July 5, 2016www2. basf.us/careers/pdfs/Vision_Values_Principles_e.pdf.

Bernard, Catherine and Alastair Macduff. "The Dealerships' Mystery Customers." *Volvo Group Magazine* (February 2015): 31.

Bessant, John, and Andrew Davies. "Managing Service Innovation," in *Innovation in Services* (DTI Occasional Paper no. 9, June 2007): Department of Trade and Industry, UK, 61–96. Accessed September 23, 2016. www.servicemanagement.cz/soubory/innovation%20 in%20services.pdf.

Bettencourt, Lance A., Robert F. Lusch, and Stephen L. Vargo. "A Service Lens on Value Creation: Marketing's Role in Achieving Strategic Advantage." *California Management Review* 57, no. 1 (2014): 44–66.

Bitner, Mary Jo, Amy L. Ostrom, and F. N. Morgan. "Service Blueprinting: A Practical Technique for Service Innovation." *California Management Review* 50 (Spring 2008): 66–94.

Bjelland, Osvald M., and Robert Chapman Wood. "An inside View of IBM's 'Innovation Jam.'" *MIT Sloan Management Review* 50, no. 1 (2008): 31–40.

Blattberg, Robert C., and John Deighton. "Manage Marketing by the Customer Equity Test." *Harvard Business Review* 74, no. 4 (1996): 136–44.

Blumenthal, Terry D. "Extraversion, Attention, and Startle Response Reactivity." *Personality and Individual Differences* 31, no. 4 (2001): 495–503.

Bowen, David E., Carn Siehl, and Benjamin Schneider. "A Framework for Analyzing Customer Service Orientations in Manufacturing." *Academy of Management Review* 14, no. 1 (1989): 75–95.

Bowen, David E., and William E. Youngdahl. "'Lean' Service: In Defense of a Production-line Approach." *International Journal of Service Industry Management* 9, no. 3 (1998): 207–25.

Bryant, Adam. "Xerox's New Chief Tries to Redefine Its Culture." *New York Times*, February 20, 2010, page BU1 of the New York edition. Accessed September 23, 2016. www.nytimes.com/2010/02/21/business/21xerox.html.

*Business Wire*. Press Release: "PetSmart Announces Fourth Quarter and Fiscal Year 2014 Results." Accessed September 22, 2016. www.businesswire.com/news/home/20150304005081/en/PetSmart-Announces-Fourth-Quarter-Fiscal-Year-2014.

Challagalla, Goutam, R. Venkatesh, and Ajay K. Kohli. "Proactive Postsales Service: When and Why Does It Pay Off?" *Journal of Marketing* 73, no. 2 (2009): 74, 76.

Chesbrough, Henry. *Open Services Innovation: Rethinking Your Business to Grow and Compete in a New Era*. Chichester: John Wiley & Sons, 2010.

Christensen, Clayton M., Scott D. Anthony, Gerald Berstell, and Denise Nitterhouse. "Finding the Right Job for Your Product." *MIT Sloan Management Review* 48, no. 3 (2007): 38–47.

Clegg, Jeremy, and Hinrich Voss. *Chinese Overseas Direct Investment in the European Union* London: ECRAN (Europe China Research and Advice Network), 2012.

Cohen, Morris A., Narendra Agrawal, and Vipul Agrawal. "Winning in the Aftermarket." *Harvard Business Review* 84, no. 5 (2006): 129–38.

Coombs, Rob, and Ian Miles. "Innovation, Measurement and Services: The New Problematique." Innovation systems. In *The Service Economy: Measurement and Case Study Analysis*, edited by J. S. Metcalfe and Ian Miles, 85–103. Boston, MA: Kluwer Academic, 2000.

Cornet, E., R. Katz, R. Molloy, J. Schädler, D. Sharma, and A. Tipping. *Customer Solutions: From Pilots to Profits*. New York: Booz Allen & Hamilton, 2000.

Dalton, Cathrine M. "A Passion for Pets: An Interview with Philip L. Francis, Chairperson and CEO of PETsMART, Inc." *Business Horizons* (2005): 48, 473.

Das, T. K., and Bing-Sheng Teng "The Risk-based View of Trust: A Conceptual Framework." *Journal of Business and Psychology* 19, no. 1 (2004): 87.

Deal, Terrence E., and Allan A. Kennedy. *Corporate Cultures: The Rites and Rituals of Organizational Life.* Reading, MA: Addison-Wesley, 1982.

Digman, John M. "Five Robust Trait Dimensions: Development, Stability, and Utility." *Journal of Personality* 57, no. 2 (1989): 195–214.

Dörner, Nadine, Oliver Gassmann, and Heiko Gebauer. "Service Innovation: Why Is It So Difficult to Accomplish?" *Journal of Business Strategy* 32, no. 3 (2011): 37–46.

Dubinsky, Alan J., and William Rudelius. "Selling Techniques for Industrial Products and Services: Are They Different?" *Journal of Personal Selling and Sales Management* 1 (Fall/Winter 1980–81): 65–75.

*The Economist.* "Top Floor, Please," March 16, 2013 issue, p. 67. Accessed September 23, 2016. http://www.economist.com/news/business/21573568-things-are-looking-up-liftmakers-top-floor-please.

Eggert, Andreas, Jens Hogreve, Wolfgang Ulaga, and Eva Münkhoff. "Revenue and Profit Implications of Industrial Service Strategies." *Journal of Service Research* 17, no. 1 (2014): 23–39.

Eppen, Gary D. "Effects of Centralization of Expected Costs in a Multi-Location Newsboy Problem." *Management Science* 25, no. 5 (1979): 498–501.

*Ericsson.* Annual Reports, 2003; 2015.

*Ericsson.* White Paper, "Managed Services' Impact on the Telecom Industry." March 2007. Accessed February 3, 2010. www.ericsson.com/technology/whitepapers/3115_Managed_services_A.pdf.

*Ericsson.* Press Release: "Ericsson Accelerates Transformation to Drive Growth and Profitability." April 21, 2016. Accessed September 23, 2016. www.ericsson.com/news/2005398.

Fang, Eric (Er), Robert W. Palmatier, and Jan-Benedict E. M. Steenkamp. "Effect of Service Transition Strategies on Firm Value." *Journal of Marketing* 72 (September, 2008): 1–14.

Feldman Barr, Terri, Andrea L. Dixon, and Jule B. Gassenheimer. "Exploring the 'Lone Wolf' Phenomenon in Student Teams." *Journal of Marketing Education* 27 (April, 2005): 81–90.

*Financial Times.* "Stephen Elop's Memo in Full." February 9, 2011. Accessed September 22, 2016. http://www.ft.com/intl/cms/s/0/37ecf3fe-3432-11e0-993f-00144feabdc0.html#axzz3RteSbbdv.

Fischer, Thomas, Heiko Gebauer, and Elgar Fleisch. *Service Business Development: Strategies for Value Creation in Manufacturing Firms.* Cambridge: Cambridge University Press, 2012.

Galbraith, Jay R. "Organizing to Deliver Solutions." *Organizational Dynamics* 31, no. 2 (2002): 194–207.

Gara, Antoine. "PetSmart's $8.7 Billion LBO Is Already Paying Off for Consortium Led by BC Partners." *Forbes,* February 18, 2016. Accessed September 22, 2016. www.forbes.com/sites/antoinegara/2016/02/18/petsmarts-8-7-billion-lbo-already-is-paying-off-for-consortium-led-by-bc-partners/.

Gebauer, Heiko, Bo Edvardsson, and Margareta Bjurko. "The Impact of Service Orientation in Corporate Culture on Business Performance in Manufacturing Companies." *Journal of Service Management* 21, no. 2 (2010): 237–59.

Gebauer, Heiko, Elgar Fleisch, and Thomas Friedli. "Overcoming the Service Paradox in Manufacturing Companies." *European Management Journal* 23, no. 1 (2005): 14–26.

Gebauer, Heiko, and Christian Kowalkowski. "Customer-focused and Service-focused Orientation in Organizational Structures." *Journal of Business and Industrial Marketing* 27, no. 7 (2012): 527–37.

Gerstner, Luis V. *Who Says Elephants Can't Dance?* New York: HarperCollins Publishers, 2002.

Grönroos, Christian. *Service Management and Marketing: Customer Management in Service Competition.* 3rd ed. Chichester: John Wiley & Sons, 2007.

Grönroos, Christian. *Service Management and Marketing: Managing the Service Profit Logic.* 4th ed. Chichester: John Wiley & Sons, 2015.

Grönroos, Christian, and Katri Ojasalo. "Service Productivity: Towards a Conceptualization of the Transformation of Inputs into Economic Results in Services." *Journal of Business Research* 57 (2004): 414–23.

Gulati, Ranjay. "Silo Busting: How to Execute on the Promise of Customer Focus," *Harvard Business Review* 85, no. 5 (2007): 98–108.

Gummesson, Evert. "Lip Service: A Neglected Area in Services Marketing," *Journal of Consumer Services* 1 (Summer 1987): 19–22.

Henkel, Carsten B., Oliver B. Bendig, Tobias Caspari, and Nihad Hasagic. *Industrial Services Strategies: The Quest for Faster Growth and Higher Margins.* New York: Monitor Group, 2004, 15.

Hill, Andrew. "The Right Fit for Doing a Deal." *Financial Times,* December 7, 2011. Accessed September 23, 2016. www.ft.com/cms/s/0/a4c428f6-1ffc-11e1-8462-00144feabdc0.html.

Hook, Leslie, and Robert Wright. "Amazon Leases 20 Boeing 767 Freight Jets for Air Cargo Programme." *Financial Times*, March 9, 2016. Accessed September 23, 2016. www.ft.com/intl/cms/s/0/6f3867e8-e617-11e5-a09b-1f8b0d268c39.html.

Hunter, John E., and Ronda F. Hunter. "Validity and Utility of Alternative Predictors of Job Performance." *Psychological Bulletin* 96, no. 1 (1984): 72–98.

*IBM*. Annual Report, 2015.

Kalyanam, Kirthi, and Surinder Brar. "From Volume to Value: Managing the Value-add Reseller Channel at Cisco Systems." *California Management Review* 52, no. 1 (2009): 94–119.

Kellaway, Lucy. "'Hello There': Eight Lessons from Microsoft's Awful Job Loss Memo." *Financial Times*, July 27, 2014. Accessed September 22, 2016. www.ft.com/intl/cms/s/0/013511fa-13dd-11e4-8485-00144fe-abdc0.html?siteedition=intl#axzz3RteSbbdv.

Kelleher, James B. "From Dumb Iron to Big Data: Caterpillar's Dealer Sales Push," *Reuters Business News*, March 20, 2014. Accessed September 23, 2016. www.reuters.com/article/us-caterpillar-dealers-insight-idUSBREA2J0Q320140320.

*Konecranes*. Annual Report, 2015.

Kotler, Philip, and Peggy H. Cunningham. Chapter 17: "Designing and Managing Value Networks and Marketing Channels." In *Marketing Management* (Canadian Eleventh Edition). Harlow: Pearson Education Canada, 2004.

Kotter, John P. "Leading Change: Why Transforming Efforts Fail." *Harvard Business Review* (March–April, 1995): 59–67.

Kotter, John P. "Accelerate: How the Most Innovative Companies Capitalize on Today's Rapid-fire Strategic Challenges—And Still Make Their Numbers." *Harvard Business Review* 90, no. 11 (2012): 43–58.

Kowalkowski, Christian. "Managing the Industrial Service Function." Published PhD diss., Linköping University, Linköping, Sweden, 2008.

Kowalkowski, Christian. "Service Innovation in Industrial Contexts." In *Service Innovation: Novel Ways of Creating Value in Actor Systems*, edited by Marja Toivonen. New York: Springer (Translational Systems Sciences, vol. 6), 2016.

Kowalkowski, Christian, and Daniel Kindström, *Tjänster och helhetslösningar: nya affärsmodeller för konkurrenskraft*. Malmö, Sweden: Liber, 2012.

Kowalkowski, Christian, Daniel Kindström, Thomas Brashear Alejandro, Staffan Brege, and Sergio Biggemann. "Service Infusion as Agile Incrementalism in Action." *Journal of Business Research* 65, no. 6 (2012): 765–72.

Kowalkowski, Christian, Charlotta Windahl, Daniel Kindström, and Heiko Gebauer. "What Service Transition? Rethinking Established Assumptions about Manufacturers' Service-led Growth Strategies." *Industrial Marketing Management* 45, no. 2 (2015): 59–69.

Kristensson, Per, Anders Gustafsson, and Lars Witell. *Tjänsteinnovation*. Lund, Sweden: Studentlitteratur, 2014.

Lemon, Katherine N., and Peter C. Verhoef. "Understanding Customer Experience Throughout the Customer Journey." *Journal of Marketing* 80 (November, 2016): 69–96.

Levitt, Theodore. "Production-Line Approach to Service," *Harvard Business Review* 50, no. 5 (1972): 41–52.

Levitt, Theodore. "The Industrialization of Service," *Harvard Business Review* 50, no. 5 (1976): 63–74.

Lieberman, Marvin B., and David B. Montgomery. "First-Mover Advantages." *Strategic Management Journal* 9 (Summer 1998): 41–58.

Lilien, Gary L., Pamela D. Morrison, Kathleen Searls, Mary Sonnack, and Eric von Hippel. "Performance Assessment of the Lead User Idea-generation Process for New Product Development." *Management Science* 48, no. 8 (2002): 1042–59.

Lovelock, Christopher, and Evert Gummesson. "Whither Services Marketing? In Search of a New Paradigm and Fresh Perspectives." *Journal of Service Research* 7, no. 1 (2004): 20–41.

Lovelock, Christopher, and Jochen Wirtz. *Services Marketing: People, Technology, Strategy.* 6th ed. Upper Saddle River, NJ: Pearson Education, 2007.

Lucas, Richard E., Ed Diener, Alexander Grob, Eunkook M. Suh, and Liang Shao. "Cross-Cultural Evidence for the Fundamental Features of Extraversion." *Journal of Personality and Social Psychology* 79 (September, 2000): 452–68.

Macdonald, Emma K., Michael Kleinaltenkamp, and Hugh N. Wilson. "How Business Customers Judge Solutions: Solution Quality and Value in Use." *Journal of Marketing* 80, no. 3 (2016): 96–120.

Malmgren, Mike. "Managing Risks in Business Critical Outsourcing: A Perspective from the Outsourcer and the Supplier." Published PhD diss., Linköping University, Linköping, Sweden, 2010.

Markowitz, Harry. *Mean-Variance Analysis in Portfolio Choice and Capital Markets.* New York: Blackwell, 1987.

Mattolini, Dana. "Xerox Chief Looks Beyond Photocopiers Toward Services." *Wall Street Journal,* June 13, 2011.

*Metso*, Annual Report, 2012.

*Michelin Group.* "Michelin, A Better Way Forward." (2015).

*Microsoft.* Stephen Elop's e-mail to employees, 2014. Accessed April 3, 2016. https://news.microsoft.com/2014/07/17/stephen-elops-email-to-employees/.

Moncrief, William C., and Greg W. Marshall. "The Evolution of the Seven Steps of Selling." *Industrial Marketing Management* 34, no. 1 (2005): 13–22.

Nie, Winter, Wolfgang Ulaga, and Athanasios Kondis. *ABB TURBOCHARGING (A): Leading Change in Certain Times.* IMD Case Study No. IMD-3-2430, available at The Case Center, UK, 2014.

Nordin, Fredrik, Danilo Brozovic, Christian Kowalkowski, and Mats Vilgon. "CASE: Managing customer relationship gaps at SKF." *Journal of Business Market Management* 8, no. 2 (2015): 455–63.

Oliva, Rogelio, Heiko Gebauer, and J. M. Brann. "Separate or Integrate? Assessing the Impact of Separation between Product and Service Business on Service Performance in Product Manufacturing Firms." *Journal of Business-to-Business Marketing* 19, no. 4 (2012): 309–34.

Oliva, Rogelio, and Robert Kallenberg. "Managing the Transition from Products to Services." *International Journal of Service Industry Management* 14, no. 2 (2003): 160–72.

Olson, Eric M., Stanley F. Slater, and Tomas M. Hult. "The Performance Implications of Fit among Business Strategy, Marketing Organization Structure, and Strategic Behavior." *Journal of Marketing* 69, no. 3 (2005): 49–65.

Ostrower, Jon. "Boeing Reorganizes into Three Parts: Airliners, Fighters and Spare Parts." *CNN Money,* November 21, 2016. Accessed

December 9, 2016. money.cnn.com/2016/11/21/news/companies/boeing-reorganization/. Boeing News Releases/Statements, "Boeing Names New Senior Leaders, Launches Integrated Services Business," November 21, 2016. Accessed December 9, 2016. boeing.mediaroom.com/2016-11-21-Boeing-Names-New-Senior-Leaders-Launches-Integrated-Services-Business.

Parker, Andrew. "Ericsson to Buy Telcordia for $1.2bn." *Financial Times*, June 14, 2011. Accessed September 23, 2016. www.ft.com/cms/s/0/1aafdc46-967c-11e0-afc5-00144feab49a.html.

Pavitt, Keith. "Sectoral Patterns of Technical Change: Towards a Taxonomy and a Theory." *Research Policy* 13, no. 6 (1984): 343–73.

*PetSmart*. Annual Reports, 2010; 2013.

*Philips*. Press Release: "Philips Provides Light As a Service to Schiphol Airport," April 16, 2015. Accessed September 22, 2016. www.philips.com/a-w/about/news/archive/standard/news/press/2015/20150416-Philips-provides-Light-as-a-Service-to-Schiphol-Airport.html.

Plouffe, Christopher R., Brian C. Williams, and Trent Wachner. "Navigating Difficult Waters: Publishing Trends and Scholarship in Sales Research." *Journal of Personal Selling and Sales Management* 28, no. 1 (2008): 79–92.

Rangan, V. Kasturi, and George T. Bowman. "Beating the Commodity Magnet." *Industrial Marketing Management* 21, no. 3 (1992): 215–24.

Raval, Anjli. "Xerox Says Shift to Services Is Paying Off." *Financial Times*, January 24, 2014. Accessed September 23, 2016. www.ft.com/cms/s/0/bac264c8-662e-11e2-bb67-00144feab49a.html.

Reinartz, Werner, and Wolfgang Ulaga. "How to Sell Services More Profitably." *Harvard Business Review* (May, 2008): 90–96.

Renault, Chloé, Frédéric Dalsace, and Wolfgang Ulaga. *Michelin Fleet Solutions: From Selling Tires to Selling Kilometers.* ECCH Case Study, 2010.

*Reuters.* "China's HNA Group to Buy Ingram Micro for $6 Billion," February 18, 2016. Accessed September 22, 2016. www.reuters.com/article/us-ingram-micro-m-a-tianjin-tianhai-idUSKCN0VQ2U0.

Rust, Roland T., and Ming-Hui Huang. "Optimizing Service Productivity." *Journal of Marketing* 76, no. 2 (2012): 47–66.

Rust, Roland T., Katherin N. Lemon, and Valarie A. Zeithaml. "Return on Marketing: Using Customer Equity to Focus Marketing Strategy." *Journal of Marketing* 68 (January, 2004): 109–27.

*Schneider Electric.* Annual Report, 2015.

Shah, Denish, Roland T. Rust, A. Parasuraman, Richard Staelin, and George S. Day. "The Path to Customer Centricity." *Journal of Service Research* 9, no. 2 (2006): 113–24.

Sharman, Andy. "BMW Sounds Alarm over Tech Companies Seeking Connected Car Data." *Financial Times*, January 15, 2015. Accessed November 21, 2016. www.ft.com/intl/cms/s/0/685fe610-9ba6-11e4-950f-00144feabdc0.html#axzz3RcmWMfOG.

Shepherd, Christian. "Volvo Seeks Edge on Driverless Car Technology." *Financial Times*, April 7, 2016. Accessed September 23, 2016. www.ft.com/intl/cms/s/0/96f256c8-fc6e-11e5-b5f5-070dca6d0a0d.html.

Shostack, G. Lynn. "Designing Services That Deliver." *Harvard Business Review* 62 (January–February, 1984): 133–39.

Shostack, G. Lynn. "Service Positioning through Structural Change." *Journal of Marketing* 51 (January, 1987): 34–43.

Shotter, James. "UK Groups Lag behind in Adding Services." *Financial Times*, May 29, 2012. Accessed September 23, 2016. www.ft.com/cms/s/0/890ae896-a1bd-11e1-ae4c-00144feabdc0.html.

*Siemens. Pictures of the Future—The Magazine for Research and Innovation*, fall 2001.

Sinfield, Joe, Ned Calder, and Ben Geheb. "How Industrial Systems Are Turning into Digital Services," *Harvard Business Review*, June 23, 2015. Accessed September 23, 2016. https://hbr.org/2015/06/how-industrial-systems-are-turning-into-digital-services.

*SKF.* Annual Reports, 2010–2015.

Sommer, Jeff. "Apple Won't Always Rule. Just Look at IBM." *New York Times*, April 25, 2015, page BU4 of the New York edition. Accessed September 23, 2016. www.nytimes.com/2015/04/26/your-money/now-its-apples-world-once-it-was-ibms.html.

Spiro, R. L., and Barton A. Weitz. "Adaptive Selling: Conceptualization, Measurement, and Nomological Validity." *Journal of Marketing Research* 27, no. 1 (1990): 61–69.

Spohrer, Jim. "IBM's Service Journey: A Summary Sketch," *Industrial Marketing Management*, 60 (2017): 167–172.

Steiner, Michael, Andreas Eggert, Wolfgang Ulaga, and Klaus Backhaus. "Do Customized Service Packages Impede Value Capture in Industrial Markets?" *Journal of the Academy of Marketing Science* 44 (2016): 151–65.

Terho, Harri, Andreas Eggert, Alexander Haas, and Wolfgang Ulaga. "Implementing Sales Strategy in Business Markets: The Role of Salesperson Customer Orientation and Value-Based Selling," *Industrial Marketing Management* 45 (2015): 12–21.

Thomas, Daniel. "Huawei Sets out Third Stage of European Strategy." *Financial Times,* February 22, 2016. Accessed September 22, 2016. www.ft.com/intl/cms/s/0/2b580046-d637-11e5-8887-98e7feb46f27.html.

Treacy, Michael, and Fred Wiersema. "Customer Intimacy and Other Value Disciplines." *Harvard Business Review* (January–February, 1993): 84–93.

Ulaga, Wolfgang, and James Loveland. "Transitioning from Product to Service-led Growth in Manufacturing Firms: Emergent Challenges in Selecting and Managing the Industrial Sales Force." *Industrial Marketing Management* 43 (January, 2014): 113–25.

Ulaga, Wolfgang, and Werner Reinartz. "Hybrid Offerings: How Manufacturing Firms Combine Goods and Services Successfully." *Journal of Marketing* 75, no. 6 (2011): 5–23.

*United Technologies.* Annual Report, 2014.

Vargo, Stephen L., and Robert F. Lusch. "Evolving to a New Dominant for Marketing." *Journal of Marketing* 68 (January, 2004): 1–17.

VDMA. *Dienen und Verdienen.* Frankfurt/Main, Germany: VDMA Verlag, 1998.

Vinchur, Andrew J., Jeffrey S. Schippmann, Fred S. Switzer, and Philip L. Roth. "A Meta-Analytic Review of Job Performance for Salespeople." *Journal of Applied Psychology* 83, no. 4 (1998): 586–97.

Visnjic Kastalli, Ivanka, and Bart Van Looy. "Servitization: Disentangling the Impact of Service Business Model Innovation on Manufacturing Firm Performance." *Journal of Operations Management* 31, no. 4 (2013): 169–80.

*Volvo Cars.* Press Release: "Volvo Cars and Uber Join Forces to Develop Autonomous Driving Cars." August 18, 2016. Accessed

September 23, 2016. www.media.volvocars.com/us/en-us/media/pressreleases/194795/volvo-cars-and-uber-join-forces-to-develop-autonomous-driving-cars.

Waters, Richard. "Semiconductor Sale a Vital Part of IBM's Strategic Realignment." *Financial Times,* February 7, 2014. Accessed September 23, 2016. www.ft.com/cms/s/0/f563bea0-8fa5-11e3-9cb0-00144feab7de.html.

Weitz, Barton, H. Sujan, and M. Sujan. "Knowledge, Motivation, and Adaptive Behavior: A Framework for Improving Selling Effectiveness." *Journal of Marketing* 50, no. 4 (1986): 174–91.

Williams, Brian C., and Christopher R. Plouffe. "Assessing the Evolution of Sales Knowledge: A 20-Content Analysis." *Industrial Marketing Management* 36, no. 4 (2007): 319–408.

*World Bank,* 2014. Accessed September 20, 2016. http://data.worldbank.org/indicator/NV.SRV.TETC.ZS/countries?page=6. Accessed May 18, 2016. http://data.worldbank.org/indicator/FB.ATM.TOTL.P5.

*Xerox.* Annual Reports, 2012; 2013; 2014; 2015.

*Xerox.* Press Release: "Xerox to Separate into Two Market-Leading Public Companies Following Completion of Comprehensive Structural Review," January 29, 2016. Accessed September 23, 2016. www.news.xerox.com/news/Xerox-to-separate-into-two-market-leading-public-companies.

Yee, Amy. "Xerox takes road towards reinvention," *Financial Times,* November 4, 2004. Accessed September 23, 2016. www.ft.com/cms/s/0/d5de5270-2e07-11d9-a86b-00000e2511c8.html.

Zeithaml, Valarie A., Mary Jo Bitner, and Dwayne D. Gremler. *Services Marketing: Integrating Customer Focus Across the Firm.* 6th ed. New York: McGraw-Hill Irwin, 2013.

# INDEX

vision   95, 110, 115-121, 170
visionary thinking   207
Voith   217
Volvo Cars   247
Volvo Group   117, 152-154, 158, 247

**W**
Wärtsilä   217
Westfalen   75
willingness to pay   25, 34, 37, 78, 127, 131, 135, 137

**X**
Xerox   4-6, 121, 122
Xiameter   77, 145
Xylem   240, 241, 246

**Z**
Zipcar   186

25974419R00178

Made in the USA
Columbia, SC
09 September 2018